TELLING STORIES

TELLING STORIES

Perspectives on Longitudinal Writing Research

EDITED BY
JENN FISHMAN AND AMY C. KIMME HEA

UTAH STATE UNIVERSITY PRESS
Logan

© 2023 by University Press of Colorado

Published by Utah State University Press
An imprint of University Press of Colorado
1624 Market Street, Suite 226
PMB 39883
Denver, Colorado 80202-1559

All rights reserved
Printed in the United States of America

 The University Press of Colorado is a proud member of the Association of University Presses.

The University Press of Colorado is a cooperative publishing enterprise supported, in part, by Adams State University, Colorado State University, Fort Lewis College, Metropolitan State University of Denver, University of Alaska Fairbanks, University of Colorado, University of Denver, University of Northern Colorado, University of Wyoming, Utah State University, and Western Colorado University.

∞ This paper meets the requirements of the ANSI/NISO Z39.48-1992 (Permanence of Paper).

ISBN: 978-1-64642-431-3 (hardcover)
ISBN: 978-1-64642-432-0 (paperback)
ISBN: 978-1-64642-433-7 (ebook)
https://doi.org/10.7330/9781646424337

Library of Congress Cataloging-in-Publication Data

Names: Fishman, Jenn, editor. | Kimme Hea, Amy C., editor.
Title: Telling stories : perspectives on longitudinal writing research / edited by Jenn Fishman and Amy C. Kimme Hea.
Description: Logan : Utah State University Press, [2023] | Includes bibliographical references and index.
Identifiers: LCCN 2023010605 (print) | LCCN 2023010606 (ebook) | ISBN 9781646424313 (hardcover) | ISBN 9781646424320 (paperback) | ISBN 9781646424337 (ebook)
Subjects: LCSH: English language—Rhetoric—Study and teaching (Higher) | Academic writing—Longitudinal studies. | College students' writings—Longitudinal studies. | Longitudinal method—Case studies.
Classification: LCC PE1404 .T45 2023 (print) | LCC PE1404 (ebook) | DDC 808/.042072—dc23/eng/20230404
LC record available at https://lccn.loc.gov/2023010605
LC ebook record available at https://lccn.loc.gov/2023010606

Cover photograph, "1-spring-vertical-eiriksmagick," © hugovk/Flickr.com.

To everyone who plays the long game of writing research
—Jenn

To Aidan and Virginia, and for their stories yet unwritten
—Amy

CONTENTS

Acknowledgments ix

Introduction
Jenn Fishman and Amy C. Kimme Hea 3

1. Storying Longitudinal Research: Relationality and Self-Reflexivity
   Brad Jacobson and J. Michael Rifenburg 14

2. Weaving Reflexivity, Relationality, and Time in a Decade-Long Study of Writing Development and Learning Transfer
   Dana Lynn Driscoll 30

3. Following Participants as Leaders in Long Research
   Lauren Rosenberg 45

4. Mission-Driven Longitudinal Research: The Public Value of Telling the Stories of Two-Year College Writers
   Holly Hassel and Joanne Baird Giordano 63

5. Understanding Imbricated Contexts: Institutional Formation and Longitudinal Writing Research
   Amy C. Kimme Hea 81

6. Researching for Capital: Longitudinal Research, Precarity, and Institutional Citizenship
   Doug Downs, Mark Schlenz, Miles Nolte, and Ashley Rives 97

7. More Simple Gifts: Labor, Relationships, and Ethics in Longitudinal Research
   Aimee C. Mapes 116

8. The Precarious Method: Longitudinal Research and Material Uncertainty in Professional and Technical Writing Studies
   Yanar Hashlamon 133

9. Radically Longitudinal, Radically Contextual: Growing Lifespan Writing Research
   Ryan J. Dippre and Talinn Phillips   150

10. Becoming History
    Jenn Fishman   167

    Epilogue: Why We Tell Stories
    Jenn Fishman and Amy C. Kimme Hea   190

Index   199
About the Authors   209

ACKNOWLEDGMENTS

As a concrete project with a title and a call for proposals (CFP), this book began in the before time, a good year ahead of the 2020 pandemics. The fact that we finished in such good time testifies to the privilege that made it possible for all of us to keep working; it also reflects the good time we had while we worked together and the great honor it was to work with everyone involved, from the colleagues who contributed their stories to Rachael Levay and her team at Utah State University Press and University Press of Colorado. The latter contributed their signature consummate support, and we benefited in particular from Rachael's steady enthusiasm and the thoughtful engagement of our anonymous reviewers.

Jenn adds her appreciation to many others, starting with the colleagues at Marquette University in the Klingler College of Arts and Sciences and the English department who made research travel monies consistently available. She gives a grateful, if sleepy, nod to the writers Stephanie Kerschbaum first gathered online in late spring of 2020 to write-on-site together at the crack of dawn, and she raises a glass to the RSA CWPAs, Jeff Ringer, Kathryn Valentine, and Kuhio Walters—grateful for their ongoing feedback, insight, and camaraderie. She saves the greatest gratitude for friends and family who have listened, over a very long time, to her stories about longitudinal research, especially Charlie, who is the most steadfast of writing partners and the Charliest in every way.

Amy is ever grateful that Anne-Marie Hall provided her expertise and insights to the launching of the UA Study, despite moving into her well-earned phased retirement. She is also grateful that Aimee Mapes stepped into a study not originally of her making, and with Aimee's expertise, the UA Study flourished. Over the six years, research assistants, writing program colleagues, the University of Arizona's (UA) provost office and College of Humanities, National Council of Teachers of English (NCTE), and Council of Writing Program Administrators (CWPA) offered financial support to this research endeavor. At all points, it has been the student writers who made the efforts possible and worthwhile—thanks to them for sticking with the long journey. Later, UA's College of Social and Behavioral Sciences provided financial support as research funds for a research assistant position that Analeigh Horton ably commanded to prepare the review manuscript of *Telling Stories*. Finally, Amy is appreciative of Steven, Aidan, and Virginia and her friends and colleagues, who consistently gave time, space, and encouragement for her administrative roles and her research projects.

Together, we acknowledge that this book began long before it was a project, and we owe much to our earliest mentors in longitudinal research, Andrea Lunsford and Nancy Sommers. We are also indebted in the best possible way to all of the co-researchers we have worked with over the years, Amy at the University of Arizona and Jenn at Stanford, the University of Tennessee–Knoxville, and Vernon College. Across drafts, time, and locations, we are most grateful to the writers who, when asked, choose to give not only their consent but also their time and attention, their trust, and their writing along with accounts of their experiences as writers to longitudinal researchers like us.

TELLING STORIES

INTRODUCTION

Jenn Fishman and Amy C. Kimme Hea

Longitudinal, adj. and n. *Pronunciation: US lɔndʒə'ˌt(j)udənl.*
Forms: late Middle English longitudinale, late Middle English longitudinel, 1500s longytudynalles (plural), 1500s–1600s longitudinall, 1500s longitudinal.

We humans have had longitudinal coordinates and muscles for a long time. For centuries, we have traced the thin line of the horizon as it extends, seemingly endlessly, toward the illusion of an origin point. In English, early modern surgeons mapped gross anatomy along longitudinal bodily axes. They also distinguished compound, transverse, and fissure-like "cissurale" fractures from longitudinal ones, while botanists and geographers described shape, distance, and dimension longitudinally. With time, we have learned to take the long view and play the long game, whether cards, golf, or politics. When someone calls "go long," we know what to do. Likewise, we have devised innumerable ways to measure and manage duration. We keep learning and relearning how to long haul, and we know when to cut a long story short and when to offer the long-form version. (This introduction, by the way, is a twenty-minute read.) Through it all, we continue to be captivated by change over time. Witness childhood height marked annually along a door frame. Google Kasmin Gallery and watch the portraits James Nares filmed at 600 frames per second—a process that renders being and time an event, if only for a moment.

On a considerably larger scale, we have been collecting longitudinal data for hundreds of years, since the first censuses were taken in the mid-seventeenth and eighteenth centuries. But it was not until the early twentieth century that we began to designate some inquiries "longitudinal research" or scientific studies "carried out or extending over a prolonged period of time" and "involving serial observations or measurements of the same individual, cohort, or experimental group"

(*Oxford English Dictionary* 2016). In one of the earliest English-language references on record, dating to 1913, J. E. Wallace Wallin (1913, 896) identifies longitudinal study as essential to clinical psychology, a necessity for the correct diagnosis and treatment of patients. A quick canvass of scholarly literature since then shows longitudinal research to be a method, a methodology, and even a quasi-field or subfield within social and behavioral sciences and the health sciences. Perhaps most usefully, several scholars including Scott Menard (2002, 2) distinguish longitudinal research as "a family of methods" defined by comparative analysis of data collected at two or more distinct periods of time. Cross-disciplinary examples run the gamut, encompassing everything from prospective and retrospective panel studies to cohort studies and, in some fields, repeated cross-sectional studies (3).

As longitudinal writing researchers, we echo the founding editors of the journal *Longitudinal and Life Course Studies*. More than a decade ago, they declared longitudinal research "the vehicle par excellence for mapping the changing human life course within a generation as development and ageing proceed" (Bynner et al. 2009, 3). They also acknowledged life course theory and research as a well-established "means of showing how the life course is both shaped and re-shaped through the interactions between changing societal circumstances, and individual and collective agency" (4). In writing studies, the focus has been on academic rather than birth cohorts and projects with Ns in the tens instead of the hundreds or thousands. Nonetheless, longitudinal research has proven to be a significant vector for improving our understanding of writing. Early examples focus on the development of school-age writers: 338 children in California followed from kindergarten through twelfth grade, starting in 1953 (Loban 1967); 100 eleven- and 100 fourteen-year-olds, whose writing development was tracked for four years starting in 1967 (Britton et al. 1975); and 8 twelfth graders interviewed in 1967 (Emig 1969, 1971). At the college level, semester-long as well as year- and years-long studies date back at least as far as the research Albert R. Kitzhaber (1963) conducted between 1960 and 1962 at Dartmouth College. Sixty years later, longitudinal research continues to serve mainly educational purposes but in an expanded sense, through studies of not only an ever-increasing diversity of writers but also writing educators and various scenes of formal and informal or independent writing instruction.

For practitioners, longitudinal research epitomizes the abundance—or superabundance—of research. Certainly, the yield from any given longitudinal study is exponentially greater than findings that circulate in formal reports, and it is not unusual for longitudinal data from a single study to inform some combination of scholarly literature, professional reports, government documents, and pedagogical materials. Less frequently, a longitudinal project generates popular commentary. A good example is the Harvard Longitudinal Study, which began in 1938. Also known as the Grant Study, the Harvard Study of Adult Development, and, most colloquially, the Harvard Happiness Study, this ongoing research has been the subject of scores of academic publications, is one of the most-watched TED talks, and is continually accruing popular references. Even a comparatively modest longitudinal study can generate a great reservoir of data rife with potential for evolving use. As this volume recognizes, longitudinal studies also contain multitudes of told and as-yet untold stories, which stand to enrich our knowledge of not only their ostensible objects of study—whether happiness or health or writing—but also affiliated sites of activity, linked networks of relations, and corresponding communities of practice.

Some of the best-known stories drawn from longitudinal research are cinematic, including the documentary series *Up*, directed by Michael Apted. Begun in the early 1960s with *7 Up!*, the series follows a fourteen-person cohort through installments filmed at seven-year intervals. A half-century into the project, Apted described the combination of patience and longevity that enabled him simultaneously to document and honor "the drama of ordinary life" ("49 Up" 2007). Although Apted asserted that "doing a documentary is one set of your muscles and doing a drama is another," some of his colleagues feel differently (Kouguell 2019). For director Richard Linklater, longitudinal filmmaking makes possible the impossible work of bringing phenomena such as relationships and childhood to the screen. Discussing his decision to film *Boyhood* with a single cast over the course of twelve years, Linklater recalls: "I just got this eureka moment of, 'Well, why couldn't you just film a little bit [at a time], and encompass all of it'" (quoted in Bishop 2014). In writing studies, Bump Halbritter and Julie Lindquist have explored the affordances that digital video lends to longitudinal research. They describe LiteracyCorps Michigan as "an oral history documentary project" designed to illuminate college students' "experiences of education in relation to [their] family histories, community life, and use of communication technologies" (n.d.). Over three stages of data collection, both they and project participants stepped behind the camera to record scenes of students' literate lives from different angles. The results challenge disciplinary conventions associated with everything from literacy narratives to empirical research, defining a methodology of looking, listening, and "strategically deferring interpretive closure" (Halbritter and Lindquist 2012, 174).

This volume is a collection of stories about longitudinal writing research told by longitudinal writing researchers. All sixteen contributors have conducted longitudinal studies at educational sites, including high schools, two- and four-year colleges and universities, and adult literacy centers. Together, we have worked on longitudinal research across career stages, starting as early as graduate school. Our ranks (at the time of writing) include one or more doctoral candidates, contingent and tenured or tenure-track faculty at two- and four-year colleges and universities, and program and university administrators. Collectively, we have designed longitudinal studies in conjunction with courses we teach (e.g., first-year composition, professional writing). We have sought IRB approval for dissertation and program research, and we have followed our longitudinal interests from our own campuses to other institutions and institution types. The stories we have chosen to tell for this occasion are related to yet distinct from the research reports and academic arguments we make elsewhere. In this volume, we tell stories about our work and the students and colleagues with whom we have worked. We tell stories about the sites that have prompted and sponsored our projects, both enabling and constraining them. We also tell stories about the scholarly conceits that we negotiate—and even seek to change—across the life cycles of our work.

We share our stories in response to a hunger for them. As Tricia Serviss and Sandra Jamieson (2017, 14) advocate, discussing the future of our discipline: "One dynamic way forward is to make the methods and processes of writing research as central as the findings reported from the research." In *Points of Departure*, they and their contributors offer a variety of tactics that support an overall strategy of greater transparency and information flow among researchers, encouraging more and more widely circulated pilot studies, changes to graduate education, and new uses of both extant data and familiar data collection and analysis tools. With similar goals in mind, others have called for resources such as an annual scholarly bibliography and a registry or census of writing research at any stage of completion (Haswell 2005; Fishman and Mullin 2012; Mullin and Fishman 2017). These arguments chime with the call Doug Downs and his colleagues (2020, 100) make in the Naylor Report, where they champion the publication of what they term "stories of discovery" as well as more conventional research findings or "discovered stories." The examples they offer, including personal narratives from undergraduate research publications like *The JUMP+*, do critical work. They offer context as well as insight into how researchers understand the rhetorical situations of their projects; they may also contain thick descriptions of and reflections on praxis. Such details make stories fair substitutes for the how-to manuals new longitudinal writing researchers often crave. They also go beyond simple instructions or models to offer commentaries on and arguments about different aspects of our discipline.

The stories we tell in this volume serve not only to illuminate longitudinal research as contributors have practiced it but also to bring attention to the places where we conduct research as well as the sites where participants in our studies write and learn about writing. Our stories portray some of the many relationships forged and tested through longitudinal research, and they shed light on different local and virtual or discursive communities of practice. In doing so, the stories we tell serve a critical purpose or, really, a range of critical purposes. Some stories give presence to facets of research frequently glossed over or ignored in our discipline, including the vital and complex, sometimes difficult relationships that form among researchers and between researchers and research participants over the course of a long project. Some stories bring attention to the powerful roles sponsoring institutions, localities, and cultural moments play in longitudinal studies of writing. Still other stories explore methodological possibilities, advocating for new uses and new kinds of longitudinal research. What all of our stories have in common is their engagement with some of the many affordances for scholarly communication that storytelling offers: opportunities for reflection and refraction, space to make associations and acknowledge relations, chances to creatively provoke and defend arguments, and so on.

In *Telling Stories: Perspectives on Longitudinal Research*, we embrace storytelling aware that the relationship between writing studies and story can be vexed. As a discipline, we have scrutinized the relationship between Greco-Roman rhetoric and poetics from antiquity onward, tracking it across genres as diverse as oratory, poetry, and medical case histories (Walker 2000; Berkenkotter 2008). Depending on our purpose and our positionality, we have chosen to trust and mistrust stories along with the narrative architectures that support them. We have recognized and even celebrated lore as a form of knowledge in composition (North 1987; Massey and Gebhardt 2011), and we have worried that stories and our enthusiasm for them contribute to wars on data-driven research within our discipline (Haswell 2005) while limiting our ability to defend our work to public audiences, including education policymakers (Anson 2008). Most problematic, we have built and provisioned grand narratives, perhaps especially (but not exclusively) in our historical scholarship, although we have also countered those stories and their undergirding methodologies. Along with critiques, correctives, and any number of additions to the historical record, we have added to our repertoire archival ethnography (Ritter 2012), retellings (Glenn 1997; Enoch and Jack 2021), counter and crooked histories (Hawk 2007; Ruiz 2016; Skinnell 2016), and, most notably, counterstory (Martinez 2020). The latter is a methodology rooted academically in critical race theory and culturally in knowledge-seeking and sharing traditions that have been long marginalized by white researchers and the predominantly white institutions that sponsor research.

The storytelling undertaken in this volume aligns with ongoing efforts to increase the number and range of stories told about writing and writing research, broadening the scope of perspectives available. To this end, we offer our stories as critical labor, reflections on and prompts or provocations to reckon with the limits of individual perspectives and the consequences of the choices we make in the various professional roles we play: teacher, researcher, writer, writing administrator. By recounting choices we did and did not make, by narrating some of our negotiations with the projects we designed and our projects' actual unfoldings, we hope to create greater conditions of possibility for future longitudinal projects. At the college level alone, we know that a great deal of recent and ongoing work is not represented directly in the chapters that follow. Indeed, we in this volume represent a small sample of writing researchers who have taken longitudinal approaches to researching postsecondary multilingual writers, STEM students, engineering students, writing center peer tutors, and graduate writing instructors. This book can be used to focus on individual courses and programs as well as different forms of assessment. Both in and beyond formal school settings, longitudinal research stands to illuminate not only writing development but also knowledge transfer and writers' resilience. There are connections to be drawn across school-based studies, K–college, and studies situated in different workplaces, in virtual spaces, and in diverse geographic locations—embracing a greater range of demographics. There are also connections to be drawn among longitudinal studies that look at writing and literacy in relation to additional activities: athletics, leadership, numeracy, spirituality, political activism, and others.

The contents of this volume might be endlessly rearranged to bring out the many connections among individual chapters. The order we chose highlights the ways longitudinal studies of writing are also studies of relationships and linked networks of relations, affiliated sites of activity, and corresponding communities of practice. Brad Jacobson and J. Michael Rifenburg, in "Storying Longitudinal Research: Relationality and Self-Reflexivity," open this collection with a central preoccupation: the relationship between researchers and research participants. Together, they introduce us to Jain, a Latinx high school student who matriculated at the University of Arizona, and Logan, a US Army cadet who attended the University of North Georgia. Drawing on Leigh Patel's scholarship (2019), Jacobsen and Rifenburg story their experiences as principal investigators of longitudinal studies to examine what it means—what it looks like, sounds like, and feels like—to take responsibility for representing other writers over time. Specifically, they story their years of work with Jain and Logan to self-reflexively examine the power dynamics within their projects and to bring to the fore "issues of power dynamics, reciprocity, and representation" that are woven into the fabric of their own and others' longitudinal projects. Their chapter juxtaposes the joys and anxieties that surround the work of building trust with research participants and striving toward reciprocity while negotiating differences of power and perception over time.

The two chapters that follow continue the close-up work of storying longitudinal relations. In "Weaving Reflexivity, Relationality, and Time in a Decade-Long Study of Writing Development and Learning Transfer," Dana Lynn Driscoll offers a retrospective on her career-long longitudinal work to showcase the interlinked dynamics of research, teaching, and mentoring. Her story—or, really, the stories within her story—give presence to some of the many personal relationships that shape her longitudinal research, including evolving friendships with former study participants, remembrances of students and mentors who have passed, and her own, ever-changing sense of self as an academic and an expert in our field. In "Following Participants as Leaders in Long Research," Lauren Rosenberg is equally reflective about her work and the ways her research has, over decades, intertwined her life with the lives of others. Specifically, Rosenberg reflects on the uniquely organic and dialogic way her work with adult literacy learners became longitudinal. Incorporating surprise and flux into the regimentation of IRB-approved research and roles, Rosenberg models what it looks like—and what is to be gained—when researchers are willing to follow participants' lead and allow their interests to guide and even drive ongoing inquiries.

The four chapters that follow tell stories about longitudinal research relations on a broader scale. They showcase some of the many ways multi-year studies of college writers and college writing are also studies of the colleges and universities in which each study takes place. Importantly, the chapters contributed by Holly Hassel and Joanne Baird Giordano; Amy C. Kimme Hea; Doug Downs, Mark Schlenz, Miles Nolte, and Ashley Rives; and Aimee C. Mapes do not tell full-blown stories of sponsorship; nor should their contributions be read as full-fledged institutional ethnographies. Instead, these middle chapters bring attention to the "ideological freight" colleges and universities contribute to campus-based longitudinal studies (Brandt 1998, 168), and in doing so they show how writing researchers bear that weight—whether as gifts or burdens—in their work.

Coauthors Hassel and Giordano as well as Kimme Hea delve into the complexities of institutional dynamics and their long-term impacts on student writers, writing researchers, and the enterprise of writing education that so much longitudinal research is designed to serve. In "Mission-Driven Longitudinal Research: The Public Value of Telling Stories of Two-Year College Writers," Hassel and Giordano outline the intense political and institutional pressures they faced as co-researchers at a community college within the University of Wisconsin System. Theirs is a story of constant negotiation with not only limited resources and accompanying rhetorics of austerity but also persistent exigences for longitudinal research and related, evidence-based revisions to college writing curricula along with the attitudes and received ideas that undergird them. The story Kimme Hea tells in "Understanding Imbricated Contexts: Institutional Formation and Longitudinal Writing Research" offers some surprising parallels. Writing from the University of Arizona, Kimme Hea stories some of the institutional and environmental factors that explicitly shaped her and her colleagues' longitudinal work, including draconian state immigration policies. Her assertion is for us researchers to consider specific institutional formations as we outline our research efforts.

The next two chapters also tell stories of institutional relations, but they look more closely at relationships among longitudinal writing researchers, paying particular attention to when and how the power dynamics of rank and role inflect longitudinal research practices and processes. In "Researching for Capital: Longitudinal Research, Precarity, and Institutional Citizenship," Downs, Schlenz, Nolte, and Rives tell a multi-perspectival tale of program-based longitudinal research and academic labor. Together, they examine ethical questions that arise when tenured writing administrators and adjunct writing instructors undertake longitudinal research meant to assess and improve writing instruction at an institution that does not support or credit faculty equally for scholarship, teaching, or service. In "More Simple Gifts: Labor, Relationships, and Ethics in Longitudinal Research," Mapes centers her story of longitudinal research on her own positionality as a non-tenure-track faculty member who joined a longitudinal study in progress as a co-principal investigator. The latter role put her in a supervisory relationship to more than a dozen graduate research assistants, creating a tricky dynamic that Mapes stories to identify and value its many gifts of "exchange, obligation, and reciprocity."

The final three chapters of this volume tell stories of longitudinal research in relation to specific communities of professional practice, where longitudinal research is—or can and should be—practiced: namely, technical and professional communication (TPC), the emerging US-based field of lifespan studies, and the rhetoric and composition/writing studies archives. To begin, Yanar Hashlamon stories longitudinal writing research as a means of advancing the social justice turn in TPC. Ostensibly, "The Precarious Method: Longitudinal Research and Material Uncertainty in Professional and Technical Writing Studies" presents classroom-based longitudinal writing studies as a means of countering the problem of determinism about workplace writing that persists in TPC research. In this chapter, Hashlamon also stories his own workplace writing, examining his role as a graduate student principal investigator of a classroom-based longitudinal study to lay bare some of the many ways precarity informs his work as much as his commitments to anti-capitalist pedagogy and ongoing critique of the corporate neoliberal university.

Where Hashlamon sees longitudinal research as a means of advancing an established area of study, Ryan J. Dippre and Talinn Phillips see it as a resource for establishing something new. Specifically, in "Radically Longitudinal, Radically Contextual," where they tell the story of "Growing Lifespan Writing Research," they also narrate some of the ways that longitudinal research can participate. As they explain at the outset of their chapter, "The diverse research methods and approaches of our fields often don't speak effectively to each other," and "even when methods do play well together, the field often lacks the structures and incentives to encourage researchers to play together themselves." Directly addressing readers who are (or may be) longitudinal researchers, they write: "Our aim here is to help those with longitudinal research experience understand how to bring a lifespan lens to existing and future projects." Jenn Fishman seems to have a very different destination for longitudinal researchers in mind when she encourages readers to head for the archives. In "Becoming History," she tells stories from her own work on the Stanford Study of Writing and Vernon Writes to explore possibilities—and possible reasons—for working in the archives of previously conducted longitudinal studies of writing. Hers is a somewhat novel suggestion, one that recalls previously collected longitudinal data to life and opens new opportunities for would-be longitudinal writing researchers. It also complements the impulse of lifespan and life course studies to capture the whole story of an individual writer or a group of writers or a particular era within the history of writing.

Of course, there is never a "whole story" to be told. Instead, there are always innumerable, ever-evolving stories that reflect the positionality, the disposition and predispositions, and the emplacement of the teller(s). The stories in this volume capture particular perspectives on longitudinal writing research; in doing so, they afford us glimpses into others' writing and researching lives. The stories also complement other forms of reflecting and reporting on research, and as such they enrich both our knowledge of writing and our efforts to share that knowledge with one another.

REFERENCES

Anson, Chris M. 2008. "The Intelligent Design of Writing Programs: Reliance on Belief or a Future of Evidence." *Writing Program Administration* 32 (1): 11–36.

Berkenkotter, Carol. 2008. *Patient Tales: Case Histories and the Use of Narrative in Psychiatry*. Columbia: University of South Carolina Press.

Bishop, Bryan. 2014. "Reliving 'Boyhood': How Richard Linklater Spent 12 Years Shooting One Movie." *The Verge*. https://www.theverge.com/2014/1/22/5332632/boyhood-how-richard-linklater-spent-12-years-shooting-one-movie.

Brandt, Deborah. 1998. "Sponsors of Literacy." *College Composition and Communication* 49 (2): 165–85.

Britton, James, Tony Burgess, Nancy Martin, Alex McLeod, and Harold Rosen. 1975. *The Development of Writing Abilities (11–18)*. London: Macmillan Education.

Bynner, John, Robert Erikson, Harvey Goldstein, Barbara Maughan, and Michael Wadsworth. 2009. "Longitudinal and Life Course Studies: A New Journal." *Longitudinal and Life Course Studies* 1 (2): 3–10.

Downs, Doug, Laurie McMillan, Megan Schoettler, and Patricia Roberts-Miller. 2020. "Circulation: Undergraduate Research as Consequential Publicness." In *The Naylor Report on Undergraduate Research in Writing Studies*, ed. Dominic DelliCarpini, Jenn Fishman, and Jane Greer, 94–105. Anderson, SC: Parlor Press.

Emig, Janet Ann. 1969. "Components of the Composing Process among Twelfth-Grade Writers." PhD dissertation, Harvard University, Cambridge, MA.

Emig, Janet. 1971. *The Composing Process of Twelfth Graders*. Champaign, IL: National Council of Teachers of English.

Enoch, Jessica, and Jordynn Jack. 2021. *Retellings: Opportunities for Feminist Research in Rhetoric and Composition*. Anderson, SC: Parlor Press.

Fishman, Jenn, and Joan Mullin. 2012. "Changing Research Practices and Access: The Research Exchange Index (REx)." *WAC Journal* 23: 7–17.

"49 Up." 2007. *POV*. http://archive.pov.org/fortynineup/filmdescription/.

Glenn, Cheryl. 1997. *Rhetoric Retold: Regendering the Tradition from Antiquity through the Renaissance*. Carbondale: Southern Illinois University Press.
Halbritter, Bump, and Julie Lindquist. 2012. "Time, Lives, and Videotape: Operationalizing Discovery in Scenes of Literacy Sponsorship." *College English* 75 (2): 171–98.
Halbritter, Bump, and Julie Lindquist. n.d. "Action." *LiteracyCorps Michigan*. https://msu.edu/~drbump/LiteracyCorps/action-recruit.html.
Haswell, Richard H. 2005. "NCTE/CCCC's Recent War on Scholarship." *Written Communication* 22 (2): 198–223.
Hawk, Byron. 2007. *A Counter History of Composition: Toward Methodologies of Complexity*. Pittsburgh: University of Pittsburgh Press.
Kitzhaber, Albert R. 1963. *Themes, Theories, and Therapy: The Teaching of Writing in College*. New York: McGraw-Hill.
Kouguell, Susan. 2019. "INTERVIEW: 63 UP Director Michael Apted." *Script*. https://scriptmag.com/filmmaking/interview-63-up-director-michael-apted.
Loban, Walter. 1967. *Language Ability: Grades Ten, Eleven, and Twelve*. [Research Report no. 18.] Champaign, IL: National Council of Teachers of English.
Martinez, Aja Y. 2020. *Counterstory: The Rhetoric and Writing of Critical Race Theory*. Champaign, IL: Conference on College Composition and Communication of the National Council of Teachers of English.
Massey, Lance, and Richard C. Gebhard, eds. 2011. *The Changing of Knowledge of Composition*. Logan: Utah State University Press.
Menard, Scott. 2002. *Longitudinal Research*. 2nd ed. Thousand Oaks, CA: Sage.
Mullin, Joan, and Jenn Fishman. 2017. "Occupying Research—Again/Still." In *Economies of Writing: Revaluations in Rhetoric and Composition*, ed. Bruce Horner, Brice Nordquist, and Susan M. Ryan, 55–67. Logan: Utah State University Press.
North, Stephen M. 1987. *The Making of Knowledge in Composition: Portrait of an Emerging Field*. Upper Montclair, NJ: Boynton/Cook.
Patel, Leigh. 2019. "Turning Away from Logarithms to Return to Story." *Research in the Teaching of English* 53 (3): 270–75.
Ritter, Kelly. 2012. "Archival Research in Composition Studies: Re-imagining the Historian's Role." *Rhetoric Review* 31 (4): 461–78.
Ruiz, Iris. 2016. *Reclaiming Composition for Chicano/as and Other Ethnic Minorities*. New York: Palgrave Macmillan.
Serviss, Tricia, and Sandra Jamieson, eds. 2017. *Points of Departure: Rethinking Student Source Use and Writing Studies Research Methods*. Logan: Utah State University Press.
Skinnell, Ryan. 2016. *Conceding Composition: A Crooked History of Composition's Institutional Fortunes*. Logan: Utah State University Press.
Walker, Jeffrey. 2000. *Rhetoric and Poetics in Antiquity*. Oxford: Oxford University Press.
Wallin, J. E. Wallace. 1913. "Clinical Psychology: What It Is and What It Is Not." *Science* 37 (963): 895–902.

1
STORYING LONGITUDINAL RESEARCH
Relationality and Self-Reflexivity

Brad Jacobson and J. Michael Rifenburg

The best longitudinal writing studies offer rich insights into the wonders and worries of a person's writing development. In many related scholarly publications, we, as readers, hear from research participants, the researchers, and people involved in participants' ongoing development. We see texts authored by participants, which invite us to enter specific settings and moments. We also find examples of data collected and explanations of how they were analyzed to reach the interpretations we are offered. In short, readers receive a complete story with who, what, when, where, why.

Amy Stornaiuolo, Gerald Campano, and Ebony Elizabeth Thomas (2019) caution against such tidy narratives. They write, "We think it is vital for researchers to make visible the histories, stakes, and geopolitical dynamics in their writing. Such a commitment to self-reflexivity in the research process involves more than being transparent about the mechanics of a research study . . . rather, it requires considering the researchers' stance and relationships to others in the study, the conceptual and epistemological foundations of their work, and recognition of what is at stake and for whom" (194). In response, in this chapter we foreground our own self-reflexive research practices by *storying* our research. We are influenced, in particular, by Leigh Patel's "Turning Away from Logarithms to Return to Story" (2019), in which she questions the ways data must become more than "mere stories" to be accepted in Eurocentric social science paradigms. Patel explains, "In my own work, which is never my own but linked to many people, it has never been enough to ask an interview question, record it, code it, and report what I perceive to be the meaning underneath what is said. That sequence should smack of individualized hubris; it does to me" (272). For Patel, this "scientific" data collection sequence arises from the lockstep logarithms forwarded by the wash of readily available qualitative research primers, handbooks, and guides. If qualitative researchers just state clearly the research processes and share some examples of the data, these sources seem to say our work will be valid. Patel rejects the assumed value of objectivity and systematicity undergirding these examples, and she pushes us to consider the counter-value of a richly situated, humanizing understanding of story: "Stories are what link us to ourselves, to each other, to the lands we've come from, go to, and return to. They take on lives of their own: we often create the version that we want rather than the version that took place" (271).

The word *story* evokes multiple meanings for us. When used as a noun, a story is a crafted final product, a narrative with a beginning, middle, and end. As fathers who read bedtime stories to our children and as researchers invested in how language and people come together to make meaning, this tidy understanding of story is central to our identities. But Patel (2019) reminds us that this version of story is incomplete, and from this perspective we begin to see story operating as a verb. *To story* describes meaning making and the construction of knowledge. It raises the idea of communally crafted communications, moments shared for a specific time and purpose and audience, words with meaning for now that arise from interactions with and a hope to serve those who sit with us.

When we read story as a verb—coupled with the question posed by Stornaiuolo, Campano, and Thomas, "*What is at stake and for whom?*"—we read story as an ongoing action. In doing so, we open the broader discussion of this volume, posing the central question of both the collection and this chapter by asking: what does it mean to story longitudinal research?

For our part, the answer lies in at least attempting to lay bare the power dynamics of our separate longitudinal research projects. Storying longitudinal research demands adopting what Stornaiuolo, Anna Smith, and Nathan Phillips (2017, 76) call an "inquiry stance," which calls for researchers to actively account for their own role in "unfolding activity" and to "routinely question their own assumptions and positionalities while remaining sensitive and open to multiple interpretations."[1] We draw particular attention to Stornaiuolo, Smith, and Phillips's use of the words *question*, *sensitive*, and *open* because we see these words pushing us toward storying our research. We storied our research during data collection where we remained sensitive and open to how we formed our interview questions, how we, in coordination with our participants, determined the when and where and how of interviews. We storied our research when we questioned and remained sensitive and open during data analysis, moments when we were often alone hunched over a laptop with piles of notes charting our trek across mountains of longitudinal research data, our research participants physically removed from *their* data. We continue to story our research when we circulate it through social media platforms, conference poster presentations, articles, and books. Though the data collection is over and the IRB application is closed, we remain sensitive and open to ongoing developments in our thinking, in scholarship, in the literate life moments of our research participants; and we offer findings that attend to these developments.

But storying isn't easy. In the accounts that follow, we highlight the tensions and possibilities that arose within our individual longitudinal research projects, reflecting on what we learn when we place our storying side by side. Brad goes first, then Michael. Brad writes of his work with Jain, a participant in a study of four Latinx student writers across the high school to college transition. Michael writes of Logan, a US Army cadet he worked with as Logan moved through the four-year ROTC curriculum at a federally designated senior military college. In our narratives we call into question—but maybe never fully answer—issues of power dynamics, reciprocity, and representation. We come together again as coauthors in the final section—confused, excited, and committed to continuing to forge a stronger understanding of how people develop as writers and how we, as researchers, can tell our research stories in all their messiness. Through reflecting on the synergies and disconnects we hear in our stories, we question what longitudinal writing research might learn if we heed Patel's words and story our research.

BRAD'S STORYING: RELATIONAL PRACTICE AND RECIPROCITY IN LONGITUDINAL RESEARCH

As Jain and I entered the third year of a research relationship that began when he was a senior in high school, it had become clear that this project meant much to both of us.[2] In addition to our monthly interviews and frequent discussions about writing, we shared text messages, emails, and phone calls. We also spent many hours just talking in my office, discussing our school and life plans; or we navigated institutional bureaucracy, as when we figured out how to find a summer class in a cumbersome online registration portal. On other occasions we talked about our families or relationships; in the span of three weeks, we realized that both of our significant others were pregnant, and we shared ultrasound pictures and updates until the babies—both healthy girls—were born within a few weeks of each other. In short, the research relationship had become a friendship.

As data collection neared completion and my own graduation from a PhD program appeared on the horizon, Jain and I agreed it would be valuable to record our experiences in the project. We each brought questions to a retrospective interview in December 2018. I draw from this interview to help me story my research. The constraints and exigencies of publication that guide researchers to findings and application often elide or confine to footnotes the messy work of building relationships and the storying such sharing entails.[3] As Jenn Fishman (2012, 175) writes, there has not been "enough attention paid to the unique types of collaboration that longitudinal studies can require, both among researchers and between researchers and study participants." In this section, I respond to this call by describing how a relational approach helped me engage productively with some of the primary tensions of the research project, including representation and reciprocity.

Positionality and Reflexivity

Even though I saw myself as a graduate student low on the academic totem pole when I started my research with Jain, the students and teacher in Jain's high school class positioned me as an expert. In an effort to encourage students to participate in my study, Jain's teacher had hyped me as a teacher and scholar from the university. I must admit, with my dark, plastic-framed glasses and limited wardrobe of button-down shirts, I did look the part. Jain told me he initially saw me as "part of the school . . . like a school official." Eventually, that impression changed, but hearing Jain say that he first saw me in an official capacity makes visible the power dynamics that undeniably infused the project and the beginnings of our relationship.

Attention to power and positionality is often central to discussions and critiques of qualitative research methodologies, especially in work with individuals from minoritized populations. As a white middle-class man working with Jain and three other first-generation-to-college Latinx students, I was particularly attentive to calls from across writing studies and related fields for self-reflexive approaches to qualitative inquiry that pay particular attention to issues of race, class, gender, and power relations (Cushman and Monberg 1998; Motha 2014; Paltridge, Starfield, and Tardy 2016). These critiques raise important concerns about how academic researchers with privilege (like me) end up appropriating the stories and experiences of students from minoritized populations for their/our own material gain (Henderson and Esposito 2019). And it's true that I have gained much from this research project. My work with Jain was part of my dissertation, and I spoke about this project at national conferences and in interviews for a tenure-track academic appointment. What could I possibly offer him in return? The glib response might be, *not enough*. I'm willing to acknowledge that is likely true. But as I discussed the research experience with Jain, I realized that elements of our research relationship went beyond transactional views of reciprocity and the kinds of benefits that can be enumerated on an IRB application. Sure, I offered writing support when asked, and I was able to pay Jain a small stipend after I earned a research grant, but as Jain keenly pointed out in our discussion, we both benefited from this project in unforeseen ways. For example, Jain told me that he feels like he "gained a mentor" by participating in the research, and he could also see the ways our relationship improved my research project. Our conversation highlights the value of relational approaches to longitudinal research as well as a need to continue discussing the ongoing negotiations of identity and authority in research relations.

Building Trust

According to Jain, the initial impression of me as a representative of the school was challenged at one of our first meetings. During the summer between high school graduation and the start of the college semester, I reached out to each study participant by text message and email to check in and to schedule a meeting if they were still interested in participating in the project. Jain was the first to respond to my messages. We met at a coffee shop near his high school—neither of us had been there before—and had a wide-ranging conversation over lunch. We talked about the upcoming semester, of course, but also his high school graduation, our families, our cars, and the upcoming 2016 presidential election, which would be his first voting opportunity. This conversation was not recorded or included in the analyzed data about Jain's writing experiences, but Jain told me later it was important for his participation in the project. He said the café environment "made it more personal" and helped him see that I was "interested" and "trustworthy." Because our conversation was not just about the research or about his writing, Jain said he saw me taking time to learn about his family and his values.

This conversation, and the many that took place before and after recorded interviews, benefited our relationship and the research project. From my researcher perspective, the project assumed a greater depth and more personalized understanding, inching closer to the emic perspective sought in ethnographically oriented research.[4] Jain seemed to recognize this, suggesting that this initial meeting and our follow-up conversations about his family and extracurricular life helped me understand "where [he was] coming from and . . . how it shaped [him] as a student." For example, Jain told me many times about his desire to make his mother proud and to serve as a positive example for his younger siblings. This understanding became central to a discussion of his writing opportunities and engagement (or lack thereof) in general education courses. I write about how Jain seemed motivated by *ganas*, which Nate Easley, Margarita Bianco, and Nancy Leech (2012, 169) describe as "a deeply held desire to achieve academically fueled by parental struggle and sacrifice" that drives the success of many immigrant and first-generation Latinx students. Importantly, the motivation associated with *ganas* draws not only from a student's recognition of parental struggle and respect and familial history and legacy but also from a social consciousness that aims to break the cycle of poverty and contribute back to their community (169–74). I wrote about how Jain told me he was interested in one of his classes because he could use the new knowledge to teach his younger brother or he could take on the role of an "activist" to teach his community. This interest in contributing to his family and community existed in tension with a teacher-centered instructional mode that valued correctness in school-based writing. In this case, our relational understanding was essential to making meaning of the data.

Member Checking as Relational Practice

Jain told me that in-process sharing and data exploration were also helpful for building trust because they gave him insight into my process and goals. For example, before or after our scheduled interviews, I would often share an excerpt of a new draft or an analysis of one of our interviews. In our retrospective interview, Jain said, "You were careful and you were discreet about what you were exposing. I saw that, and that's why it made me trust you. And then you would always ask me, like, 'Is this okay if I put this on the paper? Is it okay if I write this about you?' Or, like, 'Read this. Does this sound like you? Like I'm portraying the correct way?' and stuff. So I think it was just that control of what exactly you were writing about me and stuff, you know?" Jain's sense of "control" is important for further consideration of validity and reciprocity. I remember one time when I shared with Jain a brief excerpt focusing on his family history. Jain read it and asked, "Who's going to read this?" While he did not ask me not to share, his question was clearly a note of caution to me, and I realized I was in danger of constructing exactly the kind of colonizing project I was trying to resist. After our conversation I removed the anecdote in question, and Jain's simple question continues to guide my writing.

Transparency as Reciprocity

In addition to sharing writing, I also attempted to create a more dialogic interview environment in which I shared my views and goals with Jain as the project evolved. As Django Paris (2011) proposes, humanizing research means creating more humane interactions throughout the process. Rather than the scripted, detached interviewing posture, he suggests that the researcher should be willing to share their own experiences and opinions. Paris acknowledges the potential for bias that may come with sharing personal views but adds that "it is equally true that participants might not say something because we do not, because they do not know whom they are sharing with" (144). A truly decentered, dialogic approach to qualitative research requires relationality and vulnerability.

With humanizing research approaches in mind, I shared my opinions with Jain in real time. Soon after talking with him about a poor grade he received on a writing task, Jain sent me a message after his next graded project that said only "I give up." I called immediately and told him why I was angry. The following is an excerpt from my research notes: "I told him there are different ways of reading student writing: one way is trying to learn from the student, the other is to look for what they're doing wrong. Obviously, this teacher is in the latter camp. He said that he understands, and we can only do what we can do. *One of the things he said we can do is make my research 'really good.'*"

Both Jain and I recognized this conversation as a turning point. In our retrospective interview, Jain told me this conversation was when he "saw how important this [research] was. I saw the importance of how it could impact, in a good way, the education system or English classes." When I shared my reaction to his experiences, Jain saw me a little bit more for who I am and what I believe in, and he came to see the ways this research could potentially help others.

Jain told me he wished I would have shared more with him like this, and sooner. He told me he worried that he wasn't "contributing much" to the study, but after this discussion about his grade, that feeling changed. Jain explained, "It was, like, this is what Brad is trying to change, you know? That's why my participation is so important." While member checking practices such as sharing in-process writing are commonly advocated as an ethical research practice, our discussions about work in progress also seemed to help in relationship building. As Jain wrote in a reflection, "We have created a trust bond that is hard to obtain from a tutor or an adviser that meets with hundreds or thousands of students." The openness and vulnerability needed to form this "trust bond" indicate that further discussion is needed about the negotiation of researcher-participant relationships and identities. "Participant-observer" may not capture the storying work of a humanizing researcher, just as "participant" seems inadequate to capture research relationships. How might we continue to acknowledge and value the relationality and storying work of longitudinal research?

Humanizing Research as Process

My position as a graduate student also seemed to benefit this study. While Jain initially saw me as a school official, when he learned that I wasn't, we were able to speak frankly about his experiences with instructors and even about the university writing curriculum without worry that I might be offended or get someone else in "trouble." Jain also enjoyed hearing about my graduate student experience and about my advisers and what they thought about the research. While Jain and I were in different educational stages, we were each jumping through institutional hoops that we hoped would lead to new opportunities.

When I shared the news of my new position with Jain, he was thrilled. "You deserve it," he told me. Whether that's true and whether I can ever repay Jain for what he's offered me, I cannot say. But in moments of doubt, I am heartened by what he told me when we shared our exciting family news with each other. Jain said of our relationship: "It got to such a level that in the future I see our kids knowing each other, you know? That's how I see it. That's crazy." While I cannot control how this research project will be received, I can, as Paris (2011, 147) writes, "control how I represent the youth as I argue for change and understanding as a result of what I learned from them." I can also control how much I invest in maintaining the friendship we've built so far.

I still have work to do.

MICHAEL'S STORYING: RELATIONSHIPS IN LONGITUDINAL RESEARCH

I work with senior US Army cadets. Each semester, the 700 or so cadets at my university, the University of North Georgia (UNG), take military science classes and learn to write in the doctrinally defined US Army writing standard: "Effective Army writing is understood by the reader in a single rapid reading and is free of errors in substance, organization, style, and correctness" (United States Department of the Army, 2013). As a writing instructor, writing researcher, and writing program administrator, this standard took up a lot of my headspace. I wondered how it was taught by military science instructors, I wondered how it was understood by cadets, and I wondered how it was assessed internally and externally. I didn't have any clear answers, but I had many wonders. And when I taught an honors first-year writing course, just a year into my time at UNG, I began forming this wonder into a study because three of the twelve students in the class were cadets ready to begin a writing development journey with the US Army writing standard as one of their lodestars. I filed an IRB application, pitched my study to the cadets during the semester, and received informed consent at the end of the semester. I coauthored a piece with these three cadets as central to the data (Rifenburg and Forester 2018), and I eventually filed a modification to my IRB application and continued my research with just one cadet, Logan, as the focus. For three additional years, Logan and I talked in my office and walked the drill field and barracks. I observed his military science classes and listened to him talk me through his various writing assignments. He has since graduated and commissioned, now serving as a second lieutenant at Fort Stewart. The work Logan and I did together became a book-length project, and as Brad and I revise this chapter on a hot June day, I'm talking cover designs with my publisher. The book I put together is one story of many that describe the relationship Logan and I developed over four years. By storying my four-year research project, I feel I can foreground our relationship in ways that are not made possible by the logarithms of research Patel (2019) describes.

Logan and I would meet at least twice a semester in my office, an audio-recorder whirling in the background as we talked. In my office—Logan sitting with proper posture and me slumped in my chair—we would talk about his classes, his various writing assignments, and his weekend training activities with the Corps of Cadets. If the weather allowed, we would walk and talk. With my recorder turned off and us just talking, he would show me the barracks and explain weekly room inspections. During our interviews, he began bringing a thumb drive of his work.

He is a dependable organizer, with writing assignments dating back to seventh grade on his thumb drive. In total, he granted me access to over sixty artifacts he authored in middle or high school. One fictional piece from seventh grade was titled "A Soldier's Will" and signals Logan's early interest in the military. As a high school senior, he wrote a seven-page research paper on the Battle of Tripoli and a three-page fictional account of his experience at the Navy Junior Reserve Officers Training Corps. He was also a prolific writer outside of school and shared five pieces of self-sponsored fiction, some of which he authored in high school and one short story he authored during his fourth year at UNG. These written artifacts complemented the US Army writing assignments he, too, completed and shared: memorandums, operations-orders, PowerPoint presentations.

We talked about his curricular and extracurricular writing. As we grew in comfort with one another, he opened up about his hopes and goals. When reflecting on the close of his first year as a college student, he told me he was proud of his accomplishments. He rattled them off in quick succession: "I wanted to get contracted [i.e., sign paperwork to join the US Army upon graduation]. I wanted to start getting paid. I wanted to do well in the Corps and make sure people know I am not normal. I want to get somewhere. And really stay on top of things and not fail college and be a statistic." Our talk wasn't always about writing, but it was always about us and the stories we carry with us.

Through this desire to show people that he is "not normal" and not a "statistic," Logan accumulated a variety of experiences. He joined the swing dance club, founded the ballroom dance club, won an essay contest on censorship, and authored bylaws for his fraternity. He studied abroad in Italy and jumped out of airplanes during the summer at Fort Benning; he proposed to his girlfriend during the winter break of his senior year and received a distinguished military graduate commendation. He asked me to advise the ballroom dance club and then to advise the swing dance club, both jobs I accepted.

As our study rolled along, we saw each other less and less. He was busy with business management and military science classes; I was busy directing a writing program spread across five institutional campuses with seventy-plus instructors and more than 200 sections a semester. But we emailed and made time to talk in person. At times, Logan would email me, the ping in my mailbox serving as an aural reminder for me to turn attention again to this longitudinal study and to pull my eyes out of a teaching observation for just a moment. We both felt committed to what we began: a journey into the writing development of a cadet. When he invited me to his commissioning ceremony and introduced me to his mom and dad, his mom took my hand in hers and asked (with what I read to be happiness) about my book about her boy. I told her it was going well, and she thanked me for being a mentor.

That comment came more than two years ago, and I still puzzle over it. How research turns into partnership and how partnership may turn into mentorship and how mentorship is reciprocal: I brought a student writer into a four-year study of writing development and a student writer brought me into a four-year study of writing development. As Brad and I wrote in the opening section of this chapter, we conceptualize *story* as a verb that attends to researchers and participants who co-labored to construct knowledge. By storying the research I undertook with Logan, I can highlight how we co-labored to build knowledge and how the interactions of a tenured civilian professor and a traditional-age cadet college student led to new knowledge about writing and its role in an undergraduate military science curriculum. By storying my research, I am beginning to learn how the research design and research data and research findings are attendant to the here and now of when and where and why I designed my study and with whom I worked during my study. By storying my research, I am beginning to learn about Logan and how the relationship we built and sustained shaped the words that eventually will make their way to the printed pages of my book and the way the findings will continually shape and re-shape the way I understand writers and writing.

In her immersive study of emergency medical services workplace writing, technical communication scholar Elizabeth L. Angeli (2019, 2) points out that published scholarship tends to start with a literature review. However, she writes, "The literature is often not where research projects begin. They begin with people—and these people have stories." My study began with the people in the honors first-year writing classroom and ended with a handshake and a grateful comment. Logan and I still email. And we still tell each other stories about writing, work, and life. By storying this longitudinal research, I highlight for myself (and readers) how the relationship Logan and I built helped sustain, challenge, and drive forward this research in ways I can now see and ways I may never see.

I still have work to do.

STORYING LONGITUDINAL STUDIES OF STUDENT WRITERS: TENSIONS AND OPPORTUNITIES

We ended each of our narratives with our commitment to more work. We address some of this future work here at the close. In our narratives, we attempted to story our research, to explore our emerging projects as ongoing action, and to make visible some of the tensions that surfaced in our longitudinal research with undergraduate student writers. The challenges of unequal power dynamics, reciprocity, and representation are central to our thinking and writing here, and we are left with more questions than answers. This is okay. Kelly Limes-Taylor Henderson and Jennifer Esposito (2019, 886) ask qualitative researchers to bring an "ethic of humility" to our projects and to position ourselves as learners of rather than authorities on our topics. This approach might change the ways we interact with research participants. As learners and storying researchers, we want to be open and sensitive to the challenges we've highlighted thus far. In the spirit of humility and with the knowledge that we will inevitably leave things out and get things wrong, we conclude with observations, realizations, and questions that have emerged for us in this reflective process.

First, operating from an inquiry stance can *open opportunities to negotiate the inevitable power imbalances of a faculty member researching with/on/for a student.* We recognize that our positions within the academy that validate our research are the same positions that grant us authority in the eyes of students and community members. Once a student writer agrees to participate in a project, how much will they or can they really question or push back against our methods or analysis? We suggest that a sensitive approach to the researcher-participant relationship based on trust and openness can shift these dynamics. In writing this chapter, Brad was struck anew by the courage it took for Jain to question Brad's writing early in their research relationship, and how sharing that writing and being willing to change it based on Jain's feedback deepened their relationship and the possibilities for the project. While Logan agreed to all of Michael's interview and observation requests and never pushed back against any of the tentative findings Michael offered, Logan chose not to share letters he wrote to his then-girlfriend when he was at the US Army Advanced Camp in Fort Knox. Without Michael asking to see the letters, Logan said they were "only between me and her." In addition, after five years of allowing Michael to use his real name, Logan asked Michael to refer to him with a pseudonym, which Michael does here.

The ongoing negotiation of the researcher-participant relationship we discuss here requires an openness that can position researchers in the valuable role of learner. As Henderson and Esposito (2019, 887) write, "If we base our careers on the idea that there are always new things to learn in our field . . . our knowledge of [a] thing is not truly comprehensive or authoritative, even if we and others think it is." This recognition of our own unknowing, they suggest, can free researchers from claims to expertise, at least in some spaces. Instead, we might recognize longitudinal writing research as a mutual learning experience. Jain seemed to recognize this opportunity when he presented Brad with questions in their retrospective interview. He asked, "What have you learned from this study?" and "Is there anything you didn't expect to gain from this study but you actually did?" among other questions. These questions explicitly positioned Brad as a learner and, for the moment, shifted the researcher-participant dynamic.

Making our learning explicit—along with all we *don't* know—seems necessary, even if difficult to negotiate. But *how can longitudinal writing researchers present our work in all of its uncertainty*? Michael's book is recently published and Brad's research will find an audience shortly (he hopes), and we presume that these projects will be perused by interested readers looking for findings or insightful discussion about topics or concepts that mean something to them. While certainly some methodologically inclined readers will focus on the discussion of methods, regardless of how many times we qualify our claims to certitude, the imprint of an academic press will lead many to see the work as final. Moreover, we hope to reach a range of stakeholders both within and outside academia, many of whom will expect clear results and linear narratives. As such, we recognize the tensions inherent in publishing.

In *Fracturing Opportunity*, education researcher R. Evely Gildersleeve (2010) offers a critically self-reflective appendix that describes some of the methodological tensions in his longitudinal study of college-going literacies among migrant youth. Gildersleeve writes specifically about his own blind spots and shares a story about taking some students out for dinner to celebrate their high school graduation, only to be reminded later that restaurant-going culture in this region was a white middle-class activity and the students were not comfortable, even if they said they had a good time. "I felt like an idiot," Gildersleeve writes, directly (215). He then shares a conversation with one of the participants, Jesus, who laughed about it with him later as Gildersleeve recognized his insensitivity aloud. To us, this follow-up is as important as the initial story. We're struck by the vulnerability Gildersleeve exposes in the appendix and the fact that this description of the messiness of his research—the storying—supports other assertions made in the text. For example, earlier in the book Gildersleeve explains that relationality was key to opening up avenues of conversation that may not have been there otherwise: "Because students knew me, knew what I was about, knew what I was hoping to achieve with this project, I could freely and directly ask questions that other researchers might need to 'cloak' or mediate in a vernacular that lost some of the deeper conceptual meaning" (52). By storying the research and taking on an inquiry stance, Gildersleeve is renegotiating the terms of the researcher-participant relationship and allowing himself to be seen as a learner.

At the same time, *we recognize the unpredictability of both the research process and the relational aspects of longitudinal research.* In both of our research projects, the student writers' interest in the projects seemed to facilitate their participation and perhaps opened up these opportunities for methodological experimentation. A student writer less interested or invested in their own writing process may not have been as open to ongoing data analysis as was Logan. Similarly, Jain was questioning educational equity before the project began; when he came to see Brad's research along these lines, his investment in the research and his investment in Brad as a friend and researcher seemed to deepen. Due to their individual interest and the relationships built with Michael and Brad, these student writers may have benefited in ways we could not have predicted when completing an IRB application. For example, they explored their writing with experienced teachers and saw their own literacies and literate development in affirmative ways. As Jain wrote in a reflection, he "enjoy[ed] the feeling of getting acknowledged for some advanced rhetorical move that I pulled subconsciously." This reflection seems to echo Christina Saidy's (2018) observation that student participation in intensive qualitative research projects might lead to a stronger connection to their studies or the institution or might help them gain a better understanding of academic writing in general.

Our respective positionalities at the time of the studies may have also benefited our relationships with Logan and Jain. For example, it's possible that Michael's civilian status and beard may have been a benefit for his work with Logan, allowing Logan to talk more freely about the US Army and the Corps of Cadets. But it may have been a challenge in other situations, such as when Michael observed military science classes and entered official Corps of Cadets spaces. And Brad's positionality as a graduate student may have allowed him to shed the "school official" label more readily than if he were faculty conducting the same research. All this is to say that much of the relative success of these projects was, in many ways, situational. Would some of the hidden benefits we've described necessarily be less likely with less invested student participants? In what ways can we or should we account for the self-selection that inevitably occurs?

The messiness we discuss in this chapter must be made more visible. Working through the tensions we've described has made us better researchers and teachers and has made the respective projects more valuable to us and, we hope, to the field. While we are certainly not the first to make this call, we would like to see more narratives of challenge and failure in writing studies scholarship that center on relationality, positionality, and reciprocity in longitudinal research. Where are the opportunities for such storying in longitudinal writing studies research? What might it look like for writing researchers to commit to storying? How can we value the messiness of longitudinal research while we acknowledge the audiences that request tidy narratives? We don't presume to answer these questions but to pose them as what may be answered by writers, researchers, and participants and answered for their (t)here and now. These questions come when we tell stories about people working with words. And they are questions that deserve our attention when we story longitudinal writing research.

NOTES

1. Thank you to Kevin Roozen for pointing us to this article.
2. An avid viewer of television procedurals when I met him in high school, Jain selected his pseudonym based on the character Patrick Jane on the television show *The Mentalist*. I have changed the spelling to ease potential confusion.
3. Suhanthie Motha's (2014) privileging of afternoon tea session transcripts to highlight community knowledge and Ryan Evely Gildersleeve's (2010) critically reflective appendix stand out to me as excellent examples of storying in education research.
4. Acknowledging the influence of feminist, critical, and postcolonial critiques of ethnography's claims to holistically understand a culture, I choose to use "ethnographically oriented" to describe writing research that adopts an emic perspective and attempts to take a more reflexive researcher stance (Paltridge, Starfield, and Tardy 2016).

REFERENCES

Angeli, Elizabeth L. 2019. *Rhetorical Work in Emergency Medical Services*. New York: Routledge.
Cushman, Ellen, and Teresa Guinsatao Monberg. 1998. "Re-centering Authority: Social Reflexivity and Re-positioning in Composition Research." In *Under Construction: Working at the Intersections of Composition Theory, Research, and Practice*, ed. Chris M. Anson and Christine Farris, 166–80. Logan: Utah State University Press.
Easley, Nate, Margarita Bianco, and Nancy Leech. 2012. "Ganas: A Qualitative Study Examining Mexican Heritage Students' Motivation to Succeed in Higher Education." *Journal of Hispanic Higher Education* 11 (2): 164–78.
Fishman, Jenn. 2012. "Longitudinal Writing Research in (and for) the Twenty-first Century." In *Writing Studies Research in Practice*, ed. Lee Nickoson and Mary P. Sheridan, 171–82. Carbondale: Southern Illinois University Press.

Gildersleeve, R. Evely. 2010. *Fracturing Opportunity: Mexican Migrant Students and College-Going Literacy.* New York: Peter Lang.

Limes-Taylor Henderson, Kelly, and Jennifer Esposito. 2019. "Using Others in the Nicest Way Possible: On Colonial and Academic Practice(s), and an Ethic of Humility." *Qualitative Inquiry* 25 (9–10): 876–89.

Motha, Suhanthie. 2014. *Race, Empire, and English Language Teaching: Creating Responsible and Ethical Anti-Racist Practice.* New York: Teachers College.

Paltridge, Brian, Sue Starfield, and Christine Tardy. 2016. *Ethnographic Perspectives on Academic Writing.* Oxford: Oxford University Press.

Paris, Django. 2011. "'A Friend Who Understand Fully': Notes on Humanizing Research in a Multiethnic Youth Community." *International Journal of Qualitative Studies in Education* 24 (2): 137–49.

Patel, Leigh. 2019. "Turning Away from Logarithms to Return to Story." *Research in the Teaching of English* 53 (3): 270–75.

Rifenburg, J. Michael. 2022. *Drilled to Write: Becoming a Cadet at a Senior Military College.* Logan: Utah State University Press.

Rifenburg, J. Michael, and Brian G. Forester. 2018. "First-Year Cadets' Conceptions of General Education Writing Instruction at a Senior Military College." *Teaching & Learning Inquiry* 6 (1): 52–66.

Saidy, Christina. 2018. "Inez in Transition: Using Case Study to Explore the Experiences of Underrepresented Students in First-Year Composition." *WPA: Writing Program Administration* 41 (2): 17–34.

Stornaiuolo, Amy, Gerald Campano, and Ebony Elizabeth Thomas. 2019. "Editor's Introduction: Toward Methodological Pluralism: The Geopolitics of Knowing." *Research in the Teaching of English* 53 (3): 193–96.

Stornaiuolo, Amy, Anna Smith, and Nathan Phillips. 2017. "Developing a Transliteracies Framework for a Connected World." *Journal of Literacy Research* 49 (1): 68–91.

United States Department of the Army. 2013. "Army Regulation 25-50 Preparing and Managing Correspondence." https://armypubs.army.mil/epubs/DR_pubs/DR_a/pdf/web/r25_50.pdf.

2
WEAVING REFLEXIVITY, RELATIONALITY, AND TIME IN A DECADE-LONG STUDY OF WRITING DEVELOPMENT AND LEARNING TRANSFER

Dana Lynn Driscoll

I began writing this piece a year ago, when I submitted a proposal to this edited collection. No, that's not entirely accurate. I've been writing this piece in my mind for the last ten years, as I collected data from student writers in an effort to understand long-term writing development and writing transfer. No, I have to go further back. Perhaps I began writing this chapter at my dissertation defense. Linda Bergmann, my dissertation director, offered me an expectant smile as she asked, "What research will you do next, Dana?" My answer was to design a longitudinal follow-up. No, not quite. Three years earlier, I remember discussing in my doctoral research methods class with Pat Sullivan how the field has a challenge with "time" in that most studies didn't offer long-term outcomes . . . I'm getting close. A year and a half before that, while completing my masters at SUNY Stony Brook, I was helping Anne Beaufort (2007) develop and test the curriculum for *College Writing and Beyond*. She was telling me stories about her own longitudinal work and her relationship with time. All three of these mentors stressed not only how important time was to understanding writing and writers but also how time substantially shaped them as scholars and people.

These moments and relationships contributed to my professional development as a researcher and to the story I want to tell about a longitudinal study of writing development and writing transfer. This research, at present, includes 272 writing samples and 97 interviews, collected over 10 years. As I reflect on this work, I recognize a set of interwoven relationships that create a larger tapestry. One major thread is my relationship with my participants and my desire to honor their

https://doi.org/10.7330/9781646424337.c002

stories and their commitment to my study. A second thread is my relationship with myself (of the past, present, and future) as a professional and as a human being. Closely related to this thread is my relationship with our field and my investment in building our understanding of writing development to create a more just world. Interwoven are the professional realities of the work I do and the ways I must perform in relation to them (e.g., tenure clocks, program expectations, publishing demands). Running through all of this are my relationships with the mentors who shaped me and whose work I seek to honor and extend with my own graduate students.

STORIES LOST, STORIES FOUND: RELATIONSHIP BUILDING AND HONORING THE ANCESTORS

I remember my first-year interview with Rebecca. An international relations major, she was engaged, hopeful, and ready to travel the world. When I asked her about career goals, she said with a big smile, "I love to travel and would love to be, like, kind of a liaison, like, discuss things, like, in France, if they needed somebody to translate things; I would love to do that and just kind of be, like, the communicator between English and French." Unfortunately, this dream was never realized. Three months after our first interview, a tragic car crash cut Rebecca's life short. I remember receiving the boilerplate email from our university administration announcing her passing. Sitting in my office in shock, I listened to her interview once again and meditated on the power qualitative research offers us, a chance to document not only someone's story but also their life while they were living it.

Rebecca was one of eighteen students I was following to learn about writing development and learning transfer from first-year writing to disciplinary writing. In publications, when I've written about the loss of Rebecca from the study, it has only ever been represented in a sentence in the methods, such as this from a recent publication: "Two students' schedules prevented them from finding time for interviews, which left eighteen participants for the first year of the study. Attrition and loss of life further reduced the participants to thirteen for the remainder of the study" (Driscoll and Jin 2018, 5). This statement doesn't represent the story *behind* the method, the story of a person who had dreams that were never realized. It also doesn't say anything about how that event shaped my other relationships with students, mentors, and participants. There are three other "unfinished" stories in those same two sentences, the three students who did not return to campus for a second year. Even though I tried to track those students beyond the university, I was not successful. These are stories that will never be told, experiences never written.

While I originally designed my study to follow students for two years as a follow-up to my dissertation, it was the tragic silencing of Rebecca's story that motivated me to persist with a longer project and invited me to reflect upon the intersection of time, relationships, and reflexivity. I became committed to the study not only as an academic pursuit but also as a human one. That is, the study was a way to honor—and give voice to—the complex challenges my student participants faced over time, the experiences they shared with me, and the voices I had already lost. This changed my orientation toward my participants, making them more than "just participants" in "just another study." And so, I followed my remaining thirteen students as they completed their first-year writing courses and moved into disciplinary writing, internships, other universities, off-campus workplaces, professional careers, new jobs in new states, graduate school, medical school, and much more. As I write, I am at the ten-year mark, still following two final participants as they navigate medical school residency and dissertation writing. I followed the other eleven participants one year past graduation into successful careers in a wide range of professions, often six to eight years in total.

A question my own graduate students ask in my doctoral methods courses is how to keep participants enrolled over such a long period of time—and I always respond that the key is relationships. It becomes too easy for participants to be lost, to fall through the cracks of life, especially if you are only talking to them once or twice a year. Keeping my participants wasn't about the twenty dollars per interview I was able to offer; rather, it was about the relationships built through the interviews themselves. After the lessons I learned in the first year of my study, I always had multiple points of contact, including a phone number for texting and an off-campus email address. Even though I was interviewing participants once or twice a year, I would make sure to touch base with them each semester to talk about when our next interview would be, see how things were going, and perhaps exchange a few email or text messages. Sometimes, they had a writing dilemma, and we could talk through it, even schedule an extra interview. On a few occasions, they also sought me out for advice: a challenge with an adviser or scheduling, questions about the writing center, or career advice. Some of them came to see me as a trusted person in their lives who was invested in their success. It was building a relationship with them that encouraged my participants to keep coming back.

Another question one of my graduate students asked recently was: "would these deep personal connections make me seem less 'objective' or keep me from accurately representing my participants and their stories?" The answer lies, in part, in my theoretical orientation. While a traditional positivist approach might privilege objectivity and suggest I shouldn't get so close, interpretivist or feminist approaches stress connection building and encourage closeness. Many feminist qualitative methods, including those outlined by Linda Thompson (1992), stress the fact that there is no such thing as "truth" or "objectivity" in longitudinal work. Rather, Thompson argues that "a separation between researcher and researched does not ensure objectivity; a closer connection between the two may reconcile objectivity and subjectivity" (9). The authoritative, objective researcher has been replaced with what Shelia Henderson and colleagues (2012, 27) describe as a "historically positioned, locally situated and a very human observer . . . at the heart of qualitative writing today is strong reflexivity and recognition of the responsibility of the researcher as a critical part of the research process, and [recognition] that we write from particular positions at specific times." These approaches stress stronger connections between researchers and participants as critical for building shared understanding and knowledge—and certainly, over the years, listening to students' stories, I would agree. In particular, the phrase Henderson and her colleagues use, "very human observer," resonates for me because I think there is great value in being "very human" when establishing and maintaining research relationships and in mourning a loss.

Further, these changing relationships, reflections, and time have also affected the way I interview. My final two participants are more than just students who signed a consent form. I have been part of their educational journeys from the beginning of their college careers a decade ago, just as they have been part of my own—and literally, their stories have helped me in a multitude of ways. I have asked them hundreds of questions; at this point, they know what I'd like to talk about, anticipate what I might be interested in, and come to our interviews ready with writing samples and stories. They want to know about the results, they want me to share articles about the study with them, and they want to provide me with feedback before publication. While I came to my first three years of interviews with a fairly rigid set of questions, those questions had relaxed quite a bit by Year Six. Now, I don't even use a pre-set script. Instead, I draw questions entirely from our previous interviews, the participants' current experience, and the natural flow of conversation. I cannot imagine having done this style of interviewing in early years of the study, due to both the students' lack of maturity and my inexperience as a researcher. But now, it seems like a natural way to proceed that honors my participants and the stories they wish to share.

Another piece of this time-reflexivity-relationship triad is also connected with loss. I'm very aware of my own academic ancestors—my mentors—and I work to honor their voices, words, and legacy by continuing this work. In particular, I feel the weight of Linda Bergmann's unexpected and tragically early passing. The last time I saw her, about six months before she passed, I was several years into my data collection; we had a long conversation about learning transfer research, longitudinal work, and what the future held for the field. I remember how animated she was in talking about the questions and new research she wanted to pursue. After her passing, I worked some of the questions she was most interested in into my own study. What is remembered lives on. This relationship, perhaps more than any external motivator such as promotion or tenure, is part of what continues to encourage me to reflect and to persist as a longitudinal researcher and to honor these stories. Part of honoring my own ancestors has also encouraged me to establish strong mentoring relationships with my own graduate students, as I'll share later in this chapter.

THE ONLY CERTAINTY IS CHANGE: PARTICIPANTS, RESEARCHERS, AND RELATIONSHIPS

Year One: Karen is a freshman undecided major, considering going into business or veterinary science. She is quiet, doesn't make much eye contact, and indicates that she's not sure why she's at college. I ask about "good writing" and Karen's definition of good writing. Karen is uncertain, so I rephrase the question.

> DANA: Could you tell me, like, what makes a good paper? Would that be a better question?
>
> KAREN: Yeah. Like, proper English, talking correctly, not using, like, slang, it's understandable, formatted correctly, talking at your, like, comprehension level, talking as you are instead of, like, being a freshman in college and talking like I'm in 9th grade [pauses]. So everything will just probably [be] more [pauses] more professional, more knowledgeable.

Year Three: Karen has chosen business as her major and is working in the dorms as a residence hall assistant. She is passionate about her work in residence life, and it starts to shape her identity as both a student and a writer.

> DANA: What do you think . . . good writing is, like, how would you define it?

KAREN: Like, the audience can clearly understand what the point [is that] you are trying to get across . . . Kind of like what my 382 [business writing class] was, everything that she did, like, between the memos, between the emails and the letters and everything that we need to do in a business world.

Year Six: Karen is in graduate school studying student affairs after being a successful residence hall assistant director. Karen is engaged and excited about the work she is doing and her growing professionalism.

DANA: How do you define good writing?

KAREN: I feel it is engaging . . . It is fun to read. But then now, when you think about it and you look at textbooks, apparently they have [to have] good writing to get published, correct? And sometimes, those are not fun and engaging . . . I feel like it depends on the type of writing. For studies and theories and everything, obviously good writing is based off of your experiment and everything that you do and showing the right information and following along and there's a point to it . . . I think that the writing styles will be different from business and student affairs. Because now that I'm looking more into student affairs, yes, you have to make sure you are writing the correct terms and what-not, but it's all based off of studies. And so is business. It's based off of studies and reports and things that are more current in business, I feel. Whereas in student affairs, it's more like all of our theories are based off the past.

In the above segments, we see Karen's growing professionalism as she moves from an uncertain college freshman to a graduate student studying residence life reflected in the way she thinks about "good writing"—these experiences and identities shape her writing development. In later years, Karen doesn't even relate to or remember what she had felt so strongly about previously (like her strong distaste for general education courses, including her writing courses [Driscoll 2014]).

This example shows the power of time: the temporal reality of longitudinal research makes each interview so critical, particularly if you want to compare a single concept or question over time. With each interview, I feel a pressing need to gather as much information as I can in the moment. The next time I speak with a participant, they might be in a very different space in their lives—physically, mentally, educationally, or professionally. Sometimes, participants wouldn't remember an earlier incident that had been so important to them a year or two before. Other times, I would bring a participant's earlier answers to an interview and ask them to reflect, and they would have a hard time believing they had ever thought that way.

As a longitudinal researcher, change is the constant you are both working to represent and, in some cases, pushing against. I have come to understand that regardless of the study's focus, the central variable I am exploring is change. In their longitudinal study of cancer patients, Lynn Calman, Lisa Brunton, and Alex Molassiotis (2013, 7) had similar conclusions: "Issues that seem very important at one time point may change with the perspective of time and processes may change the way experiences are viewed." Thus, each data collection moment in a longitudinal study is central to representing and documenting who that participant is in that moment, for that moment will never come again. I've had many specific research questions over the years, and largely, I've abandoned them. I do still keep to my broad theme of studying writing transfer and long-term writing development but have learned that I need to explore these concepts in a much more flowing and dynamic way to best represent a dataset of this length and a central variable of change.

With each interview I completed, the participants grew more confident and comfortable with me, our rapport deepened, and I became more committed to their stories. The first two years, Karen was very difficult to interview: she was disengaged and offered very short responses, and it was hard to get her to elaborate. She was simply there for the twenty dollars and told me so directly. But by the third year, we had developed rapport. Her answers were longer and more detailed, she offered more eye contact, and we had begun to develop a genuine connection. I could ask the Karen I had known for six years questions she never would have answered her first or second year in the study because I had a deep connection with her—it was a combination of relationship and time that helped us grow together.

One of the questions I struggle with is this: is Karen in the above segments growing in her understanding of writing, adding elements of audience (Year Three) and genre awareness (Year Six), as I would be initially led to report? Or is it that she's more comfortable and willing to talk with me in ways she wasn't as a freshman? Or is it that I asked her the same question for six years, and she's had more time than an average student by Year Six to consider it, that my question itself may have shaped her over time? How do I represent that complexity of time and relationship? The nuance of this representation makes it difficult to know—and my suspicion is that it is a combination of all three and perhaps of more possibilities that I haven't yet considered. There are things I will never know about Karen. Part of it is my own limitation as a researcher. When I reread her interviews years later, I think of all of the questions I should have asked. On the other hand, because I have limited contact with her, I may never know the underlying motivations that encouraged her change over time and to make her critical move into the profession of student affairs. Sometimes I feel like I am looking into the window of a student's life; there are many rooms, but I can only ever see the one the student has allowed me to look into or maybe part of another adjacent room. Thus, longitudinal research is complex in part because I can never fully understand what I'm trying to study. While asking good questions can lead me to deeper insights, it can never fully resolve this challenge.

Change happens not only for my participants in the study but also for me. I can see change reflected in my own development as a researcher and an interviewer. Even in my first interview question above, which I asked in three parts in Year One (Does good writing exist? What is good writing? What makes a good paper?), I can see myself as a novice interviewer struggling to get the right question at a deeper concept I hadn't yet quite articulated. When I look at my earlier interviews, at the questions I asked or didn't ask, I see an earlier version of myself, a slice of the Dana-who-was, the new assistant professor fresh out of graduate school working to get tenure and who valued quicker approaches to research as they led to the necessary articles for tenure and promotion. Now, these questions are read and analyzed by the Dana-who-is, a full professor twelve years into my career with a lot more experience and confidence. This is a person who teaches doctoral courses on research methods, directs dissertations, mentors many of her own graduate students, and directs a writing center. This Dana has grown to value a much more fluid and reflexive approach because she has the affordances to do so and because key experiences have led her to value reflexivity and "slow research" over other things. Someday, perhaps, these words and interviews may be revisited by the Dana-who-will-be, in yet a different place and time. Part of this is my own development as a researcher; doing almost 100 interviews over ten years changes you, certainly, and makes you a much more reflexive, adaptive, and skilled researcher.

Another thread of change and reflexivity in my research and interview questions has to do with the broader field's understanding from which my study was drawn. In my early interviews, taking place in 2011–13, I asked questions based on the field's limited understanding and exploration of a new and challenging concept—writing transfer, or students' ability to use or adapt previous learning for new learning situations (Anson and Moore 2016). The field's understanding of the central concept under investigation has gone through considerable representational change and challenge in the years of my study. Through the stories of my students and the research of many others, the field has a much richer understanding and nuance of the concept of transfer; thus, the focus and conversations must change. Some of the questions I asked in my study are no longer relevant, appropriate, or wise; they have been debated and discarded or reframed in new ways. You can't expect that the field will sit idly by while you collect so much data—but it does make it more challenging to find your own footing in this ever-shifting landscape.

Thus, I can trace the interplay of change in terms of participants and relationships as well as my growing expertise as a researcher and through the shifting scholarly conversations in which I participate. Longitudinal research encourages this multiplicity and complexity in ways other research practices, with much shorter durations, simply cannot. A shorter study, collected over a few weeks or a single semester, is a slice-in-time: of your participants' lives, of your life as a scholar, a response to a point in time in the field's knowledge. But a longitudinal study, particularly one that spans a decade, has to constantly adapt: each data collection moment forms part of a larger woven tapestry among your participants, you and your own experiences, and the larger conversations that inform your work. This puts you in a very unique, I dare say temporal, position. The only constant in this kind of work is change, and being able to understand that change, document it, and flow with it is critical.

While this is certainly an exciting place to be in, it is also a challenging one. Everything about a longitudinal study is in a continual process of change. The field won't stop while you are collecting years of data, and neither will the tenure clock. Likewise, your data collection is ongoing and, thus, always in a state of change. Rachel Thomson and Janet Holland (2003, 237) have noted the challenge of a lack of closure in data collection and the importance of "always provisional" analysis and results. That is, longitudinal work requires flexibility and attention to time. Thus, you find yourself adapting to change and ongoing conversations—and hoping this work will still have a voice, even as the field shifts and as you feel pressed to start to write about data you don't yet feel are complete—because when is a story ever complete? Is "completeness" a myth in such work? Probably, but I still feel the pressure of wanting "complete" data.

GRADUATE STUDENT COLLABORATION, DEEP MENTORING, AND RELATIONSHIPS IN PUBLICATION

I remember my first week in my new faculty position at Indiana University of Pennsylvania. My research assistant, then-second-year doctoral student Roger Powell, was sitting eagerly with me, ready to dig into the data I had brought with me. I said to him, "I have been looking at this material all summer. There's so much in it. I still don't know where to even start." And there was much embedded in that statement. I had delayed my analysis of my longitudinal data for a few reasons: other writing commitments and collaborations, feeling the data weren't yet "ready" due to their ongoing nature, and not having the space or time to do the kinds of exploratory work the data needed while I was in a publish-or-perish situation in my previous faculty position. After achieving tenure and promotion and then moving to a new job as an associate professor, I finally felt I had the space, time, and resources to tackle my then-five-year dataset. I didn't have to churn out publications. I had time just to "sit" with the data. And I had a research assistant eager to help.

As I expressed to Roger, I had done three months of initial coding of the undergraduate data in the dataset to try to understand the data in broad strokes, starting with Johnny Saldaña's (2003) analytic memo strategy and open coding. Despite these methodological supports, I emerged overwhelmed: there were so many stories emerging that I wanted to tell, and the magnitude of the interviews and writing samples was already more than a single researcher could reasonably handle (it was, as we joked together, "analysis paralysis"). Thus, over that first year, Roger and I began looking at various pieces of the data together, sometimes quite successfully (as with our publication in *Composition Forum* on the long-term impact of emotions on development and learning transfer [Driscoll and Powell 2016]) and sometimes unfruitfully, such as our long and frustrating attempts to understand, code, and track writing development through students' writing samples (a problem I have yet to solve). Roger's perspective provided that critical balancing force of seeing the data from a fresh perspective and helped me manage the growing enormity of them.

While I shared much about relationships among myself, my mentors, and my participants above, establishing relationships with my graduate students as coauthors is another critical part of that interwoven tapestry, and is important to this story for a few reasons. Over the years in which I had gotten to know my participants, I grew so close to the data that sometimes it was hard to step back from those data, and their perspectives were very useful. Calman, Brunton, and Molassiotis (2013, 8) articulate the importance of having "different perspectives . . . brought to bear on the analysis[,] making it richer and generating new insights," and inviting researchers who are not involved in the data collection process to participate in analysis in order to benefit from those multiple points of view. By inviting my graduate assistants into this dataset, we were able to negotiate between my close, connected perspective as the longitudinal researcher and their distant perspective as someone who had never met my participants and, thus, did not have the same kind of emotional investment. My graduate students also brought their own interests and expertise, which helped us shape investigations into the data that would be useful and relevant to them and offered me different foci through which to explore. While I could come at the data as one who had very close relationships with participants, Roger could offer a fresh and new perspective—see the data through his own experiences, expertise, and perspective. This "layering" of perspectives, then, offered me a critical stance I could not achieve on my own.

But there's another reason to invite my graduate students into this work, which is tied to my desire to continue Linda's legacy through mentoring students of my own. One of the effective ways I do this mentoring is through Peter Smagorinsky's (2008) collaborative coding and research apprenticeship for his own graduate students. Smagorinsky describes his collaborative coding process as sitting with a graduate student and coding most, if not all, of the material together, which results not only in deep conversations but also in 100 percent inter-coder agreement and a deeper awareness of how to form conclusions from data. Smagorinsky's method is very slow, methodical, and extremely effective. For many of the projects from this dataset, we used this method—meeting weekly for several hours during the regular term to discuss the data, refine our codes, code together, and talk about nuanced aspects of the data. We also used Google Docs to collaboratively write articles from the data, each of us taking parts of the writing, sharing, and commenting.

At this point, I've worked with five different research assistants over five years, and each collaboration has resulted not only in successful publications or pieces under review but also, for my research assistants, in literacy sponsorship, developing research trajectories, cultivating key data analysis and article writing skills, and growing their professional identities. Most important, it also offered them a new relationship with research: understanding and adapting one's relationship with data, writing with collaborators, and learning to hone in on a story in a much larger dataset. These collaborations often led to jumping-off points for their dissertation projects in terms of topics, methods, or analysis strategies. My graduate students' interests helped pave new ways to reflect, engage, and shape this larger project and "get into" the data in various ways so the most compelling stories were told. As graduate students listened to my participants' stories and worked with the data, they were able to help shape their own deepening understanding of key concepts. They helped me "re-see" the data—and we ended up chunking off the data in ways that were meaningful to them and that fit their own growing research interests. For example, Roger was interested in mindset theory, which he used for his dissertation (Powell 2018), and we recently published an article on two participants in graduate school using mindset theory in the *Journal of Response to Writing* (Powell and Driscoll 2021). Daewoo Jin (Driscoll and Jin 2018) was interested in epistemology, so we explored epistemological positions over time as they related to learning transfer; again, Daewoo recently completed his own dissertation study on student epistemology in first-year composition.

Thus, these collaborative opportunities did more than help tell stories from the data; they also shaped my doctoral students' trajectories, offering them valuable experience in working with large amounts of data and composing stories from those data. Collaborative analysis and writing of these results allowed me to offer professional research apprenticeships through publishing (as Diane Belcher [1994] describes) and mentoring. I want to stress that longitudinal research is a particularly good strategy for those who are interested in inviting students into their data: it is so rich and meaningful that there is much excitement and possibility.

Finally, I've told my students about my own mentors. I've shared with them the importance of our relationships not only with our data but also with each other. I teach them about honoring our academic ancestors through the work we do and how we continue to build on their work after they are gone.

WEAVING A TAPESTRY OF REPRESENTATION, RELATIONSHIPS, AND TIME

In developing these deep relationships with graduate students and participants, I am also able to model the challenge of bringing together so many different strands in terms of relationships with participants, data, perspectives, and the broader field. And so, in developing research projects from this dataset, my graduate students and I spend a good deal of time reading the interviews, sitting with the data, and thinking about possibilities. There is an art in how to take the step from the individual strands to a clear path forward in weaving a particular story. I find this is something I can't really teach in a methods class effectively but that I can certainly model one-on-one with these data.

Part of this is that I recognize that different stories have different values to readers, and part of telling a variety of stories is in managing your own relationships. Some stories aren't those that would lead to deep insights about writing that the field would find important; rather, they had personal meaning to me because of relationships I had forged with my participants. Other stories are clearly of interest to writing teachers, administrators, and researchers; and the impetus to share them is strong. When I read others' work, I often wonder if other researchers experienced these challenges, even in book-length manuscripts: What were Anne Beaufort's 2007 unwritten experiences in working so closely with Tim? What kinds of conversations and connections did Marilyn Sternglass (1997) have over her six years of data collection? How do they make these decisions? As Shelia Henderson and colleagues (2012, 28) note of their own longitudinal qualitative research, "There is so much to include and acknowledge, so much to condense and leave out. While chronological time, at one level, gives the telling of the narrative a structure, dates and time sequence cannot carry the weight of the story alone." There truly is so much to think about and consider with such a large and complex dataset. This requires, more than anything else, taking the space to be reflexive about your data—to understand them, work with them, and weave yourself in and out of the data in various ways.

Finding that path is relational: it is a combination of gut instincts; getting the pulse of the field through recent conversations, publications, and conferences; and drawing upon the motivation of personal interests and curiosity. There are thousands of stories in this dataset, and choosing the moments, the participants, and the stories that will resonate with broad audiences and representing them in a way that is appropriate is the difference between publication and rejection. It is the difference between a good publication that can help jumpstart a graduate student's career and a messy set of rejections and resubmissions. This "inviting in" work allows me to teach and model these deep methods where we dig in, hash through, and experience months of uncertainty and eventually share the story with the field.

As an example, one of Linda S. Bergmann and Janet Zepernick's (2007) original interview questions in their groundbreaking work on writing transfer was about framing writing transfer as a "box under the bed" where at the end of a course, students might metaphorically put knowledge under the bed to gather dust or to save for later use. As part of a weaving of many strands together, my student Daewoo and I began exploring that particular question over time to understand how this concept might get at underlying issues of epistemology—his core research interest. Everything came together in a stunning tapestry for our "Box under the Bed" article (Driscoll and Jin 2018): it continued Linda's work in a very direct way, it honored the path Daewoo wanted to travel, it contributed to our field's understanding of writing development and how learner epistemologies are shaped over time, and it helped me explore yet another piece of the larger dataset that was critical to my core research questions surrounding writing transfer.

THE NEVER-ENDING STORY

Perhaps the story I've told in this chapter should have a beginning, middle, and end. But my story as a researcher is far from over, and as I am still exploring the stories of my last two participants, I'm not sure I can offer such neat closure. One of my remaining two participants is deep in her dissertation research, and I plan to continue to follow her well into her career as an epidemiologist. My second remaining has just completed medical school and moved into residency, a process that takes three to five years to complete. And I have more eager graduate students who want an opportunity to study writing development, so I plan on continuing, in some form, what I've been doing my whole career: listening to my participants' stories, tracing their development over time, and figuring out how to best share these stories with the field. My graduate students will pick up their own strands, with some of them continuing to invest in similar questions and explore them as their careers take shape and others going off in other directions. I feel the support of my academic ancestors behind us, guiding us forward.

As a way of offering a conclusion to this chapter, however, I would invite readers interested in longitudinal research to reflect on some of the tensions, limitations, contradictions, and challenges present in the story I've just shared and how they may apply to work they are doing or are considering doing. Specifically, I think about these questions: How can I build a productive relationship with my participants over time? How do my material circumstances and limitations on time impact what I can collect, analyze, and write about? How can I effectively document changes in participants over time? How much time of my own career might I want to commit to this project? How might I build reciprocal mentoring relationships with student collaborators or assistants? How do I continue to honor my academic ancestors and those who have passed?

REFERENCES

Anson, Chris M., and Jessie L. Moore. 2016. *Critical Transitions: Writing and the Question of Transfer*. Fort Collins, CO: WAC Clearinghouse.

Beaufort, Anne. 2007. *College Writing and Beyond: A New Framework for University Writing Instruction*. Logan: Utah State University Press.

Belcher, Diane. 1994. "The Apprenticeship Approach to Advanced Academic Literacy: Graduate Students and Their Mentors." *English for Specific Purposes* 13 (1): 23–34.

Bergmann, Linda S., and Janet Zepernick. 2007. "Disciplinarity and Transfer: Students' Perceptions of Learning to Write." *WPA: Writing Program Administration* 31 (1–2): 124–49.

Calman, Lynn, Lisa Brunton, and Alex Molassiotis. 2013. "Developing Longitudinal Qualitative Designs: Lessons Learned and Recommendations for Health Services Research." *BMC Medical Research Methodology* 13: 1–14.

Driscoll, Dana Lynn. 2014. "Clashing Values: A Longitudinal Study of Student Beliefs of General Education, Vocationalism, and Transfer of Learning." *Teaching and Learning Inquiry* 2 (1): 21–37.

Driscoll, Dana Lynn, and Daewoo Jin. 2018. "The Box under the Bed: How Learner Epistemologies Shape Writing Transfer." *Across the Disciplines* 15 (4): 1–20.

Driscoll, Dana Lynn, and Roger Powell. 2016. "States, Traits, and Dispositions: The Impact of Emotion on Writing Development and Writing Transfer across College Courses and Beyond." *Composition Forum* 34. https://compositionforum.com/issue/34/states-traits.php.

Henderson, Shelia, Janet Holland, Sheena McGrellis, Sue Sharpe, and Rachel Thomson. 2012. "Storying Qualitative Longitudinal Research: Sequence, Voice and Motif." *Qualitative Research* 12 (1): 16–34.

Powell, Roger. 2018. "The Impact of Teacher and Student Mindsets on Responding to Student Writing in First-Year Composition." PhD dissertation, Indiana University of Pennsylvania, Indiana, PA.

Powell, Roger, and Dana Lynn Driscoll. 2021. "How Mindsets Shape Response and Learning Transfer: A Case of Two Graduate Writers." *Journal of Response to Writing* 6 (2): 42–68.

Saldaña, Johnny. 2003. *Longitudinal Qualitative Research: Analyzing Change through Time*. New York: Altamira.

Smagorinsky, Peter. 2008. "The Method Section as Conceptual Epicenter in Constructing Social Science Research Reports." *Written Communication* 25 (3): 389–411.

Sternglass, Marilyn. 1997. *A Time to Know Them: A Longitudinal Study of Writing and Learning at the College Level*. Mahwah, NJ: Erlbaum.

Thompson, Linda. 1992. "Feminist Methodology for Family Studies." *Journal of Marriage and the Family* 54 (1): 3–18.

Thomson, Rachel, and Janet Holland. 2003. "Hindsight, Foresight, and Insight: The Challenges of Longitudinal Qualitative Research." *International Journal of Social Research Methodology* 6 (3): 233–44.

3
FOLLOWING PARTICIPANTS AS LEADERS IN LONG RESEARCH

Lauren Rosenberg

After a few unsuccessful attempts to reach a former research participant, we connect by phone. I ask George[1] if he remembers me. It has been about four years since we have spoken. "No, I don't remember," he replies quickly. So I keep talking, reminding him of the research we did together, first in 2005 through 2006 when he participated in a qualitative study I conducted on the writing practices of adults who were acquiring literacy later in life. Of the four case studies that were the center of that research, George was the participant with whom I worked the longest, extending our research relationship over a period of more than four years after the first project during which we continued to discuss his writing and literacy experiences. At this point, we have been out of touch for another four years. I have finished the monograph that reported on the original study. George has left the adult learning center where he was a student for eight years. I am certain that he must recall our occasional informal conversations, structured interviews, and time spent poring over his writing samples. There is a pause, and then, "Oh, I think I remember now." His reticence reminds me that George is characteristically guarded and careful, reluctant to commit. I tell him about the book I have published, and he tells me he wants it. I ask him if he would like to get together so I can give him a copy, and he says, "Yeah, that would be fine." George suggests meeting at the library-based learning center where he was a student and I was a researcher. He is the only one of the four participants who has never invited me to his home, choosing instead the public space of the literacy center every time we have met.

George participated in my original research on the writing practices of older adult learners, a project that was designed as a dissertation study without the intent to become longitudinal. During that project, I attended the Read/Write/Now Adult Education Center in Springfield,

Massachusetts, weekly as a researcher and volunteer, and I formed relationships with students and teachers that I did not sever when the research period ended. Conveniently, my first university appointment was within commuting distance. I was awarded small research grants each year; these grants, combined with my geographic proximity, allowed me to continue meeting with people at the center to find out periodically what they were writing and studying and what was going on in their lives. As an early career researcher, it made sense for me to bite off small chunks of additional research each year as I worked toward publication and tenure. In this way, unintentionally, I maintained connections with students and teachers at the center, and through our ongoing interactions, my research became longitudinal.

Ten years after I began this research, my monograph was published (Rosenberg 2015). I had promised the participants that I would share findings with them, and I had promised myself that if I ever published a book, I would give them copies, fulfilling my obligation as an ethical feminist researcher and community literacy practitioner. Because the participants had been stigmatized as "illiterate" most of their lives and had only had the opportunity to become students later in life (three of the four were retired on disability, including George), it was deeply meaningful to me to give them a book that was about them, that featured their reading and writing experiences and their words. I was clear about my gesture as an expression of reciprocity and gratitude; however, I could not have predicted that my personal and moral objective would lead my research along a new pathway.

In a chapter on approaches to lifespan writing research, I describe the experience of connecting with former participants: "After the book came out, I contacted the participants to give them each a copy . . . Would the four people be as I remembered them? Would they want to speak with me? I deliberately visited without a recorder or prepared questions, without the premise of approaching them as 'research subjects'" (Rosenberg 2020, 98). My conversations with the participants during these *revisits* led to long studies of their writing lives. I could not have expected our informal discussions to go in this direction, but I have been open to (and fascinated by) the trajectory my research has taken since it has become participant-led (see Rosenberg 2018). The learners whose writing practices I study—unschooled adults who were raised in poverty and have become literate later in life—come from communities that are underrepresented in writing studies. They have been explored in terms of transfer of contexts and discourses but rarely in regard to their own motivations and ongoing pursuit of writing. For this reason, it has always mattered to me to build my research on the insights I gain from participants in each phase of our work together. As I explained in "Revisiting Participants after Publication":

> Participants' responses to the published text contain possibilities for expanding the way they continue to interpret their stories. We can challenge the conventions of research when we foreground the insights of participants as they continue to reflect on and analyze their experiences . . . I propose that we extend the research tradition by paying greater attention to the ways we are informed by the people we study. Researchers can learn from participants about how they value the published text and how it might potentially circulate within their networks in ways unknown to academic researchers. We can deepen our research and our understanding of the nature of writing partnerships by following pathways that are determined by participants' interests and life course . . . Thus, I advocate for . . . a kind of writing partnership rooted in ongoing interactions between writers and moments of collaboration that create possibilities for engagement. (Rosenberg 2020, 99–100)

By highlighting the continued interrelations with research participants, I want to show the organic way my research with adult literacy learners has become longitudinal. Our research relationships have transformed into more casual revisits across time and the changing conditions of our lives; with each conversation and check-in (by phone, on social media), the personal updates combine with research updates: tell me about your grandchildren. Tell me what you are writing. The surprises I find through ongoing, participant-led research occur because I haven't approached them with a fixed design. Instead, I am guided by participants' comments and the texts they select for our conversations during informal revisits. In this way, what I find emerges from the participants' interests and our ever-shifting researcher-researched relationship.

INTRODUCING THE IDEA OF RELATIONAL, PARTICIPANT-LED LONG RESEARCH

In an article on the combined writing trajectory of Chief and Shirley, an older married African American couple in which one partner has participated in my research for fifteen years and the other for about three years, I observed that "it is important to contextualize their activities among the overall interactions of daily life that involve maintaining the self, care for family and community, as well as nurturing intelligence" (Rosenberg 2018, 22). Understanding changes in participants' lives cannot be separated from studying their ongoing development as literate individuals. Looking at our dialogic relationship involves the cooperation of researcher and researched building on previous exchanges through new configurations of our words and current encounters.

Paul A. Prior (2018, para. 9, original emphasis) makes a similar observation about writing development occurring as part of the repertoire of ordinary life activities: "From a *trajectories-of-semiotic-becoming* perspective, learning happens not *in* domains but across the trajectories of a life. It may turn out that music is important to becoming a biologist, that home is the primary site of academic work, that laboratories are teeming with social relationships, that rational stories of the progressive acquisition of knowledge need not apply." Prior's description makes clear that "domains" of learning are inseparable from one another, that the environments and contexts in which we learn inform one another, and that we rarely (if ever) function in a single role. Our experiences and ways of forming knowledge are relational.

Similarly, Deborah Brandt (2018, 245) explains that "development comes to people through the roles they play or are expected to play at different times of life; the historical events to which they are exposed; and the reconfigured meanings and potentials that accumulate around these experiences." Drawing on life course scholarship in sociology, psychology, and other disciplines, Brandt defines development "in terms of changes that occur in relationships between people and their life worlds over time, changes that gather lasting consequence for the workings of those relationships going forward" (245).

I streamline Prior's and Brandt's ideas to focus on shifting researcher-participant relationships when the subject of that interaction is writing development. In this chapter, I take a lifespan development of writing approach—informed by a methodology of *revisiting* and insights from Mikhail M. Bakhtin (1986)—to suggest that qualitative studies of writing, when they become longitudinal, can change direction and purpose in ways that determine the trajectory of the study, its meaning, and its conclusions. One telling of a story is not sufficient. When we get to know participants as leaders, our research more honestly reflects their intentions, interests, and reinterpretations rather than the researcher's agenda.

For example, Shirley, the spouse of my longtime participant Chief, has become somewhat of a collaborator in my work because of the way she claims our research together as part of a larger relationship. Since Shirley became active on Facebook in the last couple of years, our roles merge as she sends photos of her family and posts on my wall. Our research relationship cannot function in isolation from the casual social connection of two women checking in about our lives. Here is an extract from one of Shirley's recent posts on Messenger that illustrates the mingling of personal and research relationships: "Chief is doing much better seems like he has a little more get up and go about himself of course I'm always pushing him to use his brain and not mine haha his group has a gospel program tonight and that is where he is I'm sure he is enjoying himself ok Lauren all is well let me know how your mothers surgery goes hugs and best wishes to you and family."

As much as I value the loosening of formal boundaries that can cause the research to be stiff or inauthentic, I am still an academic researcher cognizant of the conventions of my discipline. Therefore, I need to be aware of the ethics of ethnographic methods and human subjects research, including the ways disciplinary expectations confine that research. In addition, I have experienced pushback from some journal editors and peer reviewers who have criticized my work for not being driven by a formal protocol or set of methods. But I have to listen to participants first because they are showing me something new about how to be a longitudinal ethnographic researcher. They are guiding me in interpreting the research. Shirley has taught me to let go of my concern about doing it the expected way. To continue with our longitudinal research, we have to do it on her terms, which means centering the relationship within the overall context of our personal lives. If this calls into question the boundaries of the IRB, then so be it. This is the direction that Shirley leads the research.

Designing longitudinal studies was not a process I foresaw; however, I find that the qualitative literacy studies I have conducted, that I have assumed to be completed, have reopened when I reconnect with participants. What starts out as a routine follow-up conversation changes shape, leading to ongoing dialogue with participants. This is one of the features of longitudinal qualitative writing research that I find compelling, the way it is organic and changeable and that what is required of the researcher is the willingness to remain open to its possibilities, simply to notice as part of the research process. Following participants as they make decisions about the research can take our studies down new pathways that suggest greater possibilities for meaningful writing partnerships.

Lifespan studies, a nascent area of research that concentrates on the development of writers from "cradle to grave" (Bazerman et al. 2018), has given me a useful approach to look at the writing practices of older adult learners as part of a continuum that crosses disciplines and life periods. Guided by the principle that writers develop throughout their lives in predictable and unpredictable ways, I have been experimenting with new methodologies and methods, influenced by the interests and needs of participants (and my own shifting life circumstances). The Writing through the Lifespan Collaboration (Collaborative) defines "lifespan" as referring to "the entirety of a lifetime—both chronologically (i.e., cradle to grave) and across the many social spheres that writers participate in (the term 'lifewide' has been used to reference this). To orient something to the lifespan is to locate change within a lifelong and lifewide perspective, up to and including multiple lifespans (i.e., across generations)" (Dippre and Phillips 2020, 5–6). The Collaborative has conceptualized the notion of a lifespan extending latitudinally as well as longitudinally, suggesting that life changes, including the ways we perceive writing development, occur across multiple planes. Lifespan researcher Anna Smith (2020, 17–18, original emphasis) categorizes lifespan research according to three "ontological orientations": "Seeing writing development as a continual, dynamic, lifewide becoming, for instance, is an ontological perspective that orients the researcher to consider not just what is developing *in* a locale, piece of writing, or time, but *across* time, space, and materials." Notice the across-ness of these definitions or orientations to the idea of learning as always deepening in multiple contexts (Prior 2018). Smith's idea of looking across is rooted in Johnny Saldaña's (2003, 8) conscious choice to use words like "across" or "through" to describe movement in time. Saldaña emphasizes the value in studying activity from a "from-through" perspective instead of the commonly assumed "from-to" way of framing time, preferring "through, 'throughout,' or 'across time'" because these words "suggest more processual immersion throughout the course of longitudinal research" (8).

Although this chapter concentrates foremost on research interplay with participants, my scholarship is also a conversation between aspects of my research, particularly now as I look "lifewide" at my own research. One piece of my studies reflects on the others and leads to the next aspect of data collection. While participants direct the research to an extent, I try to follow as the academic writer who observes their directions, records them, reflects on the turns and stops, the intersections, the side roads and detours. I see my scholarship over the last few years as the products of these observations of dialogic exchange.

Therefore, in this chapter, I am interested in the idea that across long-term relationships, our research together becomes woven in with the life course of participants and the researcher. While these relationships are often unbalanced in terms of measurable effects—the researcher surely benefits professionally in ways that may be irrelevant, even unknown, to participants—something else of worth develops. The research relationship becomes part of our lives, a thread we pick up and put down as we check in to schedule a follow-up interview or write back to a holiday card or a message on social media.

INTERACTIVE ETHNOGRAPHY, BAKHTIN, AND PARTICIPANT-DIRECTED STUDIES

I wondered how best to illustrate my claim that participants were leading the inquiry. The years I had spent analyzing interview transcripts had shown me that there was something in the dialogic process wherein a close reading might reveal subtle shifts in lead, not only in who asked a question (typically me as the researcher) but in the participant's response as well. I was already accustomed to yielding the floor during interviews and while discussing writing samples with the participant-authors; my practice has been to "linger" with participants' words (Royster and Kirsch 2012, 146) and observe as their narratives of experience "wash over" me (Ratcliffe 2005, 28). My approach to data collection and analysis is informed by the feminist ethics promoted by Jacqueline Jones Royster, Gesa E. Kirsch, and Krista Ratcliffe—composition scholars whose principles for ethical communication can be applied to all of our scholarly practices, whether we are speaking together in real time or reflecting back on a previously collected text.

Initially, I looked toward interactional ethnography, a framework used in some educational studies of literacy, as a method that might offer insight into interpreting back-and-forth exchanges between researcher and researched. The research task, as interactional ethnographers Maria Lucia Castanheira, Teresa Crawford, Carol N. Dixon, and Judith L. Green (2001, 356–57, emphasis added) describe it, is to follow the words and actions of "members of particular groups": "the interactional ethnographer examines *what members count* as literacy, literate processes, literate actions, literate practices, and literate artifacts." I was drawn to this approach because it centers the participant as the primary knowledge producer whose perspectives guide the researcher. Put into practice, however, Castanheira and colleagues maintained what appeared to be traditional research methods in which a distant team of academics analyzes subjects' experiences and writing samples. "What members count as literacy" seemed to be the *idea* that members decide on the meanings and uses of literacy within their communities.

My misgivings about this version of interactive ethnography as an analytical model led me back to the classic work of Mikhail M. Bakhtin (1986), who Castanheira and coauthors (2001, 395) credit for offering them a means of explaining the "notion of the reflexive nature of speaker/hearer (reader/writer) relationships to frame our view of the dialogue of talk and action." I wanted to see whether Bakhtin's concept of the utterance as speech unit might inform longitudinal research interactions in which the researcher and researched continually shift in their positions as speaker and interlocutor. If the unit (the utterance) can be as large as a novel or as small as a phrase, it can also be as large as an interview transcript or recording or participant's writing sample. I wondered how Bakhtin's theory that one utterance leads into the next, into the next, forming a chain of linked thought expression, might help longitudinal writing researchers understand long-term research relationships in which projects continue, changing direction and re-shaping as researched and researcher negotiate them individually and together. Bakhtin's assertion that every genre, including everyday genres, has certain dialogical functions intrigued me as I considered how the researcher-researched relationship is established and advanced through moments of dialogue. I was also interested in how my interpretation of previously collected and analyzed texts (both spoken and written) would be different years later when I returned to them in light of more recent conversations with participants.

As an example of Bakhtin's (1986) theory put into practice, I turned to my longtime participant George, with whom I have had many informal discussions and formal recorded interviews. I wanted to do a close reading of the dialogic interchange between us to see how George sometimes determines the path of our conversation and whether his lead mediates my interpretation. In this section, I consider two interview extracts in which George teaches me about his motivations for becoming more literate and explains his perspective on how literacy functions as a social force. These extracts are texts I have studied previously for their content. Now, I consider them as examples that illustrate our research relationship, rooted in our history of discussing George's literacy experiences. I notice, as Bakhtin suggests, that "each utterance must be regarded primarily as a *response* to preceding utterances of the given sphere . . . Each utterance refutes, affirms, supplements, and relies on the others, presupposes them to be known, and somehow takes them into account" (91, original emphasis).

By reexamining George's and my interaction through a Bakhtinian lens, I reopen the research as I consider it retrospectively. The recursive process of looking back into past conversations allows me to gain new insights because the analysis is new. The current analysis helps me reflect on our research relationship and understand George as someone who continues to develop his relationship to literacy on the terms he chooses. Thus, I argue that an aspect of the longitudinal researcher-researched relationship is the value of reconsidering one's interpretations in another moment. While the utterances I consider reveal our dialogical pattern, they also demonstrate that George and I have related to one another through dialogue across a long period of time and know how to cue and respond to one another.

In an exchange with George, he expressed his view that education is sometimes withheld and that the educated person should not flaunt their literate ability; rather, a person with an education is obliged to help less-literate others. He brought up this theme in many of our discussions. As someone who has become more literate later in life, he takes responsibility to be aware of the situation of non-literate people.

> GEORGE: Everybody—just like I said before—everybody wasn't able to get an education. And because you got it, that don't mean you supposed to put somebody else down because you have it; you know what I mean? If anything, you do anything; you try to do something to help somebody else. You know, help somebody else. Pull them up, not try to, you know, push them down. You know?
>
> LAUREN: That's really interesting. There's something that I was reading. Um. I'm not going to describe too much. But where this person talks about, how in this country sometimes people use literacy—reading and writing—almost as a weapon. It's almost like—
>
> G: Mm hmm.
>
> L: —I think that's what you're talking about.
>
> G: Yep.
>
> L: Like, it's used to divide people—
>
> G: Mm hmm, yeah.
>
> L: —and to divide, like, haves and have-nots.
>
> G: Yeah.
>
> L: And to give some people power and take away power from other people. It sounds to, it sounds to me that that's what you're talking about.
>
> G: Yup. Yep.
>
> L: And some people get to have it [literacy], and some people get it taken away.
>
> G: Mm hmm. Yep.

When I listen to George's opening utterance, I expect to respond as an interlocutor who is in an interviewer's role. I hear George expressing views very similar to those articulated by J. Elspeth Stuckey (1991) and Paulo Freire (2001), two scholars who theorize about how literacy can be used as a weapon for social violence. I respond to George with words aimed to draw him out further, yet I deliberately temper my enthusiasm when I hear him offer an analysis of literacy education that aligns with professional theorists but is voiced by someone whose knowledge comes from his lived experience as an African American man who grew up on a sharecropper's farm in the Jim Crow South. I practice restraint as a move that encourages George to elaborate on his understanding of literacy as a power relation because I want to hear George theorize about how literacy is operating rather than intervene by suggesting that his position is one that is already known to academics. I respond by suggesting that literacy can be viewed as a "weapon," but I also limit my response by stating that "I'm not going to describe too much." I want the interpretation to come from George. I know he has been thinking about the politics of literacy education for much of his life, even though he wouldn't name it in those terms. Although I deliberately yield my words to his, I am still very much in control of the dialogue in my role as questioning researcher. Yet George is the storyteller who can decide to interpret my gesture of yielding as an invitation to reveal more from his perspective. Bakhtin (1986, 68) explains:

> The fact is that when the listener perceives and understands the meaning (the language meaning) of speech, he simultaneously takes an active, responsive attitude toward it. He either agrees or disagrees with it (completely or partially), augments it, applies it, prepares for its execution, and so on. And the listener adopts this responsive attitude for the entire duration of the process of listening and understanding, from the very beginning—sometimes literally from the speaker's first word. Any understanding of live speech, a live utterance, is inherently responsive, although the degree of this activity varies extremely. Any understanding is imbued with response and necessarily elicits it in one form or another: the listener becomes the speaker.

It is a matter of shifting roles, and through that movement, meaning is created in a collaboration of listener-speaker and speaker-listener. One yields and shifts in relation with the other. This collaboration occurs in the moment, and I believe it can also occur retrospectively when we interpret again. Knowledge making builds on the whole of what preceded it, including the conversations that preceded it, or what Bakhtin would call "a responsive action based on this understanding" (71).

As our exchange continues, George's utterances become short expressions of agreement: "Mm hmm . . . Yep . . . Mm hmm, yeah . . . Yup. Yep . . . Yep," in which he responds to my somewhat longer, continued interpretations of the initial back-and-forth. My comments are aimed at extending the critique, checking in with George to find out whether our views are aligned, and offering Stuckey (1991) for him to revise or resist. With each of these retrospective responses to George, he confirms my words. His words/sounds/phrases, all of them short affirmations, effectively communicate his alignment with me so that we become two speakers in agreement with each other. My longer utterances remind him of and repeat what George is certain he already knows. He demonstrates the rapport between us in this moment as speaker and listener move back and forth, giving one another a place to lead the speaking and responding. As collaborators in the conversation, we negotiate the flow of the dialogue and what it means.

In a second conversation on a related topic, the interaction is different. Together (though initiated by me), we revisit a comment George made in a previous interview, as I shape a new utterance that folds in a previously expressed one. In his response, George intervenes in this process, taking control of the conversation away from me as he holds forth. His interruption of my question shows his agreement as well as his excitement to pick up the idea I have introduced and steer the discussion in the direction he chooses as he reinterprets his own former words in a new moment. Because I am aware of his interruption as a gesture to show our rapport as equals in a conversation and also to teach me something, I choose to restrain my utterance so that George may extend his.

> LAUREN: When you say here, you say, "Education for everybody help to make a better world"—
>
> GEORGE: It does.
>
> L: Is that, is that sort of what you're thinking?
>
> G: Yup. You know, if everybody in the world have an education . . .
>
> L: Uh huh.
>
> G: . . . it'd be less crime. There'd be less people on welfare. There'd be less people in, in the shelter.
>
> L: Mm hmm.
>
> G: And this country would feel better.

The conversation proceeds with George elaborating on his views of the "person who got an education." He remarks on the educated person as someone who "thinks before they act" and "react." In this example, George speaks with the intention of establishing his views, expressing a common narrative of education creating a "better world," while I mostly utter "mm hmm" as a sound of agreement that doesn't break the flow of his talk. Here, the speaker has definite intentions for what he is going to say next. Bakhtin (1986, 77, original emphasis) calls this the speaker's "*speech plan* or *speech will*," observing that it "determines the entire utterance, its length and boundaries." George speaks until he has moved through his "plan," which he eventually concludes with "yeah, yeah, yeah," an indication that the utterance is complete and I can now initiate a shift in topic in response.

The interplay between speakers is built from our own words in combination with our interlocutors': "Our speech, that is, all our utterances (including creative works), is filled with others' words, varying degrees of otherness or varying degrees of 'our-own-ness,' varying degrees of awareness and detachment. These words of others carry with them their own expression, their own evaluative tone, which we assimilate, rework, and re-accentuate" (Bakhtin 1986, 89). I understand this process of construction as social and collaborative. What we know as researchers comes from the influence of the participants in relationship with us, not only through their choice to share information and experiences but also through the language that expresses their thinking, that both mingles and merges with our own. This exchange illustrates the speech dynamic between George and me. At the same time that it demonstrates our interaction as a sequence of linked utterances, those units of dialogue also reflect our familiarity with one another's cues, as well as our common understanding of the purpose of the dialogue—which is to provide interview data for my research.

Looking toward Bakhtin to guide my retrospective analysis of these exchanges with George helps me notice more precisely how relationship is developed in a dialogic dance in which participants shift and yield to one another because they want to connect in conversation together. We respond to one another's utterances through the expression of complex ideas ("if everybody in the world have an education . . . it'd be less crime. There'd be less people on welfare. There'd be less people in, in the shelter") as well as through sounds that remind us of our rapport ("Yup. Yep"). The easy flow of dialogue allows the research to advance also. Ultimately, this close reading of a bit of George's and my discussion demonstrates the way our words merge and separate as two participants moving through a project. The Bakhtinian analysis accentuates the rapport George and I already have because of our history of working together focused on developments in his literacy practices; that is, we can observe the cueing and yielding, suggesting and restraining as moves that help us recognize how we construct meaning. As longitudinal researchers, we can learn more about how we relate to participants by studying our dialogic negotiations, especially when we reconsider the dynamics manifested in previous conversations.

REVISITING: "I TRY TO READ A LITTLE SOMETHING EVERY DAY"

By the time George and I meet at the literacy center for our revisit, I have seen two other participants. I've established a routine that involves socializing about our lives over the last few years, then looking through the book together. I read aloud the acknowledgments that express my appreciation for the participants' contributions. I remind them of their pseudonyms (George cracks up when I tell him his name is George, a name he chose). Then I show them their major passages and read with them. I mark certain sections with sticky notes while we are together so they can locate their parts later on their own. I read a range of their comments from transcripts, my interpretation of their narratives, and a few interview exchanges; and I point them to examples of their writing. I show George that the book opens with him, and I read the first scene. He follows along with keen attention. As I read George's sections, he exclaims, "that's true" and "I sure did!" There is a lot of laughter. George especially likes the descriptions of himself in the classroom and his interplay with his classmate Chief.

As we look over passages together, he remarks, "It's good to review, even though it's in the past," referring to the research process as well as the experiences we discuss, even though "it was a long time ago." It has been ten years since our initial interviews. He is the only participant in my research to reflect about the time that has passed from research to publication to this moment and how the conversations remain relevant. George understands the act of reviewing; he makes his remark confidently because he has always reviewed events in his life orally. I have listened to him do so many times during our interviews and informal conversations. His comments remind me how important those actions are for him. Stepping back to review and reflect gives him authority and control over his own experiences. I am also reminded of the value George places on reflection. He is cautious and analytical. He likes to distance situations from himself so he can contemplate them. When George remarks on the importance of reviewing and reflecting and when I ponder his words over the next seven years from the time of our revisit until the publication of this chapter, I understand that his process of cycling through thoughts and actions is vital to his sense of self as a literate individual. Through the process of reviewing and reflecting on his literacy experiences and decisions, he gains literacy agency. He can be even more confident in himself as someone who reads and contemplates world events and happenings in his communities. George is particularly aware of how he performs in public. It would matter to him to present as well-informed, something that reading has made possible. The conversation with George allows us both to see how his literacy agency continues to develop. Our deepened awareness is a result of the revisit. George helps me understand that in future research I can be more mindful of topics such as control of one's experiences and how reviewing enables continual revision of one's most significant narratives.

I read George the section of the book where he describes his longtime job at a drop forge, and he joins his own narrative, building on his already documented words: "The job's got to be just right. Like, you got golf clubs," and he is into it again, presenting himself as storyteller and experienced, skilled worker while he composes a new story in this moment spun from the already published narrative. It goes something like this: if you're making golf clubs, they can be five-thousandths of an inch off because you can shave that down, but beyond that, you've got to be precise. When he extends his narratives, George claims the book as he sees it. These are *his* experiences with literacy and work that he can recast as he chooses. His recasting is one of the ways he claims ownership and creates new meanings. When I listen to George re-spin his narratives, I am reminded that participants' words in the book represented specific moments when they spoke about their literacy experiences or interpreted decisions they had made in their writing samples. Their reflection and analysis shaped my reflection and analysis as the researcher-author. Now, in the moment of our revisit, George has an opportunity to cycle back through his already documented transcripts and writing. The stories he told in the book blend with the ones he tells during the revisit, becoming part of George's narrative repertoire. New narratives layer onto older ones, shifting the stories and opening up spaces for him to interpret his experiences again and, perhaps, to reflect on them differently. He shows me that the analyses I did previously are not complete. I looked at George one way during the period of my study; later, that interpretation changed as he participated in follow-up interviews. The analysis in my book is not the same as what I am hearing from George during the revisit. He models a process of weaving and stitching in which he selects the topics, carries them into new configurations, turns them in unexpected directions, and cuts off some threads and ties in others—teaching me that what I can know about him as an always developing literacy learner depends on where he takes the research. He offers multiple readings and rereadings, extending the possibilities for how I interpret my work.

After we read the section of the book about the gun factory where he worked after the forge closed, George tells me about a new industry opening in the city run by a company that makes train and subway cars. He says, "If I was young enough . . . if I wasn't too old . . . I'd go and get a training right now . . . and what I would do, I would be ready . . . When they open, I apply for the job, get me a job, make a good living for me and my family." This is the rhetoric of George: practical and direct, work-motivated.

I ask George whether he reads. "Oh, yes!" He is emphatic. "I try to read a little something every day," usually in the afternoon. He describes his daily practice of reading the newspaper and which sections he prefers, sports most of all: "I just want to read what's going on." He doesn't like obituaries, but he'll read them because he wants to know if there's a funeral if someone he knows died. I ask about writing, and George reminds me that he doesn't like to write, though he does it when he needs to. We talk about his friend Chief, who does like writing, and together we look over some of Chief's writing from the book. Until this moment, George hasn't seen the spoken and written texts I collected from other participants. He nods and laughs as he reads some of his peers' essays and interview transcripts, and I can see that their texts can be useful for George as evidence of a period in his life when he and the others were students together. He can know his peers differently through their published texts.

We speak this way for about an hour until abruptly, George taps the book, his hand spread across its cover, and says: "I'm going to read it. I can't tell you that I'll understand all of it, but I'm going to read it." Then he stops the conversation and ends the visit: "Well, I'm going to have to leave y'all," and he swiftly exits.

From George, I learn about the extension of knowledge making as he draws connections across communities. His experiences, removed from the present moment and documented in writing, allow him additional possibilities for thinking things through. George reveals a layer of collaboration I didn't know about until our discussion. In his roles as author of his own texts and as participant in the study, he reviews his experiences and reflects back on his words, applying his lenses of analysis to the published academic one I offer. His comments on reviewing and extending remind me that research can continue to be loose and fluid, that I can continue to learn from George about his ongoing purposes for literacy.

The revisit gave him a chance to layer new meaning onto his old stories, a pattern that demonstrates the idea that literacy is accumulated throughout a person's life (Brandt 2001). He experiences literacy as accumulated when he speaks of future industry opportunities in language he joins with his already expressed narratives about economics. Yet, he goes further than looking at literacy as cumulative when he speaks of reflecting and reviewing. For George, the object of the book provides literal and literate material for contemplation. He can take the book and decide how he wishes to think about it every time he chooses to engage. George can recognize his home and learning communities within the book; he can consider whether the stories it contains are pertinent to him and worthy of further contemplation. The book, which carries a certain weight as social and material object, is a container for the participants' written and spoken narratives about their literacy histories, and it is the text in which their previous acts of restorying are documented. Looking back on his spoken and written narratives from a time when he was a research subject gives George the chance to decide what he wishes to do with the book and whether he might want to continue our literacy work together one day. He probably won't reach out to me, but our style of interaction will change when we do speak. From this moment on, he will treat me as a longtime acquaintance, as someone who knows an important piece of him and his history.

FOLLOWING GEORGE

The greatest lesson I learned from revisiting former participants was that they wanted to continue our conversation. It was not an unusual gesture for me to contact them after many years had passed to share the results of my earlier study; that is a typical practice of ethnographic researchers who return to close their studies. What I was not prepared for was the participants' response when they reviewed the published text with me. All four of them wanted to re-engage with their own narratives, picking up those stories again and continuing them in light of new experiences. George did this enthusiastically when he reflected on his former work experiences and then speculated on a new business opening in the city that he envisioned as offering the economic promise he would pursue if he were still actively working. More so, George's practice of reviewing and reflecting, his consideration of new texts and new experiences in relation to previous ones, revealed his sustained interest in his ongoing literacy development. He remains curious and open to experiences. The conversations with George demonstrate the flexibility of interpretation as well as the power imbalance implicit in the research process. Despite our efforts to view this longitudinal relationship as a collaboration between equals, it is I who always benefits professionally while we both enjoy the ongoing personal communication, especially now that we have been talking together for many years.

I have not seen George since our visit, but we have spoken on the phone a few times. Most of what I hear about George comes through his friend Chief. I have accompanied Chief to a learning center where, until recently, he went weekly; while there, I learned that George had also been attending individual lessons for more than five years. Knowing that George maintains his commitment to his own development as a reader and writer gives me perspective on where this research might go next. I will wait to find out where George leads.

While composing this chapter, I decide to call George. It has been a while, and I want his consent to continue writing. This time, I reach him right away. George is happy to chat. He asks after my husband and wants to know what he is driving these days. (This is a conversational gesture he often makes, demonstrating his connection with me and respect for my husband.) Giving me permission to publish takes less than one minute of our fifteen-minute conversation. The rest of the time we talk about George's health and current activities. He's seventy-five now. His wife passed away over a year ago. He no longer does maintenance for his church, and he is critical of the ways the repairs are being made without him there. George tells me that the literacy instructor he was working with for years one-on-one recently retired. Despite all of these changes, he says, "I'm moving around . . . I'm not complaining."

NOTE

1. Participants' names are pseudonyms.

REFERENCES

Bakhtin, Mikhail M. 1986. "The Problem of Speech Genres." Translated by Vern W. McGee. In *Speech Genres and Other Late Essays*, ed. Caryl Emerson and Michael Holquist, 60–102. Austin: University of Texas Press.
Bazerman, Charles, Arthur N. Applebee, Virginia W. Berninger, Deborah Brandt, Steve Graham, Jill V. Jeffery, Paul Kei Matsuda, Sandra Murphy, Deborah Wells Rowe, Mary Schleppegrell, and Kristen Campbell Wilcox. 2018. *The Lifespan Development of Writing*. Urbana, IL: National Council of Teachers of English.
Brandt, Deborah. 2001. *Literacy in American Lives*. Cambridge: Cambridge University Press.
Brandt, Deborah. 2018. "Writing Development and Life-Course Development: The Case of Working Adults." In *The Lifespan Development of Writing*. Charles Bazerman, Arthur N.

Applebee, Virginia W. Berninger, Deborah Brandt, Steve Graham, Jill V. Jeffery, Paul Kei Matsuda, Sandra Murphy, Deborah Wells Rowe, Mary Schleppegrell, and Kristen Campbell Wilcox, 244–71. Urbana, IL: National Council of Teachers of English.

Castanheira, Lucia, Teresa Crawford, Carol N. Dixon, and Judith L. Green. 2001. "Interactional Ethnography: An Approach to Studying the Social Construction of Literate Practices." *Linguistics and Education* 11 (4): 353–400.

Dippre, Ryan J., and Talinn Phillips. 2020. "Generating Murmurations: Tackling a Massive Research Object." In *Approaches to Lifespan Writing Research: Generating an Actionable Coherence*, ed. Ryan J. Dippre and Talinn Phillips, 3–11. Fort Collins and Boulder: WAC Clearinghouse and University Press of Colorado.

Freire, Paulo. 2001. "'The Adult Literacy Process as a Cultural Action for Freedom' and 'Education and Conscientização.'" In *Literacy: A Critical Sourcebook*, ed. Ellen Cushman, Eugene R. Kintgen, Barry M. Kroll, and Mike Rose, 616–28. Boston: Bedford/St. Martin's.

Prior, Paul A. 2018. "How Do Moments Add Up to Lives: Trajectories of Semiotic Becoming vs. Tales of School Learning in Four Modes." In *Making Future Matters*, ed. Rick Wysocki and Mary P. Sheridan. Logan: Computers and Composition Digital Press and Utah State University Press. ccdigitalpress.org/book/makingfuturematters/index.html.

Ratcliffe, Krista. 2005. *Rhetorical Listening: Identification, Gender, Whiteness*. Carbondale: Southern Illinois University Press.

Rosenberg, Lauren. 2015. *The Desire for Literacy: Writing in the Lives of Adult Learners*. Urbana, IL: NCTE and Conference on College Composition and Communication.

Rosenberg, Lauren. 2018. "'Still Learning': One Couple's Literacy Development in Older Adulthood." *Literacy in Composition Studies* 6 (2): 18–35.

Rosenberg, Lauren. 2020. "Revisiting Participants after Publication: Continuing Writing Partnerships." In *Approaches to Lifespan Writing Research: Generating an Actionable Coherence*, ed. Ryan J. Dippre and Talinn Phillips, 97–110. Fort Collins and Boulder: WAC Clearinghouse and University Press of Colorado.

Royster, Jacqueline Jones, and Gesa E. Kirsch. 2012. *Feminist Rhetorical Practice: New Horizons for Rhetoric, Composition, and Literacy Studies*. Carbondale: Southern Illinois University Press.

Saldaña, Johnny. 2003. *Longitudinal Qualitative Research: Analyzing Change through Time*. New York: Altamira.

Smith, Anna. 2020. "Across, Through, and With: Ontological Orientations for Lifespan Writing Research" In *Approaches to Lifespan Writing Research: Generating an Actionable Coherence*, ed. Ryan J. Dippre and Talinn Phillips, 15–26. Fort Collins and Boulder: WAC Clearinghouse and University Press of Colorado.

Stuckey, J. Elspeth. 1991. *The Violence of Literacy*. Portsmouth, NH: Boynton/Cook.

4
MISSION-DRIVEN LONGITUDINAL RESEARCH
The Public Value of Telling the Stories of Two-Year College Writers

Holly Hassel and Joanne Baird Giordano

OUR RESEARCH STORY: LOOKING BACK

In 2005, we were teaching English in Wausau, Wisconsin, at the University of Wisconsin–Marathon County, which was part of the multi-campus University of Wisconsin (UW) System's statewide two-year institution. The campus was located in a small city and served students from local urban high schools, surrounding farming communities, and dorm residents from both larger cities (including Milwaukee) and rural towns. Wausau has one of the largest per capita Hmong populations in the United States, which meant UW-Marathon County served second-generation bilingual Hmong speakers as well as recent immigrants who had grown up in refugee camps in Thailand. Though the campus was small (about 1,400 students at its highest enrollment), the student population was surprisingly diverse in terms of students' literacy experiences and preparation for college writing. The writing program served exceptionally well-prepared students (including high school valedictorians) who were starting college close to home to save money as well as significantly underprepared students who, based on their admissions profiles, would have been excluded from higher education outside of an open-access campus.

At the time, we were both relatively new to the campus. Holly was working toward tenure, and Joanne was developing the campus basic English skills program (developmental reading, learning skills, and English as a second language [ESL] courses). We came together first as departmental colleagues and then later as research partners after noticing gaps between the diverse learning needs of campus students and the writing program curriculum. The existing curriculum was modeled after

https://doi.org/10.7330/9781646424337.c004

the University of Wisconsin–Madison's course catalog, and approaches to teaching drew from the programs at the selective research institutions where almost all faculty in our department had attended graduate school. Many students struggled academically as they transitioned from developmental writing[1] (English 098) to first-year writing (English 101) and then to a second-semester research-based writing course (English 102), which fulfilled the writing requirement for a college degree both at our institution and across the state system.

Neither of us had the institutional capital required for initiating changes to the writing program on our campus or to our wider statewide English department's curriculum. We also lacked the evidence required for understanding and then addressing our students' complex literacy needs. We started by bringing colleagues together for a reading circle with regular meetings in which we discussed writing studies scholarship and talked about strategies for creating a more cohesive writing program. During those meetings, it became apparent that there were questions about our students that we didn't have clear answers for beyond knowing that many of them arrived at our campus without the experience required for doing the kinds of reading and writing instructors expected them to do, not only in writing courses but also across the curriculum. Much of the scholarship we had been reading and discussing was useful in shaping our understanding of writing studies as a field, but it was conducted at sites unlike our own; as a result, it offered limited help. Ultimately, we realized that we weren't going to have an accurate picture of our students' needs without engaging in some kind of systematic inquiry on our own, open-access campus. We also knew that we needed to find out what was happening to students over time, throughout their entire experience in our writing program, which meant designing research or doing assessment across more than one semester.

We decided to design a small-scale scholarship of teaching and learning (SoTL) study to trace students' development as critical readers and writers across their first college year as they transitioned from English 101 to English 102. We hoped to find out whether redesigning English 101 to focus on source-based writing would improve our campus students' success outcomes in English 102. We worked with a colleague to redesign her English 101 course around source-based writing assignments and then collected and analyzed the work that twenty-one of her students produced in both their first and second semesters. Our study (Hassel and Giordano 2009) revealed that students reverted to rhetorical strategies from high school (including five-paragraph essays) in the second-semester research-based course when faced with new writing tasks that were different from their prior academic experiences. Although we began the project with an open mind about what we might find out about student writers, we didn't anticipate how challenging it would be for some of them to adapt their writing strategies to the demands of research-based writing.[2] We were only just beginning to reflect on the extent to which our own professional training and published scholarship provided us with an incomplete picture of the literacy development of two-year college writers and the teaching practices to support their growth.

This first collaboration became the starting point for both subsequent research studies and rethinking our own assumptions about what it means to be a college writer. The students in our initial study were placed in credit-bearing composition (by the state-mandated standardized placement test), and yet many of them seemed to be doing reading, writing, and learning in a complex borderland between underprepared and college-ready. At the same time, our work together was also revealing that our prior professional experiences left us inadequately prepared for helping those students transition to college-level reading and writing. We didn't use the word *longitudinal* to describe how we began to rethink and re-shape our approach to research, but we started talking about how to investigate our students' experiences over time, which led to a number of different collaborative research projects tracing students' development over multiple semesters.[3] Our work then became formally longitudinal (and ultimately, we hope, made contributions to two-year college English studies) because our analysis started at the point of placement and then documented students' experience over multiple semesters.

We also categorize our longitudinal work—and our story—as mission-driven because we were motivated by more than a practical need to gain an evidence-based understanding of our students' readiness for college reading and writing and the experiences they had in our writing program. We were also driven by the social justice function we ascribe to open-access college pathways (see Jensen et al. 2021).

Initially, we didn't have a goal to publish our work. In institutions that have a contractual structure that rewards research (or in positions that have contractually allocated time for research and publication), what is called a "research agenda" may have driven our investigative efforts. However, as faculty with 4/4 loads and minimal contractual professional development expectations even in a tenure-line position (Holly) and in a non-tenure-line, full-time teaching position (Joanne), scholarly activity is motivated differently. Our primary concern in our early years as writing studies researchers was to learn more about our students' experiences in first-year writing for the purpose of assessing ways to create a more equitable and inclusive local writing program for students from communities that have been historically marginalized in higher education. Over time, as we worked on additional projects, we saw a need for scholarship that would support teaching and program development in writing programs at other open-access institutions.

We asked ourselves challenging questions, for example, what do we need to know to make practical, informed decisions about curriculum and instruction that would help students develop as writers? Become more critical readers? Complete our writing program? What curricular and pedagogical approaches increase the likelihood that students will make progress toward attaining a college degree? We needed clear evidence that changes we made to our placement process, writing program curriculum, and support for instructors were working. But we also needed evidence to convince administrators at the statewide and local campus levels that our two-year institution needed support programs in place for students who were admitted to our institution without the literacy experiences and cultural capital for staying in good academic standing and receiving an associate's degree, preparing for transfer to a four-year university, or both. Our research helped our colleagues expand a writing studio program beyond our own campus to the entire statewide institution, with increased writing course completion rates for participating students. The changes we made to our writing and developmental support courses with department colleagues earned a Conference on College Composition and Communication Writing Program Certificate of Excellence (2017) and a Diana Hacker Two-Year College English Association Outstanding Programs in English Award (2016).

However, while we were achieving professional success and witnessing an incredible response to program changes from hard-working colleagues across the state, our institution was slowly devolving through a series of punishing cuts to state funding that left our already cash-strapped institution unable to continue offering even basic support services for students. In March 2015, the newly appointed chancellor (who started in January of that year) announced that a new "regional" structure would be put in place that would result in the elimination of on-campus support staff and leadership positions, replaced with a centralized and regionalized structure. This meant that many campuses had no academic or other leadership directly onsite on the campus much of the time. Further, our students (the most at-risk in the UW System) had reduced or eliminated opportunities to pay tuition on campus, receive academic advising from professional staff, get help with financial aid, or have sufficient information technology support available. As we were both involved in our shared governance structure, a tumultuous no-confidence vote led by department chairs and the senate in an effort to forestall the reduction in services absorbed an enormous amount of our time.

The subsequent two years resulted in both of us taking on leadership roles in the UW Colleges Senate, Holly as chair of the Steering Committee (the executive group of the faculty senate) and Joanne as the chair of the Academic Policy Committee, working to lead changes that would benefit students and staff. Both roles included a time-consuming revision to the associate's degree, movement of the Student Surveys of Instruction to an online format (also necessitated by the reduced support staff after the regionalization) (see Van Slooten, Giordano, and Hassel 2019), advocating for an equity adjustment for non-tenure-line instructors, and spearheading an assessment of the new regionalized structure (met with resistance by administrators). The reduction in support for students and instructors also meant that Joanne's role as the developmental reading and writing coordinator was under additional strain as more and more instructors faced emotional and pedagogical labor associated with diminished resources for students (see Kalish et al. 2019). With so many of our work hours focused on governance and administrative responsibilities, our ongoing research projects fell to the wayside while new project ideas languished.

Just two years later, in October 2017, the University of Wisconsin System announced that our institution would be dismantled, and our thirteen campuses and online programs would merge with four-year universities under a new regional structure—even though the two-year institution had the third-highest enrollment in the entire state system. These changes meant that we would be resigning our accreditation as an institution; no longer have authority to manage the curriculum and programming we had built; and be subsumed under the curriculum, hiring and mentoring practices, and departmental and institutional policies of the "receiving" four-year institutions—most of which had little interest in adopting new campuses that would require oversight and integration. As our institution fell apart, we no longer had access to some of the institutional research required for tracing students' academic progress for a final statewide project, many participating instructors faced employment insecurity, and the program we were researching no longer existed.

After three years of disrupted work, we reached a critical crossroads and realized that we would no longer be able to continue our research on two-year college writers if we stayed in Wisconsin, especially given that our campuses would be affiliated with a four-year institution with administrators who had clearly stated that they had no interest in continuing open-access education. We subsequently left Wisconsin so we could continue doing research. In this chapter, we explore what we learned from studying the experiences of open-access student writers over time and reflect on what longitudinal research about two-year college students and teachers can offer the field of writing studies. We have been committed to this work in part because of how limited systematic research studies have been in tracing the literacy journeys of students at two-year colleges.

In the remainder of this chapter, we reflect on our own work as teacher-scholar-activists during our fifteen-year collaboration, setting our own stories alongside those of the college students who participated in research projects we conducted. In this reflection, we consider how the story of our professional relationship doing longitudinal research aligns with previous studies that have sought to capture the literacy development of students starting their postsecondary education at two-year colleges and how disruptive the effects of austerity and disinvestment in public higher education can be on scholars' lives, careers, and learning.

LONGITUDINAL RESEARCH AT TWO-YEAR COLLEGES

Though we didn't initially intend to undertake a longitudinal research project when we began doing systematic inquiry into our diverse students' college journeys, the nature of the investigations we undertook led to studies that ultimately traced students' experiences through multiple years. Likewise, we came to see how limited the published scholarship that is relevant to program development and classroom research was. Paul Rogers (2010), for example, offers an overview of longitudinal research in writing studies. His synthesis illustrates how longitudinal knowledge of writing development in postsecondary contexts contains inadequate representation from work in open-admissions contexts with students who would be excluded from higher education at other institutions.

We acknowledge some of the important research that has informed our work through explorations of the literacies of college students, like Elizabeth Chiseri-Strater (1991) and Anne Herrington and Marcia Curtis (2000), each a focused study of a small group of students and the latter tracing students from basic writing courses through their subsequent coursework. These studies and other, similar research take place at research-intensive public schools (Yancey, Robertson, and Taczak 2014; Gere et al. 2017) or at elite or private colleges and universities (Carroll 2002; Sommers and Saltz 2004). All of these studies offer useful starting points for understanding how students evolve and grow as they pursue postsecondary reading and writing goals; but they don't tell us how marginalized, structurally disadvantaged, and low-income students at open-access, primarily two-year, colleges can and do make transitions to college literacies. When it came to the work of trying to make sense of how our own two-year college students fared as college writers, largely from marginalized groups, the existing literature was limited.

We certainly drew from the few studies that focused on students who began their schooling in open-access two-year colleges and adult basic education programs (Sternglass 1997; Tinberg and Nadeau 2010; Wilson 2017). Howard Tinberg and Jean-Paul Nadeau (2010) focus on student writers over the course of a single academic year; studies published more recently, such as Annie Del Principe and Rachel Ihara (2017), contribute to the body of knowledge using longitudinal methods that trace students' literacy experiences as they begin their college coursework at open-access institutions, and they reinforce our own experience in reflecting the challenges of conducting longitudinal research in community college contexts. The researchers struggled to retain participants, and both studies show how the students who have the greatest underrepresentation in research and scholarship on literacy development are the same students who have the most tentative relationship to higher education and, typically, the least exposure to college culture and literacy practices.

INSIGHTS ABOUT LONGITUDINAL RESEARCH FROM STUDENTS' STORIES

Our own story of spending a decade conducting multi-semester research projects is intertwined with the stories and educational experiences of the nearly 140 college writers whose work we studied (which does not include dozens more students who participated in a statewide research project we conducted with additional research partners). Our students' development as writers, their educational successes and setbacks, and their often winding and unexpected pathways toward a postsecondary degree demonstrate the challenges of conducting longitudinal research at two-year colleges while also highlighting the need for more longitudinal studies conducted in open-admissions contexts. The project we started in 2011, which we only recently returned to for data analysis, helps us illustrate some of the stories we think can help us know more about future two-year college teachers and students and understand how the challenges of retaining participants in open-access research projects over time (such as those experienced by Tinberg and Nadeau [2010] and by Del Principe and Ihara [2017]) can make such work difficult. We hope that experiences of students in our study can provide readers who do not work and teach in these contexts with a richer understanding of the complexities of teaching and learning in open-access writing programs. We also hope that teacher-scholars at two-year colleges and other access institutions might identify ways they might contribute to longitudinal work in the field.

We can't tell all of their stories, but a few, we think, can make their lives and learning more visible. Quantitative data provide an introduction to their story. For example, our thirty-nine participating students had low standardized test scores (15 or lower in reading and/or English on the ACT, the benchmarks for which are 21 and 18, respectively, for placement into degree-credit coursework) and were placed into a developmental reading or writing course (typically both). None would have been admissible to a four-year university with any academic admission requirements beyond a high school diploma. Most of them would have taken more than one semester of developmental English at a campus with multiple levels of required basic skills coursework, but they took only one semester before enrolling in a credit-bearing English 101 course at our institution. Typically, the data institutions use to drive decisions about acceleration (or how quickly underprepared readers and writers are expected to engage in college-level learning) are linked to writing course success outcomes in the first semester. In contrast, we looked not only at students' grades and pass rate in their composition course but also at their writing and grades across multiple semesters in multiple courses. Most participating students had difficulty successfully completing reading-intensive courses in other disciplines, which suggested that they were most likely underprepared for college learning not just through our placement measures but also through their actual experiences as college students. From here, the texture of students' stories is what interests us in helping to understand how their life circumstances intersect with their literacy learning needs. The experiences of almost all of the students in our study raise concerns for us about the national push for accelerating students to more advanced college reading and writing courses and tasks, and they show that attending to students' stories as much as to the data about them serves an important complementary function—especially when assessments of effectiveness of acceleration initiatives are based on grades in a single course and a single semester (Jaggars, Edgecombe, and Stacey 2014; Hassel et al. 2015). This pressure is exerted almost exclusively on two-year colleges.

Ying's academic and extra-academic story illustrates the need for a long-term perspective in understanding students' literacy growth over time. She was a Hmong speaker who first started learning English when she was eleven years old, and she had been in the United States for only about seven years before starting college. She was a high-achieving high school student but was still enrolled in an ELL course late in her postsecondary education. She made rapid progress over the course of our study and eventually became one of the most advanced writers in the group of participants. However, she clearly needed a semester of basic skills coursework to prepare for English 101. She describes the gap between her prior learning experiences and her developmental writing course: "At the beginning of this semester I did not have an idea and I was not sure of how to write an academic paper. In high school I did not follow the academic writing paper rules. It was a struggle for me and I was not sure if I could make it through this course." With minimal experience as an academic writer, Ying needed a semester to help her transition to college-level writing. Ying used successful reading strategies (like annotation and taking notes to summarize key points in a text) early in her first semester but needed extra time to study texts as an L2 reader. For a self-assessment, Ying wrote, "It took me a while to read a chapter because there were many words that I didn't know—I use an online dictionary for an example that is easier to understand." By tracing the development of students like Ying over time, we were able to learn more about the needs of second-language readers and writers who have been explicitly taught about how the English language works—and the distinct ways their learning needs differ from those of developmental writers who have less experience with strategies for learning about and discussing language.

Joanie is another example of a student who stuck with summarizing and reporting on information without adapting her writing strategies for assignments that required analysis of sources even though she and the other students showed some growth as college writers. In her first semester of developmental courses, Joanie's writing revealed a misunderstanding of texts, and her reflective pieces about her own work focused on her lack of confidence in writing rather than discussing her development as a writer. However, she learned to structure her work based on outlines and noted that "when it comes to actually starting my paper, I can count on the outline and go off of that. Honestly, I personally think that is the best thing the English department has ever invented in school." It was much easier for her to learn the basics of how to use an outline and follow the conventions of academic writing than it was to complete the parts of assignments that required her to engage first with texts and then with research sources.

By following Joanie's literacy development over time, we were able to identify how issues with reading made it difficult for her to transition to research-based writing in her second year in ways we would not have been able to notice if we had looked at her work for a single course or just the first year. In a second-semester midterm reflection, she describes her challenges with writing about reading: "I read a lot, but I still cannot grasp those new vocab words in my reading to put into my essays. I am not trying to make me sound smarter, but I know it would help improve my essays more by making it sound more professional. I guess that leads to critical thinking due to all the thinking I have to do." Joanie continued to use sources in an informational way throughout the writing program, discussing the content of an assigned text for a rhetorical analysis essay in developmental writing and summarizing the plotline of the movie *The Blind Side* for an analysis assignment the next semester in English 101. She eventually encountered a major problem in her final writing course in which she was accused of plagiarism for using a few sentences from a text in a way that (at least in our professional judgment) seemed more like patchwriting than deliberate plagiarism. By following her academic progress and analyzing Joanie's work over her three semesters in our writing program, we were able to identify the multiple ways her limited experience with academic reading and challenges with comprehension affected her work as a writer.

Further, longitudinal research about college students' literacy experiences is complemented by understanding how students' extra-academic contexts (particularly those of low-income and first-generation students) are helped or hindered by curricular approaches or pedagogical practices in a writing program. Ying faced responsibilities and workload issues that made spending time on academics more challenging for her in comparison to students at selective residential campuses who can reserve more time for study. In an essay for her developmental writing course, she described how she balanced the demands of a complicated home life with school:

> As the oldest child, I have many responsibilities at home and that is why I had limited time for sports. I prepare dinner, do household chores, and assist with school work. My parents were not educated and they do not

know the English language so they cannot help us with our homework. Every day, I have to make sure that my younger siblings are doing their homework, and I help them with their homework before I do my homework. I translate for my parents, and every week I look through our mail to make sure all the bills are paid.

Other students in our study faced similar issues that required them to balance school with complex life responsibilities. For instance, one student lost her housing three times in the two years because of a fire, a breakup, and conflict with a family member who had trouble understanding the time commitment for her schoolwork while also working long hours at a big-box store. Another student was a primary breadwinner for his family even though he was still a teenager. These life experiences are inseparable from students' academic trajectories and their literacy development. Including the stories of such students in the body of research in writing studies will allow for a more robust understanding of who college writers are.

We see our story and our students' stories as illustrating three key takeaways. Open-access instructors and students have distinct academic experiences that are valid parts of higher education and should be represented. In addition, open-access students have complex extra-academic material situations that strongly influence their classroom engagement in ways that are not about their potential for success; persistence in both the general and the specific sense (retention from fall to fall from one academic year to the other) takes on special importance for open-access campuses.

To explain these takeaways further: undertaking longitudinal research is, itself, challenging in gathering robust and valid data. For example, the research story we tell here was shaped deeply by the life experiences and academic experiences of students in our study. Five of the thirty-nine students in the cohort were on our campus for one semester or less, so we were unable to chart their development as writers over time. For example, one student, Jim, moved out of state (from Wisconsin to the Southwest) after attending for two weeks but did not realize he needed to withdraw from college formally until the instructor called him. Another participant, Doris, was unable to accumulate any college credits (degree or non-degree) in her only semester on our campus. We were unable to follow nine additional students after the first year. One of them, Maggie, made exceptional academic progress and was able to transfer to the four-year university of her choice (and subsequently graduated within four years of starting college—the only student in our study to finish a degree within that short traditional time frame). Her experience illustrates the potential challenges of working with research subjects who enroll at a two-year college because they are inadmissible anywhere else and then leave when they are eligible for admission to a school of their choice. Another highly motivated student, Frances, transferred to a neighboring two-year technical college after having difficulty completing math courses on our campus, explaining to one of us that it seemed unlikely that she would be able to complete the math requirement by the end of her second year but that she could receive an associate's degree at an institution with more flexible quantitative learning requirements. A year later, she reported that she was thriving at her new campus and had received a scholarship based on her academic performance.

However, of the fourteen students who left the campus after the first year—or 36 percent of our study participants—three were on academic probation and three were suspended. Of the students who stayed for a second year, another five had problems with academic standing, and one was suspended for academic misconduct. One challenge of conducting longitudinal research with subjects who begin college in developmental English is that their limited experience with academic reading and writing makes it less likely that they will remain in college long enough to complete the research study: the life circumstances that made developing as academic readers and writers more challenging for them in K–12 education typically haven't changed when they go to college.

We think it's important here to emphasize that English 102, the transfer research course, is *the starting point* for first-year writing for a well-prepared college writer at selective institutions in Wisconsin, and most higher education systems have a similar course that fulfills a writing or communications requirement. The course matters because success in it is required for graduation with an associate's or bachelor's degree and thus has the potential to be a significant barrier to college success. There is an *entire year of learning* at many community colleges in the US that will *never be represented in longitudinal writing studies research at selective campuses*, literacy education that is primarily the responsibility of writing instructors and programs. At the same time, because these students are less likely to stay in college (as our data and prior scholarship such as Tinberg and Nadeau [2010] show), it is more challenging to do that research.

What this means is that if we assume, as much of the scholarship in writing studies does—such as work by Deborah Brandt, Mike Rose, Andrea Lunsford, Min-Zhan Lu, Jacqueline Jones Royster, Victor Villanueva, Geneva Smitherman, and many others—that people's literacy is shaped by their identities, contexts, and access to literacy-rich environments, entire literacy stories are not being told because students who are learning in open-admissions environments are simply not part of the narrative. We need to know more about how pathways to college look for the many students who want to pursue higher education but for whom the "direct from high school to college" route has already passed them by; these are nontraditional-age students who have jobs and families or who are place-committed or who simply have too precarious a relationship with higher education to invest in the expense and logistical risks of relocation for college attendance. Longitudinal examination of such students and their growth as writers (as well as the curricular and pedagogical opportunities that provide them with the greatest chance of success) is an important component of expanding access to college credentials—perhaps the single most significant way to social and economic mobility—to more diverse students.

OUR RESEARCH STORY: LOOKING AHEAD

To return to our story, the dissolution of the institution and the accompanying dissolution of the research-based program development work on which we had spent so many years required us both to make difficult decisions. We had seen a shifting of statewide and system-wide priorities starting in 2010, when Governor Scott Walker was elected and Act 10 disemboweled public unions; before that, we saw furloughs and reductions in take-home pay as the result of increased contributions for retirement and healthcare. We saw in 2012 the change in funding allocated at the UW System level for Undergraduate Teaching and Learning Grants—the sole source of teaching and learning funding available to us as instructors working at an under-resourced and teaching-focused institution with little available capital to invest in research projects, even those that are teaching-focused. In that year, the UW System launched a massive "Growth Agenda" campaign aimed solely at recruiting students, with minimal attention paid to retention or graduation. The dollars previously allocated for undergraduate teaching and learning (and administered by our system-level Office of Professional and Instructional Development) were swept into a single large pot of funding that was available only by submitting pre-vetted proposals through the administration of each individual campus, eliminating the "straight line" from teacher-researchers to even the small amount of grant funding support previously available and instead requiring an intensive middle-manager review process.

For Joanne, remaining in Wisconsin would likely require her to leave higher education. Her stable, permanent-contract position as the statewide developmental English coordinator for all of the UW System's two-year colleges was eliminated, and her only option was to take a semester-to-semester contract teaching situation at a four-year institution where administrators seemed intent on eliminating ESL programs and outsourcing developmental English (her two areas of expertise) to a local technical college, even though the tech school didn't have the structures in place to offer those courses. She reached the inevitable conclusion that the only way to continue doing research and the kind of teaching she valued was to leave the state. She subsequently returned to Utah, her home state, and took a tenure-line position at Salt Lake Community College. In many ways, she started her career over by moving from working as a program coordinator to an assistant professor position, but she found not only more stability but also a richer set of resources for supporting teaching, professional development, and students. However, she also left her husband and teenage daughter behind for an indeterminate amount of time after weighing the choice between leaving the profession and living away from her family.

For Holly, it meant reevaluating assumptions about being place-bound (due to custody arrangements for her two children) and looking seriously at other institutions for the first time in fifteen years, as well as thinking carefully about her professional priorities for the last part of her career. She had become steadily more involved in national service, and an employment opportunity that presented itself within a day's drive of central Wisconsin (and nearer to her family in northern Minnesota) became a hopeful and positive option—but it was not without challenges, including the enormous logistical and emotional labor required to move her family and reorient to a new job, as well as a substantial shift in workload and focus. The new job also required renegotiating a custody arrangement and spending long periods of time away from her school-age children during the summers. Equally important, however, it meant that Holly stopped working with open-admissions students, which she considered the most valued and sustaining part of her professional responsibilities. Opportunities to teach basic writing and writing studio courses were not in her future at the four-year university she joined, and though she helps prepare new teachers (graduate students in English) for careers in writing programs on open-admissions campuses and two-year colleges, the direct work with student populations at two-year colleges has ended.

Though we are both much happier in new positions that are more stable, this change was not without sacrifices. In retrospect, we would not have been able to refocus our professional lives on research even if our institution hadn't been dismantled because the punishing effects of budget cuts on our program work and institutional service left us without the time and emotional energy required to conduct multi-semester studies.

It's true that dissolving an institution rarely happens, particularly long-established public two-year colleges. That being said, the effects of austerity measures on higher education are re-shaping our profession at many institutions, and we see no end in sight to what is a mounting assault on accessible and affordable public higher education (see more about our story in Kalish et al. 2019). One only needs to look at the daily news headlines. As we wrote this, for example, the governor of Alaska had just announced a massive, impossible-to-absorb 41 percent cut to the budget of the University of Alaska System, and those in the education community are reeling to consider what programs and campuses to close, already planning for declaration of a fiscal emergency that would enable the layoff of tenured faculty with just sixty days' notice. Some higher education institutions' ability to endure the pandemic and succeed post-pandemic is questionable, and two-year colleges have seen sizable enrollment drops as the student populations who attend them grapple with employment, childcare, and housing precarity that was already significant but has been exacerbated by the pandemic (see St. Amour 2020). We see our own institution's demise in this story and expect similar circumstances to emerge regularly in the future.

One thing we know is that our story will look different than what we imagined it would be prior to 2017. In some ways, we have been surprised by the ways that being in different states has actually enabled us to do *more* intensive project planning and to pursue new longitudinal research projects than we could when we were physically collocated at our old campus. In part, this is because seeking out more stable environments has made it possible to spend less time on the all-consuming work of putting out program fires, shared governance, and classroom fires and to think intentionally and mindfully about the ways we want to spend our professional time. Now that we have the reflective moments to do that—returning to projects that were put on hold, like the one we discuss in this chapter—we see even more clearly how the research questions we pursued speak to larger concerns we have about the field and to larger questions about the purpose for, value of, and access to higher education. We will always mourn the end of the institution that brought us together and gave us a shared professional vision, but we are hopeful about the work we can now do together that will contribute to the larger discipline of writing studies.

NOTES

1. At most, 20 percent of students began in English 098, with the majority of the students at the time placing into English 102.
2. At the time we conducted our first research project (2007–2008), there was very little empirical research in writing studies focused specifically on transfer. Scholarship on the TFT movement (Teaching-for-Transfer) had not yet been published. Transfer-focused research at open-access institutions (where students come from a much wider range of linguistic backgrounds and previous secondary school literacy experiences and who often have large gaps in their educational history) was even rarer. Our *TETYC* article (Hassel and Giordano 2009) pre-dates Linda Adler-Kassner, John Majewski, and Damian Koshnick's (2012) article (one of the first we can find) by three years.
3. We subsequently designed additional studies that would help us learn more about students' learning needs and how they developed as readers and writers across more than one semester of coursework in an open-access learning environment. Our work included an exploration of the college literacy experiences of students who self-identified as Hmong speakers (Giordano and Hassel 2015), an analysis of students' progress through the writing program and general education coursework based on their multiple measures placement profiles (Hassel and Giordano 2015), and research that traced underprepared students' journeys through the writing program and first two college years (Giordano and Hassel 2016). For our final project in Wisconsin, we collaborated with colleagues to draw from what we learned in our research to revise our writing program (Phillips and Giordano 2016), engage in intensive faculty development work (Giordano et al. 2017), and investigate the success of our program changes by analyzing the work of student writers collected at every level of our writing program across our thirteen-campus statewide institution (Phillips et al. 2019).

REFERENCES

Adler-Kassner, Linda, John Majewski, and Damian Koshnick. 2012. "The Value of Troublesome Knowledge: Transfer and Threshold Concepts in Writing and History." *Composition Forum* 26. https://compositionforum.com/issue/26/troublesome-knowledge-threshold.php.

Carroll, Lee Ann. 2002. *Rehearsing New Roles: How College Students Develop as Writers.* Carbondale: Southern Illinois University Press.

Chiseri-Strater, Elizabeth. 1991. *Academic Literacies: The Public and Private Discourse of University Students.* Portsmouth, NH: Boynton/Cook.

Del Principe, Annie, and Rachel Ihara. 2017. "A Long Look at Reading in the Community College: A Longitudinal Analysis of Student Reading Experiences." *Teaching English in the Two-Year College* 25 (2): 83–206.

Gere, Anne Ruggles, Lizzie Hutton, Benjamin Keating, Anna V. Knutson, Naomi Silver, and Christie Toth. 2017. "Mutual Adjustments: Learning from and Responding to Transfer Student Writers." *College English* 79 (4): 333–57.

Giordano, Joanne Baird, and Holly Hassel. 2015. "Critical Reading, Rhetorical Analysis, and Source-Based Writing." In *Teaching US-Educated Multilingual Writers: Pedagogical Practices from and for the Classroom*, ed. Mark Roberge, Kay M. Losey, and Margi Wald, 244–62. Ann Arbor: University of Michigan Press.

Giordano, Joanne Baird, and Holly Hassel. 2016. "Unpredictable Journeys: Academically At-Risk Students, Developmental Education Reform, and the Two-Year College." *Teaching English in the Two-Year College* 43 (4): 371–90.

Giordano, Joanne Baird, Holly Hassel, Jennifer Heinert, and Cassandra Phillips. 2017. "The Imperative of Pedagogical and Professional Development to Support the Retention of Underprepared Students at Open-Access Institutions." In *Retention, Persistence, and Writing Programs*, ed. Todd Ruecker, Dawn Shepherd, Heidi Estrem, and Beth Brunk Chavez, 74–92. Logan: Utah State University Press.

Hassel, Holly, and Joanne Baird Giordano. 2009. "Transfer Institutions, Transfer of Knowledge: The Development of Rhetorical Adaptability and Underprepared Writers." *Teaching English in the Two-Year College* 37 (1): 24–40.

Hassel, Holly, and Joanne Baird Giordano. 2015. "The Blurry Borders of College Writing: Remediation and the Assessment of Student Readiness." *College English* 78 (1): 656–80.

Hassel, Holly, Jeffrey Klausman, Joanne Baird Giordano, Margaret O'Rourke, Leslie Roberts, Patrick Sullivan, and Christie Toth. 2015. "TYCA White Paper on Developmental Education Reforms." *Teaching English in the Two-Year College* 42 (3): 227–43.

Herrington, Anne, and Marcia Curtis. 2000. *Persons in Process: Four Stories of Writing and Personal Development in College*. Urbana, IL: National Council of Teachers of English.

Jaggars, Shanna Smith, Nikki Edgecombe, and Georgia West Stacey. 2014. "What We Know about Accelerated Developmental Education." New York: Columbia University, Teachers College, Community College Research Center. https://ccrc.tc.columbia.edu/media/k2/attachments/accelerated-developmental-education_1.pdf.

Jensen, Darin, Carolyn Calhoon-Dillahunt, Brett Griffiths, and Christie Toth. 2021. "Embracing the Democratic Promise: Transforming Two-Year Colleges and Writing Studies through Professional Engagement." *New Directions for Community College* 194: 55–66. https://onlinelibrary.wiley.com/doi/10.1002/cc.20452.

Kalish, Katie, Holly Hassel, Cassie Phillips, Jennifer Heinert, and Joanne Giordano. 2019. "Inequitable Austerity: Pedagogies of Resilience and Resistance in Composition." *Pedagogy: Critical Approaches to Teaching Literature, Language, Composition, and Culture* 19 (2): 261–81.

Phillips, Cassandra, and Joanne Baird Giordano. 2016. "Developing a Cohesive Academic Literacy Program for Underprepared Students." *Teaching English in the Two-Year College* 44 (1): 79–89.

Phillips, Cassandra, Holly Hassel, Jennifer Heinert, Joanne Baird Giordano, and Katie Kalish. 2019. "Thinking Like a Writer: Threshold Concepts and First-Year Writers in Open-Admissions Classrooms." In *(Re)Considering What We Know: Learning Thresholds in Writing, Composition, Rhetoric, and Literacy*, ed. Linda Adler-Kassner and Elizabeth Wardle. Logan: Utah State University Press.

Rogers, Paul. 2010. "The Contributions of North American Longitudinal Studies of Writing in Higher Education to Our Understanding and Development." In *Traditions of Writing Research*, ed. Charles Bazerman, Robert Krut, Karen Lunsford, Susan McLeod, Suzie Null, Paul Rogers, and Amanda Stansell, 365–77. Oxford, UK: Routledge.

Sommers, Nancy, and Laura Saltz. 2004. "The Novice as Expert: Writing the Freshman Year." *College Composition and Communication* 56 (1): 124–49.

St. Amour, Madeline. 2020. "Who's Up, Who's Down, and Why." *InsideHigherEd*, November 19. https://www.insidehighered.com/news/2020/11/19/community-college-enrollments-down-nationally-not-everywhere.

Sternglass, Marilyn. 1997. *A Time to Know Them: A Longitudinal Study of Writing and Learning at the College Level*. Mahwah, NJ: Erlbaum.

Tinberg, Howard, and Jean-Paul Nadeau. 2010. *The Community College Writers: Exceeding Expectations*. Urbana, IL: National Council of Teachers of English.

Van Slooten, Jessica, Joanne Baird Giordano, and Holly Hassel. 2019. "Better Living through Policy: Feminist Shared Governance and Equitable Evaluation." In *Academic Labor beyond the College Classroom: Working for Our Values*, ed. Holly Hassel and Kirsti Cole, 81–94. New York: Routledge.

Wilson, Smokey. 2017. "What Happened to Darleen? Reconstructing the Life and Schooling of an Underprepared Learner." In *Teaching Composition at the Two-Year College: Background Readings*, ed. Patrick Sullivan and Christie Toth, 37–53. Boston: Bedford/St. Martin's.

Yancey, Kathleen Blake, Liane Robertson, and Kara Taczak. 2014. *Writing across Contexts: Transfer, Composition, and Sites of Writing*. Logan: Utah State University Press.

5
UNDERSTANDING IMBRICATED CONTEXTS
Institutional Formation and Longitudinal Writing Research

Amy C. Kimme Hea

It is fall 2010, and the University of Arizona (UA) Writing Program is reeling from two intersecting concerns: impending shifts in leadership and extensive budget cuts. Over the course of this semester, all three of us with "director" as part of our titles faced profound professional changes: our then-director, Anne-Marie Hall, announced her impending phased retirement; our then–assistant director, Chris Minnix, found another position at a different university; and I, associate director, participated in ongoing negotiations with our department and college to assume the director role while at the same time considering an offer from another institution. As writing program administrators (WPAs), we knew these changes were connected to larger institutional forces at play. In this moment, we also understood that we had to build a strong case for the ongoing needs of the UA Writing Program and its integral roles in the department, college, and university. In particular, we desired to push back against dominant narratives about the writing program as merely functional and student writers as deficient or lacking. In this time of loss and transition, Anne-Marie and I discussed at length opportunities to make visible our program and its work and to reframe how the program and students were represented. One afternoon during a conversation in her office, which would later be my office, we decided, "let's draft a strategic plan."

As I think back on this time, I want to emphasize the value of telling this story in a book on longitudinal writing research, which is by nature intimately bound to persons and places. In this chapter, I stress the need to understand local institutional formations, arguing that doing so is vital to longitudinal research. For myself and my colleagues, learning this lesson involved shifting from collecting concerns to engaging in strategic action, including the University of Arizona Longitudinal Study

https://doi.org/10.7330/9781646424337.c005

of Student Writers (UA Study). Our story illustrates how and why strategic planning for the UA Writing Program led to the design and development of a five-year mixed-methods study of student writers, but this chapter also showcases what we gained as scholars, researchers, teachers, and WPAs. Begun in 2012, the UA Study has amassed more than 2,700 data points along with deep-data cases of twenty-two student writers who started in our first-year writing classes. As a prequel to forthcoming reports on the UA Study by myself and Co-Principal Investigator Aimee Mapes, this chapter makes a strong case for longitudinal researchers to perform some form of preliminary and systematic environmental scan (Lapin 2014; Albright 2014)[1] of their own institutional locations, even while acknowledging that such work is always dynamic, partial, contingent, and fraught. This call is not meant to suggest that all researchers must pursue a single protocol. Instead, using my experience as an example, I want to advance the value for longitudinal researchers to undertake systematic institutional reviews in order to build more responsive studies, inquiries more genuinely designed both to address the local needs of students, teachers, and administrators and to craft new knowledge for our field.

PAYING ATTENTION TO INSTITUTIONS

As researchers and rhetoricians, we know the value of context. While it is nothing new to suggest that we address context in a thoughtful way, I strongly advocate that we think of it in an institutional way, making sure to consider how the changing nature of our institutions impacts research at all levels of a project. That is to say: institutional formations are imbricated in our research from our own educations as researchers to our IRB offices, available resources for research support, and the many other material layers of our work. While those of us at UA did not set out consciously to conduct an institutional ethnography (IE), for my own part, as I tell this story, I want to emphasize my agreement with Michelle LaFrance (2019, 134), who foregrounds "relationality" as "one of the most powerful gifts of IE." In particular, LaFrance (12) defines IE as "a process of inquiry [that] can help writing researchers study the complexities of institutional locations and the experiences and practices associated with writing, shifting the focus of the study from what writers do 'naturally' to account more fully for how writers, writing instructors, and writing administrators negotiate their institutional contexts and material actualities."

I do not claim IE as the specific methodology we deployed in the UA Study—as our process preceded LaFrance's publications—but I intend in my work here to outline the location of the UA Writing Program as a site for research, attending to the specifics of the place, space, and people. I also suggest that it is fitting to think of the context of our research as a participant of sorts, since the histories, actions, and discourses of our location have profound impacts on the whole of our research. In particular, the UA Writing Program's institutional positioning over time, its geographic location in a Southwest borderland, and its students all factored into the program's strategic plan—which, in turn, ushered in our longitudinal study. I want to point, then, to the ways institutional ethnography as methodology and the UA Study share a common purpose: to understand institutions more thoroughly (even knowing that they cannot be wholly or singly unified) and to insist that our locations are not empty stages where work unfolds but rather are actors in the dynamic contexts of our research and teaching.

As an alum of Purdue University, I am familiar with, and certainly subscribe to, the ways institutional formations are always already part of our work—thinking here of my colleagues James E. Porter, Patricia A. Sullivan, Stuart Blythe, Jeffrey Grabill, and Libby Miles (2000), all of whom argue for institutional critique as a means for material interventions and transformation. As I was lucky enough to know these scholars in graduate school, I took value from their work, but I also framed my own graduate research in critical theory, which is still my theoretic tendency. I wholly ascribe to the ways institutional formations have their own pedagogic function, teaching us and reflecting back to us narratives and practices of what literacy means, what writing should be, and perceptions of student writers. This pedagogic function is not one that is fixed or monolithic but instead dynamic as it is made and remade, with some articulations more deeply entrenched, intertwined, and imbricated with cultural and social inequities. Those articulations are made in language and action; as the pedagogic function of institutions is certainly connected to issues of power, it takes effort to challenge and dislodge inequities that otherwise are taken as normative or continually reasserted as truths.

For me, institutions are rooted in sets of articulations. For LaFrance, IE is grounded in the contributions of Dorothy Smith, and it is Smith who connects institutional ethnography in sociology to the work of noted Birmingham cultural studies scholar Stuart Hall, who deploys articulation theory as a means to redress discourses and practices of oppression in non-essentialist and non-reductivist ways (Hall 1985; Grossberg 1986). Articulation theory aims not merely to describe institutions but also to intervene against the dominant and inequitable relations they produce, to do the work of challenging and rearticulating (Haraway 1985, 1988, 1997; Deleuze and Guattari 1987). While not a unified theory (as most are not), articulation theory ultimately challenges dominance, including the ways institutions and the persons co-constituted by them subordinate others through their narratives and their actions (Slack 1996; Johnson-Eilola 1997; Kimme Hea 2007; Kimme Hea, Pack Sheffield, and Walker 2017). Because the resulting inequities are entrenched in both discourses and actions, articulation theory addresses struggle and a continual need to rearticulate systems of oppression. Thus, in my own work I situate every study—including my own longitudinal research—in the imbricated nature of persons, institutions, language, and actions. All of these have historical, material, social, cultural, political, and affective dimensions that inner-animate. Articulation theory is not an exact science or method, but as Hall describes it to Lawrence Grossberg (1986, 55) in their interview, "a theory of articulation is both a way of understanding how ideological elements come, under certain conditions, to cohere together within a discourse, and a way of asking how they do or do not become articulated, at specific conjunctures, to certain political subjects." Here is the aim of the practice: to dismantle and act on systems of oppression and to intervene in those forces, understanding them as available for change but also dynamic, leading to an ever-vigilant set of actions against these forces.

CONTEXTS OF THE UA STUDY

My intellectual commitment to articulation theory prompted me to see fall 2010 as an opportunity to account for the dominant narratives at play at UA. In particular, I wanted to do more than trace my and others' personal relations; I also wanted to tease out the broader contexts of those relations as they were cast in dominant narratives about the program and the people who participate in it (students, teachers, and administrators). I was especially interested in articulating value: budget cuts and lack of job security—although differential experiences—come from somewhere and from some kind of thinking and acting. After all, I was about to become the director of a writing program with eleven different writing courses, more than 11,000 undergraduate student enrollments in any given academic year, and hundreds of instructors. For myself and my colleagues, strategic planning offered a means of inquiry as well as a means of reframing the program agenda to better address our collective expertise, accomplishments, and needs as well as to represent our concerns to other stakeholders.

We made these decisions as UA budget cuts threatened to make our situation in the writing program even worse. As Anne-Marie Hall and I explained in the 2011 Writing Program Academic Program Review Report (1): "While we [the UA Writing Program] lost a total of 34 percent of the faculty and staff (from 23 to 12), our number of students served increased by 3.4 percent (from 11,877 in 2005 to 12,298 in 2011)." This single line implies a great deal more than it states outright about the program and precarity, but the genre of the report we were drafting did not invite unpacking such statements. The report also did not accommodate an articulation of needs. When Anne-Marie and I turned to strategic planning, we did so with the conviction that a strategic planning process would help us get at the assumptions belied by such data points and potentially generate support for the program. In addition, strategic planning offered us a way to assert agency: to declare our mission, to work with stakeholders across the program, to chart our needs, and to address inequities of budget as well as misperceptions about student writers and teachers.

In fall of 2011, we began our strategic plan with a review of our context—a systematic process of investigating the local, regional, and national landscapes and collecting insights from all stakeholders in the program. The process covered several months and included a simple SWOT (Strengths, Weaknesses, Opportunities, and Threats) assessment, which was crafted with faculty supervisors—long-term colleagues in the writing program (WP) who led teacher development, assessment and curriculum projects, and service work, from our custom textbook publications to community engagement projects. This assessment continued through all levels of the program, including our WP committees and open sessions for teachers. What arose from this process was our strategic plan. Over five years, we aimed to achieve six broad goals: (1) create opportunities for continued, research-focused training for our leadership team; (2) leverage our collective writing expertise and experience to support campus-defined strategic areas of growth; (3) implement a wider program assessment and revise program components; (4) seek out more access to digital technologies to ensure that our curriculum reflects needs of multimodal twenty-first-century writers; (5) develop and conduct short- and long-term research projects that have local significance and professional impact on the field; and (6) develop a public relations/communication focus to feature the program's strengths and contributions and to build and strengthen our community relationships.[2] The first two years of implementation involved a variety of projects, including technology refresh and increased professional development for faculty supervisors and WPAs, the establishment of writing program postdoctoral fellows, and a program-level assessment of student learning that would become our longitudinal study.[3]

Throughout the process of conducting the strategic plan, we discussed the importance of telling or retelling the story of our writing program to change campus perceptions of it. As Anne-Marie and I worked to implement several aspects of the strategic plan, we saw an opportunity to connect assessment, the new priority we placed on research related to the program, and our campus presence. Inspired by Harvard's and Stanford's longitudinal projects, we found ourselves designing the UA Study in conjunction with program-level assessment that had gained sponsorship from the vice provost for academic affairs. For us, a longitudinal study introduced an opportunity to understand the writing experiences of students who entered UA through the broadest academic writing door: our English 101 and 102 sequence. Specifically, we wanted to better understand their meta-cognitive and affective relationships to writing over time and to learn how they characterized their writing lives. Unbeknown to us, the UA Study would also reveal some of the complex ways in which some Arizona college students' literacy experiences are shaped by regional politics and laws such as SB1070 and HB2281.

As I turn in this chapter to the contexts informing our work, I note that the UA Study became a means for us to redefine the program for campus audiences through our investment in a highly visible research project. This move represented a significant rearticulation, given the overall local institutional invisibility of the program's already robust research, which included contributions from many in the program to academic conferences and peer-reviewed publications. From the start, the UA Study enabled us to shift our campus identity from that of a merely functional program to that of a unit actively engaged in contributing to the university's research mission. At the same time, we also sought to change the campus discourse about student writers. Our strategic planning process made plain how frequently they were defined through discourses of deficiencies (Valencia and Solórzano 1997), and we hoped that longitudinal study would enable us to place their experiences as college writers into broader social, political, and literacy contexts. In other words, we embarked on the UA Study not only to produce findings but also, through the activity of publicly conducting the study, to change the culture of writing on our campus.

Context One: Asserting Writing Program Value
Then and now, economic forces undergirded the challenges we faced at UA—as a campus, as a program, and as individuals, whether WPAs, faculty, or students. What I hope comes through in my story is how related choices—for example, how budget crises were managed—are profoundly yoked to assumptions of value, risk, and precarity. On our campus and across our state, narratives about where to invest—or, more often in the rhetoric of continuous budget crisis, what to protect—loom large for students, teachers, and administrators of writing programs. Such narratives are fully vested in assumptions about what and who counts most relative to institutional asset management. In writing programs, we operate within economies that value literacy and activities that support its acquisition and development. All too often, however, our programs are embedded in larger campus and community (e.g., state, federal) economies that conflate the importance of literacy with false ideas about the ease of literacy learning. The result is all too familiar to WPAs and other literacy educators: namely, perpetual struggles against assumptions that written literacy is easy to learn, easy to teach, and easy to orchestrate programmatically. Despite decades of critical pedagogy, social turns, and antiracist praxis, we in writing programs continue to hear echoes of ease that confound our work.

At UA, we connected assessment and research, even though, as Chris M. Anson and Robert L. Brown Jr. (1999, 151) suggested some years ago, "the educational role often blurs or subverts the research role, creating a loss of credibility in spite of internal scholarly prestige." We took seriously this rejoinder that the very assessments we craft may subvert our being seen as researchers and scholars, but we also believed the risks involved were worth taking. In fact, we were building on other longitudinal studies that also have included a program assessment as part of their projects (Carroll 2002). Invoking our research expertise in conjunction with our campus identities as teachers and administrators offered us a unique and powerful means of intervention into high-stakes conversations that our other available means did not allow. That is to say, we were often performing assessments and submitting related reports, but those activities were constrained by individuals and occasions that requested or required them. Considering our research design and next steps, we were reminded of Sharon James McGee's (2005, 62) argument that "by thinking beyond the local writing program, we can become aware of the way that the university forms and organizes power both locally and institutionally. By doing so, we can begin to uncover ways to deal with the kinds of problems that often confront a writing program." The study was giving us a chance to "look beyond the program" and allowed us to claim our own expertise and begin to actively change narratives about the students and the program, but it also would be true that this vista sheds light on pain, stress, and uncertainty.

The first year of our study looks different when we observe the work from different angles. As WPAs, we see that our efforts to administer surveys, coordinate research assistants and holistic ratings, and wrangle data despite server crashes yielded our program assessment report. (This report was also produced with much support from Aimee Mapes, who came into the project as co-principal in the close of that year and who crafted the statistical analysis the initial team had struggled to make clear.) The report demonstrated modest gains in four of our writing measures, and it won a university-wide assessment award, which raised the writing program's campus profile. In particular, this sequence of events showcased student success measured in terms of rising writing scores, even while inside the program we discussed the limited insights such measures can ever offer and began to think of the study as getting closer to the students we served. Moving away from program evaluation, our research team looked for ways to use the UA Study to engage local stakeholders and discuss the UA student writer community (Mapes 2013, 2014a; Mapes and Kimme Hea 2014; Kimme Hea et al. 2015) and to talk about the UA Study with other writing scholars (Kimme Hea and Pack Sheffield 2013; Mapes 2014b). We drew inspiration in our annual meetings and teacher development sessions to discuss what students enjoyed in their writing classes, and we provided UA Study updates to the associate vice provost who had supported our first year. This activity helped us construct the UA Study as part of the new "long game" of our strategic planning priorities, giving us a way to articulate our goals and to begin, in language and actions, to challenge assumptions about student writers, teachers, and administrators at the university.

Context Two: Politics of Location

Despite all our work to design, launch, and provide Year One data from the UA Study, we also could not ignore the reality that literacy and learning are always inflected in a particular place, unfolding in a specific context; at UA, the narratives of our region are rife with xenophobic and racist discourses. We are geographically closer to Mexico than to our state capital, Phoenix, and our daily lives are bordered ones. In fact, the University of Arizona is 113 kilometers from Nogales, Mexico, with its sister city, Nogales, Arizona, just due north. Prior to the coronavirus pandemic,

"More than 3.4 million people as well as more than 325,000 train and truck containers crossed between Nogales, Arizona, and Nogales, Mexico" every year (United States Department of Transportation n.d.). But living in a borderland, cultural affordances are not equally distributed or experienced (Anzaldúa 1999). For example, for the Tohono O'odham Nation whose lands are bisected by the US-Mexico border, there are mainly constraints where others enjoy the commerce "because immigration laws prevent the O'odham from crossing [the border] freely" (Tohono O'odham 2016, para 5). The year before we launched the UA Study, Governor Jan Brewer intensified anti-immigrant sentiment by passing SB 1070, which was later dubbed "the-show-me-your-papers" legislation and which intensified anti-immigrant sentiment rather than immigration reform (Johnson 2012). As Randal C. Archibold (2010, para. 6) reported when the law went into effect, "proponents and critics alike" recognized it as "the broadest and strictest immigration measure in generations," criminalizing the failure to carry immigration documents and authorizing the police broad power "to detain anyone suspected of being in the country illegally." This law produced fear and pain, and it gave a platform to figures like the infamous Sheriff Arpaio whose legacy of racial profiling still looms for the terror and physical harm he waged on the Latinx community in Arizona (BBC News 2020).

At nearly the same time, Superintendent of Schools Tom Horne was actively working to dismantle ethnic studies across the state, pointing specifically to the Mexican American Studies Program at Tucson High School, which had demonstrated success in terms of positive learning outcomes for students (Cammarota and Romero 2014). With the passing of HB 2821 in 2010, as Nicole Santa Cruz (2010, para. 3) expressed, the state sought to "ban schools from teaching classes that are designed for students of a particular ethnic group, promote resentment or advocate ethnic solidarity over treating pupils as individuals. The bill also bans classes that promote the overthrow of the U.S. government." Tucson High School sits directly kitty-corner from the University of Arizona, at the corner of Euclid and 6th Streets where UA actively recruits students to come to campus. It is only twelve meters from the university. Whether from Tucson High School or other local and regional schools in Arizona, students who find their way into UA English 101 and 102 may be native speakers of Spanish or other languages. These students also progressed through K–12 in a state that in 2000 passed Arizona Proposition 203, which promotes English-only classrooms and separates English speakers from all other language learners (Heineke 2016). In this context, the geographies of our campus are defined not only by place and space but also by discourses and actions that seek to promote some literacies and cultures and erase or destroy others. In fact, the University of Arizona resides on lands we have only recently (in 2021) begun to acknowledge are historic tribal lands of the O'odham and the Yaqui peoples (University of Arizona 2021, para 1).

The UA Study positioned itself early on as a way to understand student writers, recognizing that many come from regional schools in Arizona or from tribal lands to become UA Wildcats. In 2012, 62 percent of the students held resident status and 43 percent of resident students self-identified as members of a minoritized population (University Analytics and Institutional Research 2022). The discourses, policies, and laws described in this chapter are all deeply intertwined with literacy and learning and are ever steeped in discourses of deficit, lack, and remediation (and at their worst, physical and linguistic violence). In terms of dominant narratives, all UA students were entering the university with ever-present news of state bills and laws involved in monitoring language, race, and ethnicity. Especially for regional students unbuffered by privilege, they were aware of new laws that could impact their families and home communities; and these pressures were systematic, layered, and an inescapable part of their everyday lives in Arizona.

The tensions of place, space, and dominant discourses impacting student lives came to the forefront between the second and third years of our longitudinal study. While the first year was about the larger reframing of the writing program itself, we quickly down-shifted from our larger numbers of participants to a small but consistently participating cohort (knowing that attrition would happen as in all studies and preparing ourselves to gather more ethnographic data from the students who continued). We also began to shift methodologically from programmatic concerns (i.e., assessment) toward getting to know, even better and differently, those students who were still with us at the beginning of Year Three. As we learned, these students well understood the stresses of racism and anti-immigrant action, which were woven through their writing experiences. In the first two years we did not pose direct questions about how their engagements with race, gender, sexual orientation, and other formations of identity shaped the stories they were sharing with us. That changed in the third year, when we worked deliberately to collect more personal stories from the individual writers who continued to invest in the UA Study.

To engage our Year Three cohort, we practically remade our approach, deploying specific research strategies to get to know our writers and their experiences. We asked students to craft video introductions, literacy videos to share their own stories of writing and reading, and to respond to text blasts that invited in situ responses to a bank of questions about literate practices. We also created a new survey—a revision of our Year One and Year Two surveys—that asked writers how their identity formation influenced their literacy activity. This survey, which marked a significant turn in our research, was designed by two research assistants, Anushka Swan Peres and Ana Ribero.[4] It was their push in the revision of the survey that created a new space for participants to connect their experiences and identities to their writing and reading. The Year Three survey invited students to open up about a host of important topics: relationships between their home languages and academic discourse, their parents' literacy levels and their own experiences as writers, the pain or the joy of being given feedback on writing they connected to their lives, and so on. Through our surveys and interviews, we learned how participants connected their first languages and first childhood writing experiences with the subsequent experiences they had through college with writing education across all the locations and positions they came to inhabit. This shift gave us first glimpses of the way our case studies of student writers could help us connect institutional formations relative to students' literate lives. We could see a means to shift discourses and practices to look locally at the specifics of our program and its position at the university and to look regionally at the dominant narratives characterizing students' home communities, language practices, and exposure to education—knowing that there is not a single narrative. Context and institutional factors came to the fore as key components in why students were framing their literate experiences.

CONCLUSION

In this chapter, I have attempted to elaborate on the value of looking institutionally at the dynamics of longitudinal work in a specific time, place, and location. As I considered how to story my own experiences, I wanted to close by suggesting that the value of longitudinal work is not only in results and findings but also in the ways research can recast assumptions about both writing programs and student writers. On campuses like mine, where the role of the writing program was instrumentalized, we were able to recast assumptions about what we contribute to the university. At the same time, as the UA Study unfolded, we confronted some of the many institutional forces that frame student literacy experiences throughout our state and region. None of this would have taken place and, indeed, the UA Study would very likely never have come to pass if not for the strategic planning we undertook. Within that process, the UA Study is most closely beholden to the environmental scan we did, which helped us understand our writing program's position within the university and engage—as well as resist—some of the most harmful narratives about our students. The in-depth, if partial, understanding of our program's institutional position did more than create the immediate site and knowledge base for our work: it gave purpose to our research in ways that complement the conventional disciplinary aims of scholarly knowledge production while augmenting our opportunities to apply what we have learned from our research.

Ultimately, however, the value of institutionally informed work is in its potential to shift narratives and to recast stories, and the value of this depth of environmental scanning—whether through a strategic plan or other means—is to think about our contributions in ways that can challenge dominant narratives that lead to oppressive practices, from budget cuts to students' lamentations as lacking writing expertise. At UA, we came to see our project as a need not merely to understand the acts of writing by students but also to attend to a complex set of factors and forces at play, ones we discussed in terms of their local and regional politics (Kimme Hea 2014; Mapes 2014a; Ribero 2014; Walker 2014; Mapes and Kimme Hea 2016, 2018). The very politics of our location compelled us to ask different questions and come to new ways of asserting our own program's value and the contributions of students and teachers. As I think of how our longitudinal work unfolded, I hope we researchers in writing studies will take a long view and make room to chart institutional formations, to challenge the dominant discourses of students, and to push against categories of student literacy that erase the social and political dimensions. For writing programs poised to launch such efforts in longitudinal writing studies, I recommend more than considerations of time and money, which we know are necessary and fraught; instead, I urge researchers to consider their local context, institutional formations, power relations, and local, regional, and national politics as they undertake their work. These latter concerns require attention to the dynamic and shifting nature of language and actions and time and consultation with stakeholders, and they might even necessitate or reveal assumptions worth challenging as we situate our studies.

NOTES

1. These articles were published after UA Writing Program's strategic plan was developed, but I note the usefulness of this approach with gratitude to Maribel Alvarez for sharing these resources with me.

2. The expanded summary of these goals is provided here as a reference: 1. Creating opportunities for continued, research-focused training for our leadership team, which included building a professional development library and resources for faculty; creating space and opportunity for informal exchange and social interaction; creating a course down-curriculum development (reduced teaching load) plan to work on a specific project need for the program (for graduate associate teachers [GATs], adjuncts, and faculty supervisors); offering travel support to all members of the leadership team to participate in conferences, study other writing programs, or attend workshops related to writing; and revising job descriptions in relation to mission statement and core objectives of the writing program and include a robust annual review process that aligns with the positions. 2. Leverage our collective writing expertise and experience to support campus-defined strategic areas of growth, including creating writing across the curriculum (WAC) and writing in the disciplines (WID) programming that can be taught by administrators, faculty supervisors, and GATs. 3. Implementing a wider program assessment and revising program components, including conducting an Annual Program Review process; completing self-study in anticipation of inviting the Council of Writing Program Administrators to conduct an outside review; and completing a strategic plan with one-, three-, and five-year stages (secure commitments from key stakeholders, pursue objectives of plan, have yearly assessments of the writing program in relationship to objectives). 4. Seek out more access to digital technologies to ensure our curriculum reflects the needs of multimodal twenty-first-century writers, including demonstrating our technology needs to administrators to build that aspect of the program. 5. Develop and conduct short- and long-term research projects that have local significance and professional impact on the field, including creating research teams to work on issues of grammar and style, ESL training for all GATs, WAC and WID, multimodal composition, and pursuing funding to support and disseminate research. 6. Developing a public relations marketing focus to feature the program's strengths and contributions and to build and strengthen our community relationships, including creating and broadcasting a public relations message; targeting populations who can be donors and/or supporters of our program; keying the PR to our mission statement, objectives, and strategic plan; making visible all research contributions that have come out of our program (i.e., fellowships) and publications; and connecting with former teachers in our program to publicize their work. One welcome revision from the first strategic plan to a draft 2014–17 strategic plan draft was to "create more equitable labor practices in relationship to hiring, retention, workload, and support of all instructors across ranks, including graduate students, lecturers, faculty supervisors, and directors." This draft plan was not fully completed before changes in writing program leadership occurred.

3. The strategic plan was also useful in arguments to financially support online writing, for hiring a staff person dedicated to placement and portfolio assessment, and in preparation for the writing program's move to the College of Social and Behavioral Sciences.

4. Both Ana Milena Ribero and Anushka Swan Peres positively impacted the UA Study with their own research interests, which are best demonstrated in their dissertations (Ribero 2016; Peres 2020).

REFERENCES

Albright, Kendra S. 2014. "Environmental Scanning: Radar for Success." *Information Management Journal* 38 (3): 38–44.

Anson, Chris M., and Robert L. Brown Jr. 1999. "Subject to Interpretation: Researching the Textual Representation of Writing Programs and Its Effects on the Politics of Administration." In *The Writing Program Administrator as Researcher: Inquiry in Action and Reflection*, ed. Shirley K Rose and Irwin Weiser, 141–52. Portsmouth, NH: Heinemann/Boynton-Cook.

Anzaldúa, Gloria. 1999. *Borderlands/La Frontera: The New Mestiza*. San Francisco: Aunt Lute Books.

Archibold, Randal C. 2010. "Arizona Enacts Stringent Law on Immigration." *New York Times*, April 24. http://www.nytimes.com/2010/04/24/us/politics/24immig.html.

BBC News. 2020. "Joe Arpaio: Former Arizona Sheriff Fails to Regain Old Job." August 8. https://www.bbc.com/news/election-us-2020-53704860.

Cammarota, Julio, and Augustine Romero. 2014. *Raza Studies: The Public Option for Educational Revolution*. Tucson: University of Arizona Press.

Carroll, Lee Ann. 2002. *Rehearsing New Roles: How College Students Develop as Writers*. Carbondale: Southern Illinois University Press.

Deleuze, Félix, and Gilles Guattari. 1987. *A Thousand Plateaus: Capitalism and Schizophrenia*. Translated by Brian Massumi. Minneapolis: University of Minnesota Press.

Grossberg, Lawrence. 1986. "On Postmodernism and Articulation: An Interview with Stuart Hall." *Journal of Communication Inquiry* 10 (2): 45–60.

Hall, Anne-Marie, and Amy C. Kimme Hea. 2011. "2011 Writing Program Academic Program Review Report." Unpublished report, October 12, electronic file.

Hall, Stuart. 1985. "Signification, Representation, Ideology: Althusser and the Post-Structuralist Debates." *Critical Studies in Mass Communication* 2 (2): 91–114.

Haraway, Donna. 1985. "A Manifesto for Cyborgs: Science, Technology, and Socialist Feminism in the 1980s." *Socialist Review* 80: 65–105.

Haraway, Donna. 1988. "Situated Knowledges: The Science Question in Feminism and the Privilege of Partial Perspective." *Feminist Studies* 14 (3): 575–99.

Haraway, Donna. 1997. *Modest_Witness@Second_Millennium.FemaleMan_Meets_OncoMous: Feminism and Technoscience*. New York: Routledge.

Heineke, Amy J. 2016. *Restrictive Language Policy in Practice: English Learners in Arizona*. Bristol, UK: Channel View.

Johnson, Kevin R. 2012. "A Case Study of Color-Blindness: The Racially Disparate Impacts of Arizona's S.B. 1070 and the Failure of Comprehensive Immigration Reform." *U.C. Irvine Law Review* 2 (1): 313–58.

Johnson-Eilola, Johndan. 1997. *Nostalgic Angels: Rearticulating Hypertext Writing*. Norwood, NJ: Ablex.

Kimme Hea, Amy C. 2007. "Riding the Wave: Articulating a Critical Methodology for Web Research Practices." In *Digital Writing Research: Technologies, Methodologies, and Ethical Issues*, ed. Heidi McKee and Dànielle Devoss, 269–86. Cresskill, NJ: Hampton.

Kimme Hea, Amy C. 2014. "Big Data and Deep Data: Situating the UA Study of Student Writers against the Either-Or Binary between Local-Global Research." Presented at the Conference of Writing Program Administration, Normal, IL, July 19.

Kimme Hea, Amy C., and Jenna Pack Sheffield. 2013. "'Going Public' with Longitudinal Research: Stakeholder Theory and UA Study of Student Writers." Presented at the Council of Writing Program Administrators, Savannah, GA, July 18.

Kimme Hea, Amy C., Jenna Pack Sheffield, and Kenneth Walker. 2017. "Figuring Programmatic Agency: The Framework as Critical Rearticulatory Practice in Writing Program Administration." In *Applications of the Framework for Success in Post-Secondary Writing: Scholarship, Theories, and Practices*, ed. Nicholas Behn, Duane Roen, and Sherry Rankins-Robertson, 21–37. Anderson, SC: Parlor Press.

Kimme Hea, Amy C., Anushka Peres, Aimee C. Mapes, and Ana Ribero. 2015. "Student Writing Enjoyment." Presented at the University of Arizona Writing Program Teacher Development General Meeting, Tucson, January 12.

LaFrance, Michelle. 2019. *Institutional Ethnography: A Theory of Practice for Writing Studies Researchers.* Logan: Utah State University Press.

Lapin, Joel D. 2014. "Using External Environmental Scanning and Forecasting to Improve Strategic Planning." *Journal of Applied Research in the Community College* (11) 2: 105–13.

Mapes, Aimee C. 2013. "A Portrait of First-Year Student Writers." Presented at the University of Arizona Writing Program Teacher Development General Meeting, Tucson, August 7.

Mapes, Aimee C. 2014a. "Lessons from Second Year Interviews: Students Don't Read Emails." Presented at the University of Arizona Writing Program Teacher Development General Meeting, Tucson, August 15.

Mapes, Aimee C. 2014b. "Our Freshman Year: Stage One Results of a Five-Year Longitudinal Study of Student Writers." Presented at the Council of Writing Program Administrators, Normal, IL, July 19.

Mapes, Aimee C., and Amy C. Kimme Hea. 2014. "Second Year Data Collection." Presented at the University of Arizona Writing Program Teacher Development General Meeting, Tucson, January 13.

Mapes, Aimee C., and Amy C. Kimme Hea. 2016. "Report on UA Longitudinal Study of Student Writing." Presented at the Council of Writing Program Administrators, Raleigh, NC, July 16.

Mapes, Aimee C., and Amy C. Kimme Hea. 2018. "Languaging as Belonging: Insights from a Five-Year Longitudinal Study—Part One." Presented at the College Composition and Communication Conference, Kansas City, MO, March 17.

McGee, Sharon James. 2005. "Overcoming Disappointment: Constructing Writing Program Identity through Postmodern Mapping." In *Discord and Direction: The Postmodern Writing Program Administrator*, ed. Sharon James McGee and Carolyn Handa, 59–71. Logan: Utah State University Press.

Peres, Anushka Miriam Swan. 2020. "Queer Ecovisual Rhetorics and Settler Colonial Landscapes." PhD dissertation, University of Arizona, Tucson.

Porter, James E., Patricia A. Sullivan, Stuart Blythe, Jeffrey Grabill, and Libby Miles. 2000. "Institutional Critique: A Rhetorical Methodology for Change." *College Composition and Communication* 51 (4): 610–42.

Ribero, Ana. 2014. "'I am not a good writer and they had told me that I do not have a voice': Patterns of Metacognitive Knowledge and Affect in First-Year Writers' Reflections." Presented at the Conference of Writing Program Administration, Normal, IL, July 19.

Ribero, Ana Milena. 2016. "Citizenship and Undocumented Youth: An Analysis of the Rhetorics of Migrant-Rights Activism in Neoliberal Contexts." PhD dissertation, University of Arizona, Tucson.

Santa Cruz, Nicole. 2010. "Arizona Bill Targeting Ethnic Studies Signed into Law." *Los Angeles Times*, May 12.

Slack, Jennifer Daryl. 1996. "The Theory and Method of Articulation in Cultural Studies." In *Stuart Hall: Critical Dialogues in Cultural Studies*, ed. David Morley and Kuan-Hsing Chen, 112–27. London: Routledge.

Tohono O'odham. 2016. "Tohono O'odham History and Culture." http://www.tonation-nsn.gov/history-culture/.

University Analytics and Institutional Research. 2022. "UA Factbook, Enrollment Data." https://uair.arizona.edu/content/enrollment.

University of Arizona. 2021. "About Us." https://www.arizona.edu/about.

United States Department of Transportation. n.d. "Bureau of Transportation Statistics Border Crossing Data." https://www.bts.gov/browse-statistical-products-and-data/border-crossing-data/border-crossingentry-data.

Valencia, Richard R., and Daniel G. Solórzano. 1997. "Contemporary Deficit Thinking." In *The Evolution of Deficit Thinking: Educational Thought and Practice*, ed. Richard R. Valencia, 160–210. New York: Routledge.

Walker, Kenneth. 2014. "Reflection in Action: Developing Complex Coding Schemes for Metacognition and Affect in the UA Study." Presented at the Conference of Writing Program Administration, Normal, IL, July 19.

6
RESEARCHING FOR CAPITAL
Longitudinal Research, Precarity, and Institutional Citizenship

Doug Downs, Mark Schlenz, Miles Nolte, and Ashley Rives

WPAs and non-tenurable (NT) writing faculty have long experienced tension between refusing and accepting opportunities that involve extra work without clear forms of compensation (that is, institutional exploitation).[1] For example, faced with a new, unpaid demand for learning outcomes assessment, some faculty might "do the bare minimum," offering grudging compliance, while others might "go the extra mile," motivated not only by personal standards of professional excellence and dedication to student learning but also by hope for institutional rewards of some kind. Patricia Stephens (2004, 45) draws from Pierre Bourdieu's thinking on social capital to explain the potential that faculty bank on when they invest against their immediate interests: "Players can and do use their accumulated capital to transform the rules of the game," whereby "over time, different kinds of capital can come to be valued . . . When players attempt to subvert the distribution of capital, to disrupt the status quo, a space for change becomes possible." Writing program administrators (WPAs) and faculty may play a similar game when they comply with (and thereby sustain) exploitative institutional structures and practices—if doing so enables them to build enough capital to make material and structural changes that benefit the precariat (Daniel 2017) by resisting and rewriting those structures.

In 2014, NT faculty, graduate students, and the tenured director of Montana State University's (MSU) Core Writing Program faced such choices as we contemplated a longitudinal research project on multi-year learning gains from our writing-about-writing first-year composition pedagogy. Given a long-standing lack of support for NT faculty and graduate student instructors (e.g., professional development, reasonable pay), we felt a real tension between their desire to conduct program research and the exploitative effect of such involvement. Even given

https://doi.org/10.7330/9781646424337.c006

what we stood to learn about pedagogy through such research, would it really *pay off* for these instructors in terms of institutional membership and well-being? Could it be ethical to engage contingent faculty, who contractually were not asked—or paid—to keep research portfolios, in such work? Could it be ethical *not* to?

In retrospect, we can frame the complexities of the decisions we made through a citizenship metaphor. At MSU and throughout American higher education, research is essential to full institutional citizenship. The membership, entitlements, privileges, permanence, and belonging that many institutions grant faculty hang on a research portfolio. Teachers without research assignments are easily reduced to disposable, at-will instructional labor and regarded, as Susan H. McLeod (2008, 166) states, as "other" and "second-class citizens." Wherever this economy is in place, teaching-intensive or teaching-exclusive positions both lower instructional costs and restrict access to the capital associated with full institutional citizenship. As we pondered conducting research together, we considered the limits and possibilities of citizenship on our campus. In particular, we wondered if longitudinal research could support contingent faculty members' bids for institutional citizenship. Recognizing that longitudinal research involves duration and rewards stability—the very opposite of precarity—we also wondered if faculty without full institutional citizenship (e.g., contractual research assignments) would be hampered or professionally harmed by conducting longitudinal research. Would undertaking volitional and largely uncompensated research be to their benefit in any way, or would it simply extend institutional malfeasance toward contingent faculty?

Our deliberations were complicated by the limited public record on NT writing faculty as longitudinal researchers. While many longitudinal research teams include NT faculty and graduate students, published accounts have tended to elide researcher identities and positionalities. Rarely are all team members even named, much less identified as tenurable or non-tenurable faculty, graduate students, or undergraduates. A literature review confirms that accounts of NT or graduate student researchers involved in longitudinal writing research are unavailable outside this volume (see Mapes, chapter 7, and Hashlamon, chapter 8, this volume). Not only have the field's research reporting practices reinscribed institutional habits of rendering non-tenurable research team members invisible, the resulting absence of data makes it impossible to estimate their contributions to our field. The flattening of research experiences also leaves no trace of the impacts researchers' institutional standings have had on their research.

On its face, we might assume that longitudinal research is solely the domain of tenurable faculty and PhD students. Who else has the assigned time for a research project that by definition goes long? Who else does the institution contractually hold in place long enough to see a multi-year project through? Who else can afford to research rather than work an additional job? Who else has the time, know-how, and professional and institutional citizenship to write and manage the grants for such research or the ensuing progress reports and publications? The reality is that longitudinal research demands resources, agency, and institutional and professional capital that are difficult to come by for all researchers, including the doctoral students and tenurable faculty most frequently cited as principal investigators. Moreover, researchers of all ranks and roles experience different kinds and levels of precarity in the contemporary university, stemming from institutional structures and motives as well as human dynamics. Citizenship, to varying degrees, counters precarity by increasing access to available privileges and providing influence within the institution. But no faculty are without precarity, and citizenship that supplies full stability and guaranteed resources sufficient to the demands and realities of teaching and researching in higher education is a myth. Longitudinal research is a reality check, fundamentally an undertaking in precarity.

Perhaps instinctive recognition of this reality is one reason we believed a longitudinal project might be possible even for our precarious team. After all, no team makeup would eliminate precarity or grant unlimited agency. Instead, we embraced the combined certainties that all research is precarious and that full institutional citizenship is beyond reach of those not researching—even while a research portfolio does not guarantee citizenship—and decided to dive in to a longitudinal project. Our team was ultimately composed of one tenured faculty and WPA (Doug), three non-tenurable faculty (Mark, Miles, and Ashley), and two MA-student instructors (Kim and Julie). In this chapter, we turn a narrative retrospective lens on the interplay of citizenship and precarity in our collaboration, seeking insight into the ways the team negotiated the complexities of precarity in relation to longitudinal research and the impact of those complexities on both the project and each researcher's institutional citizenship.

CITIZENSHIP AND PRECARITY

Citizenship is a useful metaphor for its entailments of membership and enfranchisement. It signals a protected status of belonging and entitlement with notes of permanence or stability, voice, and participation in governance, implying due process and equity. Metaphorically, citizenship further entails access to forums for contribution and conversation and thus rights to participate in "substantive interactivity" (Spinuzzi et al. 2003, 172). Citizens are also vested with certain agency and autonomy (Stephens 2004, 48), enjoying a range of uninspected activity not accorded to non-citizens. The metaphor is painfully loaded in the current US political moment, given the continual burden on non-white bodies to, in effect, "show their papers." Faculty, by analogy, show their papers in annual reviews, with NT faculty frequently having to reapply for their own jobs.

Citizenship also entails civic duty and responsibility; Eileen E. Schell (1998, 119, 117) emphasizes "the responsibility to be informed" and the "academic citizenship" responsibility to advocate for one another. Some literature uses *only* this civic responsibility entailment, such as the Modern Language Association (MLA) Commission on Professional Service's report (1996). To argue for service as intellectually valuable and thus meriting greater institutional credit, the MLA made intellectual work and "professional citizenship" poles of an axis—demonstrating what we *don't* mean by "citizenship" and unintentionally emphasizing how integral research actually is to full institutional enfranchisement. For the MLA, "intellectual work" is "ideational work" that "must explicitly invoke ideas and explore their consequences," and it requires intellectual accomplishment that can only emerge from scholarly or professional expertise (175). Intellectual work "contributing to the development and use of knowledge is primary in the academic value system: it is the defining character of faculty work in an institution of higher learning and a prerequisite for its highest rewards" (174). Thus, research, teaching, and service can all be intellectual work.

By contrast, "professional citizenship"—in which excellence "is expected as a sine qua non of faculty citizenship, necessary but not sufficient for professional achievement and the most significant academic rewards" (Modern Language Association Commission on Professional Service 1996, 179)—involves the "many faculty tasks and responsibilities that do not constitute or demand substantive intellectual contributions . . . yet they are useful, even essential . . . in order to create, maintain, and improve the infrastructure that maintains the academy" (174). For the MLA, then, "citizenship" entails duty alone, obligation to serve, and infrastructure only, with intellectual work standing as superstructure upon—neither contributing to nor rewarded by—"citizenship." We prefer to understand citizenship rather as the whole of academic life and membership, including but not limited to those "most significant academic rewards" merited only by intellectual work. In our view, access to, inclusion in, and expectation of intellectual work constitutes institutional citizenship. Intellectual work and its paragon, research, cannot be bifurcated from citizenship.

The Council of Writing Program Administrators (1998) affirms our position, premising intellectual work as the coin of the higher-ed realm. Further illustrations are prominent in the literature of our field, where the concept of citizenship often exists even if the term is absent. William J. Carpenter (2002), for example, captures a citizenly interplay among faculty roles, privileges, and responsibilities: "a rightful member of a professional community . . . capable of participating in and shaping the conversations and activities that define the community and its members . . . to analyze and critique the community and the actions of its members" (158). Numerous contributors to Theresa Enos and Shane Borrowman's 2008 collection *The Promise and Perils of Writing Program Administration* speak to citizenship as well. Nita Danko (2008, 138) uses the touchstone "without title" to mark disenfranchisement, distinguishing between working *for* the community but not feeling invited to work *in* it. Claire C. Lamonica (2008) recounts her department's attempt to help her by shielding her from research requirements while administrating, rendering her non-promotable and non-competitive in the job market. Emily Isaacs (2008, 177) notes how much weight is given to "what have you published," excluding "what have you researched? What have you written? How have you used your expertise and research to further the interests of teaching writing to college students," which better encompass a teacher-scholar's role. Suellynn Duffey (2008, 144) speaks of her institution drawing a direct line between intellectual property and faculty standing as "the naturalized paradigm," in which non-tenurable faculty and staff were to "know their place."

By these definitions, NT writing faculty are almost always less than full institutional citizens. Our field, in fact, prototyped the academy's present revelry in precarity, which often excludes NT faculty from professional engagement and cuts them off from teacherly growth, participation in research, and even conversation with one another. Ann Penrose (2012, 109) says the material conditions of NT labor suggest that "NTT faculty are not members of the professional communities in which they work"; Randall Bowden and Lynn P. Gonzalez (2012, 5) conclude that contingent faculty are generally excluded from "the historical function of higher education to promote inquiry and advance the sum of human knowledge." This exclusion is so de rigueur that even some scholarship devoted to NT faculty well-being fails to notice it (e.g., Baldwin and Chronister 2002; Kezar and Sam 2013). Professional isolation and the stresses of precarity, particularly "a loss of linguistic and discursive agency" (Daniel 2017, 64), inveigh against entailments of citizenship crucial to faculty empowerment, particularly communication and networks (Kezar and Sam 2013).

As we have observed, an inverse correlation between precarity and citizenship does not mean they are binary poles of an axis whereby full institutional citizenship eliminates precarity. Some precarities are baked into institutional structures and systems by managerial forces (both within a given institution and in outside systems like state governments and agencies) to control and direct faculty agency. These precarities might include artificial constriction of resources, credentialing that creates gatekeeping, and limits on shared governance, due process, equity, and agency such as illusory faculty input, elimination of faculty ombuds, and capricious application of policy. Other precarities emerge in balancing teaching, research, and being human. These binds, shortages, and instabilities relate to workload management and time resources, divided attention and competing priorities, strains relating to interpersonal interaction (including favoritism and exclusion), and advancement and recognition pressures such as ladder climbing and rat racing. None of these precarities is exclusive to researchers who are NT faculty or students; none is escaped by tenure or research contracts.

Rather, citizenship demarks paths and privileges that help teacher-researchers *negotiate* inescapable precarities. For example, no one has enough time, but instructors also tasked with research (that is, in our construct, treated as full citizens) may at least have access to time-sharing measures (workload proportion adjustments, sabbaticals, research leaves) and aids (research assistants, grant-writing offices) to help manage that particular precarity. It is those precarities that result from inadequate access to or exclusion from such facilitative and protective privileges for citizens as exist within institutional structures that we emphasize here.

While our retrospection emphasizes negotiating precarity in longitudinal research, we choose this lens of institutional citizenship as a hopeful take on a disturbing reality. We have continued to see our individual choices to conduct longitudinal research as a needful and valid optimism, an effort not just to make an intellectual contribution to writing studies and build a sense of professional engagement and accomplishment but to reduce our institutional precarities as well—even though our results were limited.

INTRODUCTIONS: INSTITUTION AND RESEARCHERS

Our drive for professional engagement and citizenship converged with the problem of our writing program's standing in the university and our desire to understand the long-term outcomes of our first-year composition (FYC) pedagogy. MSU is Montana's R1 university, with a STEM/Ag focus. Required writing instruction and accompanying infrastructure are vestigial compared to those of peers: the gen-ed writing requirement is one first-year course (exempted by 30 percent of students) with no required upper-division writing instruction. Writing assignments beyond short daily homework are the exception rather than the rule across campus.

Most FYC is taught by NT faculty, whom MSU has had a rich history of neglecting. NTs are limited to one-year contracts, and compensation is slender for the locale. We struggle for and rarely secure steady funding for professional development or NT faculty meetings. NT faculty have thus been starved for development, even organizing their own reading group prior to Doug's becoming WPA in 2013. Contracts are teaching-only (no service or research assignment) even though the faculty handbook requires teachers to engage in professional development and contact with students beyond the classroom (e.g., in mentoring and writing recommendations). Not only, then, could funded research increase NT faculty's financial compensation, but it would significantly increase their professional engagement. Of course, such research participation would thereby undermine the entire point of teaching-only contracts, which relegate NT instructors to "deliver" curricula rather than systematically build the knowledge on which curricula might be based.

What we sought to study through longitudinal research was how a writing-about-writing (WAW) pedagogy (Downs and Wardle 2007; Bird et al. 2019; Wardle and Downs 2020) fueled students' learning about writing semesters after their FYC course. We used a pre-/post-metacognition assessment in WAW and non-WAW FYC courses to see whether students were gaining a metacognitive perspective, and then we recruited a subset of assessed students for the study's longitudinal phase. Our plan was to interview each student once per semester while collecting their school writing until they earned their undergraduate degree. In practice, we struggled and largely failed to keep students engaged in the study beyond their first year of participation, a problem we attributed to both the limited writing assigned across the university and the logistical difficulty we had scheduling interviews with our own limited time.

As noted earlier, "we" were six writing teachers in various roles in our Core Writing Program. The project was conceived by Doug and

Mark in winter 2013. Mark was our most experienced NT researcher. A high school teacher in the late 1970s and the 1980s, he participated in the original National Writing Project site and in the 1990s earned a PhD in environmental literature at the University of California, Santa Barbara (UCSB). There, he served as a non-tenure-track (NTT) WPA and in 2001 wrote a composition textbook (Kirscht and Schlenz 2001). After leaving UCSB to run a publishing house, he joined MSU in 2010 to teach literature and composition. During our study (in 2017), Mark also became assistant director of our writing program, based on his fire for and expertise with NTT faculty development. Doug began as WPA in his sixth year at MSU, immediately following achieving tenure and promotion to associate professor. He had published regularly on college-level writing, research, and reading pedagogy, helping develop WAW pedagogies and the textbook *Writing about Writing* (Wardle and Downs 2020). At the end of Doug's first semester as director, his and Mark's conversations centered on two problems: studying the value of the program's WAW pedagogy for learning transfer, and engaging NT instructors with the profession in the absence of funding. While Doug, like the rest of the team, had no experience with longitudinal research, he was a full faculty citizen. As such, MSU supported his engagement with the Conference on College Composition and Communication (CCCC) and the Council of Writing Program Administrators (CWPA), which were sources of guidance, funding, and resources for conducting longitudinal research. Mark and Doug were the two team members on the project from beginning to end. (Mark retired in 2019.)

The original team also included Miles Nolte, NT faculty, and Kimberly Hoover, a graduate student instructor in our English MA program. Doug and Mark recruited them based on their desire for professional engagement (even at the cost of additional workload and time), their interest in writing pedagogy, and their engagement with our program's WAW pedagogy. We shared a convivial work history. Miles had been an NT instructor since completing his MA in English in 2012. Lacking seniority to land a full-time teaching schedule, he taught part-time while maintaining careers as a fly-fishing outfitter and a freelance magazine writer and columnist. Thus, Miles was not only an excellent, experienced pedagogue; he was also a natural anchor for collaborative work, including writing. Miles worked on the project from its inception in 2014 until fall 2016, several months after he had left MSU for writing work in New York City. Kim also started with the project in spring 2014, in the second semester of her MA program. She was studying metacognition for her thesis and had read more extensively on the subject than the rest of us. After completing her MA the following year, Kim spent 2015–16 as an NT instructor in our program before departing for Pittsburgh to begin a PhD. She separated from the project in early 2017 as her doctoral work intensified (and she elected not to take part in this retrospective).

With Miles's and Kim's departures, we needed two more researchers for the project's final year. In early 2017 we used the same criteria for recruitment, seeking an NT and a graduate instructor. Ashley Rives Engler had completed her MA in English at MSU in 2014 and became an NT instructor that fall. She published a portion of her MA thesis research on Common Core State Standards in the *Journal of Adolescent and Adult Literacy* (Rives and Olsen 2015) and was interested in further research. Ashley worked on the project through its end in spring 2018 and taught at MSU through spring 2020. Julie Christen also joined the project in spring 2017, at the end of her first year of MA studies. As in Kim's case, Julie was studying composition pedagogy, was innovative with WAW pedagogy, and was eager both to build research experience and to see further inside our particular study. She worked on the project until its end and began a PhD at Arizona State University in fall 2018. (While Julie contributed to our retrospective, she opted not to coauthor this chapter.)

ABUNDANCE, SCARCITY, DELIGHT, AND FRUSTRATION

To build our reflections, Doug coordinated and recorded retrospective conversations with team members. In the following accounts, individual researchers' voices are preserved in quoted material and paraphrases, while "we" and "our" represent the team's joint thinking. Our experience was typical of much reported longitudinal research, with highs and lows, discoveries and confounds, hits and misses. We see the complexity of our experiences in parallel with the complexities of our various institutional precarities and citizenships, as this section describes.

Abundances and Delights

In many ways, being able to design and carry out a longitudinal research project was just *neat*. As each of us hoped, longitudinal work fed our professional curiosities and interests. We got to interact with each other and build our program by engaging our profession through reading and conference presentations. We were able to join the academically and institutionally valued activities of grant writing, team-based long-term research, and building on and contributing knowledge to pedagogy and learning outcomes. And in some ways, it was indeed useful for building institutional capital—status toward fuller citizenship (particularly for the WPA and graduate students).

While the university excludes an entire class of teachers (NT faculty) from research, both their teacherly instincts and their own experiences as graduate students make research's value to teaching indelible. Mark expressed this directly: "My whole orientation to pedagogy is based on research. If you're going to know this thing, you're going to know it by contributing to what's known or questioning what's known—you're not going to know it otherwise." Ashley noted the role of research in the belonging and substantive interactivity aspects of institutional citizenship: "It's just so hard and isolated, unless you do spend time talking to others or going into classrooms or reading, to know if what you're doing is aligning." As a researcher seeing other teachers' assignments and students' work, she gained perspective on her own students. Especially striking is the sustaining aspect of such engagement. Ashley noted several times the persistence of thinking the study generated: "Something I did two summers ago is still popping into my head when I'm doing final grading—I'm still learning and still trying to grow my own awareness and thinking about teaching. Having those conversations with Mark is still affecting my teaching. As NT there's very little space for that—it's really all I have to go on, is thinking about these various projects that I've been in." Ashley found value in "just being in the room—like, Mark and I may have different perspectives, but hearing his and hearing him talk about teaching always leaves me with something to think about." In our writing program, "spaces for those conversations just don't exist."

Ashley's pleasure at being included in significant work was echoed among the team. Miles, after delineating "higher-level" reasons that motivated his research, added, "On a personal-interest level, *cool*—I'm happy to be asked! That feels good!" Mark, comparing our research collaboration to his other faculty interactions, saw a rare communication. "Our collaboration *to begin with* was exceptional" within our department, he suggested. Doug shared that perspective, seeing how research and scholarship in the humanities often fosters monkish solitude. This project was the first time instructors in our program, working across tenure and degree lines, were able to spend summer mornings on a backyard deck or winter afternoons by a coffee shop fireplace talking *research*. This convivial aspect of university citizenship was a delight and a relief. The same was true of the opportunity longitudinal research created for funding NT faculty and graduate students to participate in national professional meetings. The energy, connection, and inclusion in our field's conferences are of tremendous value for writing teachers; increasing the number of teachers in our program able to attend and contribute to them was a huge win from our project.

Doug, as a tenured researcher, was excited at the opportunity for "big inquiry" that team-based longitudinal research provided, bolstered by a CCCC Research Initiative Grant. For him as for the rest of the team, the project provided career highlights. It also amplified his already significant citizenship privileges, which he hoped to leverage for institutional change. As a WPA concerned with instructor equity, Doug hoped the value of the study would at least partially offset its insufficiently compensated workload. In Miles's words, the hope was that he might "gain some capital in the program" and incent the department "to keep me around and pay me more." Both Miles and Mark particularly felt their contingency, which factored directly into Miles's eventual departure. "Were my position more stable and substantive," he reflected, "that would have allowed me to invest in this project in a different way, and it would have made the leaving decision way harder. I'm not sure it would have changed it, but had MSU been more interested in keeping me around, that whole math on where I was going and what I was doing would have changed." The connection between research and citizenship was also reflected in Mark's thinking: "I just really see being involved in research as part of our labor advocacy. Research is essential to labor conditions." In a community that grants full faculty citizenship only to researchers, all faculty jobs must permit research. This conviction drove Mark's constant rejoinder to whether we could afford to have NT faculty researching: "Can we afford not to?"

Our project also built our senses of *agency* in satisfying personal professional curiosity. Miles in particular expressed personal investment in "figuring out ways of programmatizing [our curricular WAW] approach—I felt some level of personal attachment to championing it." Mark expressed similar investment in writing with Kim and Doug on a *CCC* article draft: "It's like dang, man! The thinking, collaborating, the mental work of it was like my life work, like a synthesis of it all." Mark also hit on a statement that covered every member of the research team. "Motivation is never what's lacking for me," he said. "Opportunity is what's lacking. Opportunity and reward, I guess." Even Doug, as a more fully enfranchised citizen, felt this sense of opportunity as well as a much-appreciated sense of focus. Longitudinal research offered a way "to track down the mental paths my work opens to me. My curiosity is to research All the Things, but without inventing the thirty-four-hour day or a responsible way to ignore everything but my own interests, I'm stuck."

Lest we overlook the obvious, these reflections on personal satisfaction make clear that the NT faculty the institution excludes from research, and thus full citizenship, are not categorically unwilling or unable to research. That said, in considering NT faculty to recruit to the project, Doug and Mark sampled a wide range of NT faculty investment in research and what it represented. "This is the difference between a job, a gig, and a calling," Mark suggested. "There is a divide: there are people who if not fulfilled, if you don't give them growth opportunities, these people don't function. And there are people who, 'No, this is just a job, and your growth opportunities are makin' me look bad!'" Our project demonstrated how NT positions allow for a greater range of vocation, literally *calling*, than universities have historically rewarded with citizenship. As post-tenure review procedures acknowledge, a similar range exists among tenured faculty, and our longitudinal research experience reinforces the need to question institutionally rigid associations of instructor type and research support.

While the rest of our account complicates the general optimism associated with our longitudinal research, our overall experience was positive. Each of us found ourselves more strongly engaged with our professional community and more fully "citizen"—regardless of whether the institution acknowledged it.

Scarcities, Vulnerabilities, and Frustrations

As noted earlier, any instructor or faculty administrator encounters precarities through structural and artificial scarcities and instabilities. Varying degrees of citizenship provide or deny means of negotiating such precarity, and conducting longitudinal research amplifies the challenges of such negotiation. Our experiences designing and conducting longitudinal research highlighted many of these quotidian challenges.

For example, people wanting more time is universal, and we did for our project. But our contrasting citizenships mediated time's scarcity. Our base teaching loads were, for Doug as WPA, 2/1 (administrative reassignment from the standard tenure-line 2/2 load); for NT faculty, 4/4; and for graduate students, 2/1. Doug, with full institutional citizenship, could have sought a one-course research buyout. However, he didn't want to further give up teaching, so he committed more of his contracted research time (nominally 40 percent of workload) to this project, or so he told himself. But teaching reassignments were institutionally impossible for other instructors—when we queried HR on behalf of NT teachers, we were memorably told, "yeah, that's not actually a thing." So we attempted to trade time for money by using the bulk of our grant funding (about $6,500/year) for NT and graduate student summer stipends. But that meant only about $2,000 per year per researcher, while paying an equivalent to one course per semester would have required about $11,000 per year (including benefits). In reality, then, NT and graduate researchers significantly increased their workload and time demands with only token compensation. For each of us, this negotiation of scarcity came down to a poor but deliberate compromise of self-care and desire. We were a crystal example of Sue Doe and colleagues' (2011, 445, original emphasis) statement that "professional activities by non-tenure line faculty are troubling *not* because these faculty members choose to participate in them, but rather because colleges and universities take advantage of the uniquely human capacity to derive satisfaction from the mere fact of functioning as a professional."

We experienced time scarcity most as frustrations with attention and prioritization. Ashley framed the problem of compensation by stipend rather than by time in terms of loyalties: "It's easier to push off the research until there's a meeting and you're like, oh crap, I really have to do something because I do value these people—but that's why it gets put off, because you have to face your *students* and you can't be, like, 'I was doing this other thing and not looking at your work.' It's just the balance of, who am I going to see next and how do I face them and make sure I have my stuff done." Failing to offset research work with fewer students meant that team members often felt they didn't have the bandwidth for both, which sometimes constrained the quality of our work. Miles reflected that "I would have liked to have been able to designate more mental resources to the writing stage of this—the conclusions I drew and the ways I drew those could have been more substantive and richer . . . But I wasn't trying to go beyond because I was just trying to get *this* thing done." As Ashley said, "It's a hard tension of wanting to be involved and yet really feeling like I'm not giving it my all—it doesn't become my top priority because the thing I *am* getting paid to do at the moment [teaching] is my top priority, even if intellectually the other part [research] informs it." And while Doug's positionality gave him more potential breathing room, his WPA commitments and other research projects were already using it all up—the effects of competing loyalties, prioritization, and divided attention were the same.

What might have been costliest to the longitudinal nature of our project, with this time and attention scarcity, was difficulty maintaining long-term relationships with students in the study. One of the most consistent trends in longitudinal research reports is the unique relationships that emerge between researchers and participants over years of contact (in this collection alone, for example, see Driscoll, chapter 2; Rosenberg, chapter 3; and Jacobson and Rifenburg, chapter 1). Having to divide our attention so much diminished our "loyalty" to active relation building with our participants in ways that hampered our ability to remain in contact and schedule interviews.

Scarcities of time, compensation, and institutional capital intensified when it seemed that citizenship capital was not actually accruing throughout the study: the institution continued to value research work from tenurable faculty and graduate students but not from NT faculty. As a result, NT researchers realistically had only personal motivation, not real career motivation, to work from. Lacking both compensation and credit, Miles acknowledged that "it was very easy to kind of blow it off a little bit because it was like 'this isn't a *real* job'—no one's really counting on us for this, nobody's really paying us very much money to do this." The unsustainability of this situation deepened for NT researchers in particular as money and healthcare pressures intensified. They might calculate, as Mark did, that research would "add to my résumé which would add to my bottom line which would make me financially more secure," but they might also be in a position equivalent to Miles's: teacher, outfitter, and writer. "I'm accustomed to keeping a lot of trains on track," he confirmed, "but I was trying to work one job—the outdoor recreation job was all-consuming, there really wasn't space for thought—and then there were other writing deadlines occupying my time and frankly paying much better. I know that I can get the writing done for this research piece in a smaller sliver of time—that probably was what suffered just due to what money I needed to make." Had we been able to "swap out coursework for research work" with equivalent pay, Miles concluded, "I would have said, *sweet*, I know how to do the math on that—I'll take X many less trips and I'll seek out X many less freelance opportunities, and I'll make that work."[2]

Our institution historically has not counted NT faculty publications toward any increased standing, so even that traditional goldmine of institutional capital offered only limited motivation. As with the time conundrum, it is difficult to tease apart the publishing difficulties inherent to longitudinal research itself or to teacher-researcher life generically, particularly those stemming from limited citizenship. Our study joins a list of major longitudinal research projects that have generated more conference presentations than publications. Difficulties with both data collection and analysis complicated our decisions about, and grounds for, what to write. But a larger problem was sustaining coordinated focus on the pieces we did work on. Kimberly Hoover's chapter in Barbara Bird and colleagues' collection (2019), along with data Doug included in invited talks (e.g., Downs 2016) and book chapters (e.g., Downs 2020), saw daylight because they were largely individual works. By contrast, our collaborative efforts suffered as divided attention and competing demands for time created what Robert Pirsig (2005 [1974], 304) called "gumption traps" or what Doug calls "headwinds," spirit-sucking drag that causes us to lose heart or interest or forces other priorities to take precedence. Academic writers well know how easy it is to lose momentum on projects; we think this challenge increases when the research is longitudinal and increases further when an institution not only complicates the means of doing such work but also lowers its rewards for writer-researchers who are less than full citizens.

How might we have better negotiated these scarcities? We might have further leveraged Doug's full-citizen privileges, having him give up some teaching through a course buyout to take up more of the project load from other researchers, thus more equitably distributing scarce time resources. But the multi-semester demand of longitudinal research would have far outstripped the institution's forbearance; a long-term reassignment from an already reduced teaching load would have been unobtainable, except perhaps with six-figure external funding over several years. The way to do such a project again would probably be to ensure an actual one-course/semester teaching reduction for NT researchers, which would require a daunting amount of funding. Being able to schedule just five hours per week of shared time for research training, data collection and analysis, and team discussion would make a night-and-day difference to such projects. A further priority would be expanding the number of researchers so we could gather additional data and do more with it, increasing the power of the study. Ultimately, the time-scarcity problem, particularly as encountered by NT faculty, is the most troublesome chicken-and-egg aspect of trying to use citizenship-demanding research methods to accrue capital toward citizenship, particularly from an ethical perspective.

Contingent researchers were also vulnerable to having their limited citizenship summarily revoked. All four NT faculty (Ashley, Kim, Mark, and Miles), as newer hires—and Mark as a rare NT faculty with a PhD that our dean didn't like to spend "extra" money per course on—were on the bubble when enrollment fluctuated. Both Miles and Mark hoped that research participation might enhance their value to the university and protect them from losing sections or their jobs. Mark worried, "I'm involved in this project, I want this project to work, I want it to come to fruition—do I have a [teaching] contract next semester? If not, shoot, I've failed the project. To me, that was a very real risk. In giving myself over completely and working on something—it's an anxiety that my subaltern status threatens the viability of the project." Two researchers did leave MSU during the project. Kim's departure for a PhD was expected, but Miles's move out of academe was a loss Doug had striven to head off. Miles saw that no matter our efforts, MSU simply was not committed to developing the writing program or its faculty, and he had good alternatives. After taking a semester to explore writing opportunities in New York City, his evolving professional and personal life—combined with MSU's lack of commitment and stability—made a return to MSU and the research project untenable.

In designing our longitudinal study, we understood that researchers could come and go, but we didn't successfully plan for continuity. As personnel changed, our lack of foresight brought confounds to our interviewing, coding, data analysis, and efforts to resolve findings. As newcomers in the project's fourth year, Ashley and Julie felt limited by not having participated in prior design and decision-making. Ashley recalled, "I kept running into moments of 'I wouldn't have coded it this way based on my own understanding and I don't understand how this happened,' which made me question, how did we get to that?" She also found that "with two people gone, we couldn't ask them questions to understand their thought process in that coding, and the remaining team members couldn't always speak to what the former members had meant." Perhaps it goes without saying that in longitudinal research design, a system to ensure continuity from departing to arriving researchers is a basic need. We think, though, that this aspect of longitudinal methods is muted in existing reports in part because more precarious and contingent researchers are so rarely highlighted there.

LONGITUDINAL RESEARCH, PRECARITY, AND CITIZENSHIP

Despite the difficulties and dissatisfactions of our longitudinal project, none of us regrets launching and participating in it; the upsides were definitely worthwhile. Even with what we've come to understand about the structural difficulties of longitudinal research, particularly with vexed institutional citizenship, the question is not, as Mark and Doug originally struggled with, whether we ought to do it but simply how. As we frame that problem in retrospect, understanding precarity through a lens of citizenship can help future longitudinal teams consider and plan wisely for the complexities they face.

Some of those complexities are the entangled nature of advantages and disadvantages, the often unclear distinctions between institutional positions (tenurable, WPA, NT, graduate) as relates to various precarities, and the limits of even full-citizen advantages. For us, participating in the study simultaneously improved (through engagement) and degraded (through overload) the quality of our professional lives. Further, *lasting* advantages accrued more to Doug and the graduate students than to NT faculty because of the way higher education differentiates citizenship, with NT faculty excluded from research and its institutional capital by design. The circular problem of experience is a case in point: our project would in many ways have gone better with more experienced (PhD-holding) researchers participating, but it is a luxury to be able to accrue such experience, and not all researchers are enfranchised to do so. And even Doug's full institutional citizenship was not proof against some structural precarities built into researching in universities. For instance, time and funding were theoretically more available, but not practically so. Our efforts did not alter these structures at MSU, though they altered us as teacher-researchers in good ways.

We therefore also conclude that while full institutional citizenship can help researchers negotiate some of the precarities of longitudinal research in limited ways, it can't eliminate them. Some privileges of citizenship, such as relative permanence and contractual space for research, make longitudinal methods easier to use; but long projects demand resources that institutions are not always willing or able to give even full citizens. The demand in higher education that full citizens be researchers becomes even more fraught when the research in question is longitudinal. The precarities college teachers increasingly face are inimical to the stability, support, and long-term commitment required by longitudinal projects. Retrospection on varied precarity in our own project exposes both the question of how longitudinal methods will continue to be viable in the current higher-ed regime and the importance of reporting and reading longitudinal projects, data, and findings through the lens of the precarities that shaped them.

Thus, we are grateful to be able to write openly about our difficulties, delights, frustrations, and pleasures in conducting longitudinal research with reference to our specific institutional positions. So many realities of longitudinal projects are under erasure in the channels through which researchers typically report such projects, and it was disheartening to find that just as NT faculty and graduate students are often invisible in our institutions, their positionalities have similarly been largely invisible in research publications. As a field, we can better advocate for citizenship and research rights for NT faculty if they are visible in our writing, fronting ways in which researchers' citizen statuses shape and constrain our projects.

NOTES

1. Due to the very time, resource, and contract constraints our chapter highlights, Doug drafted the chapter alone based on the other authors' input and incorporated their feedback in revisions. While in the humanities it's unusual for non-"writers" to receive author credit, here science-based author credits are warranted. Mark, Miles, and Ashley's contributions in focusing the piece, providing so much of its text orally, reading and commenting on multiple versions, and coming to key insights across those drafts make them authors.
2. Yet we don't want to oversimplify. By the end of our study in 2018, the writing program *was* able to negotiate NT course reassignments for small-scale, one-year research projects. NT researchers still found it difficult to balance priorities, which Ashley suggests was because experience, such as one builds earning a PhD, is at least as big a factor as time. Miles similarly notes that while the lack of institutional resources limited our longitudinal project, a lack of experience with research broadly also strongly limited the project. Their provisos call us to consider at greater length how English MA students build empirical research experience.

REFERENCES

Baldwin, Roger G., and Jay L. Chronister. 2002. *Teaching without Tenure: Policies and Practices for a New Era*. Baltimore: Johns Hopkins University Press.

Bird, Barbara, Doug Downs, Moriah McCracken, and Jan Rieman, eds. 2019. *Next Steps: New Directions for/in Writing about Writing*. Logan: Utah State University Press.

Bowden, Randall, and Lynn P. Gonzalez. 2012. "The Rise of Contingent Faculty: Its Impact on the Professoriate and Higher Education." *Journal of Applied Research in Higher Education* 4 (1): 5–22.

Carpenter, William J. 2002. "Professional Development for Writing Program Staff." In *The Allyn and Bacon Sourcebook for Writing Program Administrators*, ed. Irene Ward and William J. Carpenter, 155–65. New York: Allyn and Bacon.

Council of Writing Program Administrators. 1998. "Evaluating the Intellectual Work of Writing Administration." http://www.wpacouncil.org/aws/CWPA/pt/sd/news_article/242849.

Daniel, James Rushing. 2017. "Freshman Composition as a Precariat Enterprise." *College English* 80 (1): 63–85.

Danko, Nita. 2008. "Without Title: One NTT's Struggle in the TT Society." In *The Promise and Perils of Writing Program Administration*, ed. Theresa Enos and Shane Borrowman, 135–39. West Lafayette, IN: Parlor Press.

Doe, Sue, Natalie Barns, David Bowen, David Gilkey, Ginger Guardiola Smoak, Sarah Ryan, Kirk Sarell, Laura H. Thomas, Lucy J. Troup, and Mike Palmquist. 2011. "Discourse of the Firetenders: Considering Contingent Faculty through the Lens of Activity Theory." *College English* 73 (4): 428–49.

Downs, Doug. 2016. "Building Sophisticated Rhetorical Awareness in Writing-about-Writing Courses." Keynote address. Presented at the Roundhouse Composition Symposium. University of Texas–Rio Grande Valley Writing Program, Edinburg, May 5.

Downs, Doug. 2020. "Double Standards and Sunshine: Exploring Expectations for Professional and Student Writing in FYC." In *Stories from First-Year Composition*, ed. Jo Anne Kerr and Ann Amicucci, 23–42. Fort Collins, CO: WAC Clearinghouse.

Downs, Doug, and Elizabeth Wardle. 2007. "Teaching about Writing, Righting Misconceptions: (Re)Envisioning 'First-Year Composition' as 'Introduction to Writing Studies.'" *College Composition and Communication* 58 (4): 552–84.

Duffey, Suellynn. 2008. "Skeletons in the Closet, Ghosts, and Other Invisible Creatures." In *The Promise and Perils of Writing Program Administration*, ed. Theresa Enos and Shane Borrowman, 139–46. West Lafayette, IN: Parlor Press.

Enos, Theresa, and Shane Borrowman, eds. 2008. *The Promise and Perils of Writing Program Administration*. West Lafayette, IN: Parlor Press.

Hoover, Kimberly, Elle Limesand, Maggie Hammond, and Max Wellman. 2019. "Writing about Writing Focus: A Roundtable." In *Next Steps: New Directions for/in Writing about Writing*, ed. Barbara Bird, Doug Downs, Moriah McCracken, and Jan Rieman, 209–19. Logan: Utah State University Press.

Isaacs, Emily. 2008. "Tenure, Promotion, and the WPA: What Is Research and Writing?" In *The Promise and Perils of Writing Program Administration*, ed. Theresa Enos and Shane Borrowman, 175–82. West Lafayette, IN: Parlor Press.

Kezar, Adrianna, and Cecile Sam. 2013. "Institutionalizing Equitable Policies and Practices for Contingent Faculty." *Journal of Higher Education* 84 (1): 56–87.

Kirscht, Judy, and Mark Schlenz. 2001. *Engaging Inquiry: Research and Writing in the Disciplines*. Upper Saddle River, NJ: Prentice-Hall.

Lamonica, Claire C. 2008. "Neither Fish nor Fowl: The Promise and Peril of Directing a Program on an Administrative Line." In *The Promise and Perils of Writing Program Administration*, ed. Theresa Enos and Shane Borrowman, 146–52. West Lafayette, IN: Parlor Press.

McLeod, Susan H. 2008. "Three Reflections and an Observation: Reflection Part I." In *The Promise and Perils of Writing Program Administration*, ed. Theresa Enos and Shane Borrowman, 164–67. West Lafayette, IN: Parlor Press.

Modern Language Association Commission on Professional Service. 1996. "Making Faculty Work Visible: Reinterpreting Professional Service, Teaching, and Research in the Fields of Language and Literature." *Profession 1996*: 161–216.

Penrose, Ann. 2012. "Professional Identity in a Contingent Labor Profession: Expertise, Autonomy, Community in Composition Teaching." *WPA: Writing Program Administration* 35 (2): 108–26.

Pirsig, Robert. 2005 [1974]. *Zen and the Art of Motorcycle Maintenance*. New York: Harper Perennial Modern Classics.

Rives, Ashley, and Allison Wynhoff Olsen. 2015. "Where's the Rhetoric?" *Journal of Adolescent and Adult Literacy* 59 (2): 161–70.

Schell, Eileen E. 1998. *Gypsy Academics and Mother-Teachers: Gender, Contingent Labor, and Writing Instruction*. Portsmouth, NH: Boynton/Cook.

Spinuzzi, Clay, Jennifer L. Bowie, Ida Rodgers, and Xiangyi Li. 2003. "Open Systems and Citizenship: Designing a Departmental Web Site as an Open System." *Computers and Composition* 20 (2): 168–93.

Stephens, Patricia. 2004. "A Move toward 'Academic Citizenship': Reading Emotion in the Narrative Structures of Part-Time Faculty." *WPA: Writing Program Administration* 27 (3): 35–51.

Wardle, Elizabeth, and Doug Downs. 2020. *Writing about Writing*. 4th ed. Boston: Bedford/St. Martin's.

7

MORE SIMPLE GIFTS
Labor, Relationships, and Ethics in Longitudinal Research

Aimee C. Mapes

HOW NOT TO CLIMB MOUNT EVEREST

Let me confess. Originally, I wanted to title this chapter "How Not to Climb Mount Everest." As everything felt daunting and precarious, overwhelmed by the *how* of the University of Arizona Longitudinal Study of Student Writers (UA Study), I gripped onto Nancy Sommers's (2008) metaphor of data as a 600-pound avalanche of student writing: what could be more precarious than an avalanche while climbing Everest? With an astounding assortment of over 2,776 surveys, interviews, writing samples, video logs, and reflections, the UA Study amassed a torrent of data. With 158 participants in 2012, the research required numerous temporary and ongoing collaborators, including graduate students, administrators, and faculty. Looking for guidance, we followed insights of previous longitudinal studies, such as Marylin Sternglass at City College (1997), Anne Beaufort (2007), Lee Ann Carroll at Pepperdine (2002), Richard H. Haswell at Washington State University (2000), Nancy Sommers at Harvard (2008), Andrea Lunsford and colleagues at Stanford (Fishman et al. 2005; Lunsford, Fishman, and Liew 2013), and Doug Hesse at University of Denver (2010). The Mount Everest metaphor captured the realities of cost (it's expensive), time (it's a commitment), and energy (it's exhausting), as well as the local and national pressures (relentless). Initially, this chapter would offer practical lessons—a type of survival guide for funding, managing attrition, and creating a base camp for data management. While a survival guide is seductive and useful—offering replicable procedures for recruitment, data collection, data analysis, and funding—it would likely flatten the embodied, lived realities into a grid of procedures, ignoring the fuller set of relations.

In writing studies, many narratives of longitudinal studies end up as partial stories: presentations of data results, case studies, snippets

https://doi.org/10.7330/9781646424337.c007

of voice in researcher reflections, sparsely narrated analytic memos, reports to institutional partners and sponsoring organizations. Scenes over time rarely cohere into a *story*, never mind a story focused on caring relations among researchers. My story is an ensemble, a series of collaborations that shaped the UA Study. I learned from the labor of/ with co-researchers. Only by acknowledging their labor can I tell my research story.

A STRANGER TO THE UA STUDY

I joined the UA Study formally in late fall 2012, the year I also became assistant director in the UA Writing Program. The only lecturer on the research team, I had an annual contract, which would be renewed over the next two years until I secured a position as a non-tenure-eligible assistant professor. A stranger to the project I joined, I listened from my peripheral role, confident in my research ability but self-conscious of my position as a lecturer. Here and there, I gleaned research goals from bits of conversation. At one meeting in fall 2012, I sat at a table, mostly observing dialogue among the UA Writing Program director, Amy Kimme Hea; the associate director, Anne-Marie Hall; and two research assistants (RAs), Kenny Walker and Jenna Pack Sheffield. These two RAs, I learned, were instrumental in data collecting efforts. I offered to perform a usability test on a survey with my English 101 students, hoping to gather a stronger understanding of the initial protocols. I felt distant from the research team, who began planning the first stage of research months before my arrival. With each year, a sense of precarity resurfaced as the UA Study faced new problems, constraints, and unanticipated changes.

Spanning six years of data collection (2012–18), the story of the UA Study is the embodied, lived experience of people doing ensemble research. The research team consisted largely of two principal co-investigators, seven research assistants, and five research fellows. Concerns over funding and participant attrition never ceased. Data collection, managing and organizing materials, loomed large each semester. Finding time to analyze data became increasingly difficult, as sustaining data collection and securing funding exhausted our energies. An abridged version, my reflection cannot capture the full extent of graduate student research relations or their activities over these years. Even so, this chapter attempts to present a multi-angle account of researcher relations when research teams undertake longitudinal studies in institutions like the University of Arizona, which boasts over 40,000 students and more than 8,000 faculty and staff. In this way, longitudinal research activities are "collaboratively enacted by people in locally grounded endeavors and tied to other material practices" (Fleckenstein et al. 2008, 413). The UA Study is a story of *people*—especially graduate student co-researchers—who ostensibly are authorized to collect data, analyze it, and report it but whose roles are traditionally subsumed in scholarship. In this chapter, I trace the messy realities of team-based longitudinal research with graduate student co-researchers, cognizant that each cycled in at different times with a different set of tensions, often woefully uncertain of where (or how) the current activity fit within the larger research trajectory.

Freshman Year: The Trials of Big Data

It's May 2013. Imagine a stack of 420 student papers in a Bankers Storage box. The research team is planning a process for scoring student papers to yield replicable, aggregable, and meaningful data (Haswell 2000). We train twelve readers (faculty and graduate teaching assistants [GTAs] in the program) to assess student papers using a six-point analytic rubric. In the final weeks of the spring semester, we meet with readers to calibrate their inter-rater reliability. Over two days, they score papers in the Sabino Room of the Student Union. RAs record scores for each of the 420 papers on a print sheet. I coordinate with a faculty consultant in the College of Education to plan statistical analysis. Together, RAs transfer scores into Excel, following a procedure of dual reporting to ensure accuracy. We check for typos or errors and then prepare the data for the Statistical Package for the Social Sciences (SPSS). This takes an RA more than fifty hours.

It's early June 2013. I visit with the associate director, and we process the raw data. Some students earned lower scores in the spring assessment than in the fall. Some students showed no change or change by only one or two points. Others improved by more than five points. But what counted as evidence of success or failure for these student writers? She asks, "Can you tell us what kind of score represents growth? Is it a change of five points or more?" According to the stats consultation, no, it's arbitrary. Oddly, none of our research team ascribes to a positivist paradigm to empirical design anyway. Despite our fears about the raw scores that summer, we carry on conducting a repeated measure analysis of variance (ANOVA) of the data to understand whether differences from fall to spring were statistically significant. Engrossed by these results and the narrative we might need to argue to upper administration depending on the outcome, we researchers remain conflicted. A pre-post assessment seemed to elide an iterative, multifaceted construct of writing development.

With every writing program administrator (WPA) I meet in the next year at the Council of Writing Program Administrators (CWPA) or the Conference on College Composition and Communication (CCCC), I hear some version of "I don't recommend that approach. You will find yourself having to demonstrate statistical progress with each assessment. It sets an expectation." When I reflect on Year One, I know our team made compromises that best fit the local needs and the time constraints. To be sure, the pre- and post-design of Year One could serve to reinscribe a system of manufactured crisis in the assessment of student writing (Gallagher 2011). It's only in hindsight that I recall that yes, in the interest of resources, time, and sanity, Year One data collection of the UA Study served as a program assessment, which intensified the pressure to demonstrate student writing gains. These behind-the-scenes moments are difficult to unpack, and it may not ever be possible to do so satisfyingly. Yet, these underreported scenes reveal the invisible labor of longitudinal research studies.

In the next years, I worked closely with graduate student research assistants, which became a key part of my role. Amy moved into an administrative post as associate dean in the College of Social and Behavioral Sciences. The associate director, Anne-Marie Hall, retired. I gained footing in the English department with increased responsibilities as assistant director of the UA Writing Program. I met regularly with RAs, especially in the final years of data collection. Graduate student co-researchers contributed tremendously to all activities of the UA Study: RAs observed. RAs interviewed. RAs collected writing samples. RAs collaborated with principal investigators on analysis and publication. At the research development phase, for instance, Jenna Pack Sheffield (2011–13) and Kenny Walker (2012–14) helped develop staggered research phases. Kenny remained on the team during the second year of data collection and was joined by Ana Ribero (2013–16). In all, we boasted seven research assistants over nine years, including Anushka Peres (2013–15), Tanya Tercero (2016–17), Amy Takabori (2017), and Emily Jo Schwaller (2017–18); the study also involved five research fellows whose exclusive role was interviewing student participants, including Lizzie Bentley, Eric House, Brad Jacobson, Devon Kehler, and Madelyn Tucker Pawlowski. None experienced the same journey. Relations with graduate students are my longitudinal story. When I invoke Paul Anderson's (1998) "Simple Gifts," I mean to magnify the UA Study in terms of relations among people and contexts across time.

Ongoing co-researcher relations of the UA Study were about care. They were gifts of exchange, obligation, and reciprocity.

Managed Attrition: Fear and Knowing in Year Two

I assumed that the first year of the UA Study would be the most precarious. I was wrong. In the second year of the study (2013–14), our sophomore year, we wrestled with participant attrition; I recall numerous, emotionally fraught meetings about, of all things, gift cards. The initial incentive of fifteen dollars didn't encourage many participants to schedule second year interviews. We couldn't be certain that it was the monetary value because students hadn't responded to emails. We were obsessed with attrition rates. How would we hit our goal over five years with so few returning in just the second year? What about the CCCC Research Grant we had been awarded?

Year Two evolved into weekly strategy meetings to curb rates of attrition. In almost every grant application, presentation, or proposal about the UA Study, Amy and I explain the power of a "planned attrition" study—a method of carefully selecting and narrowing participants (and their data) over time. But managing attrition was no easy method. A fictive narrative of control, managed attrition covers up elements of fear, anxiety, and fettered relations. Entangled with a story of attrition is another tale. It is about the success of Year Two, which resulted in completing sixty-two interviews thanks to a tenacious cold-calling campaign. RAs Kenny Walker and Ana Ribero regularly called students' mobile phones. They left voicemail messages. They caught students walking to class and invited them to schedule an interview. Soon, students began responding. Through RAs' actions, the UA Study finally connected *with* students, setting the foundation for further relations. Much longitudinal research attests to the necessary attachments between participants and researchers (Sternglass 1997; Beaufort 2007; Roozen 2009; Lunsford, Fishman, and Liew 2013). Building trust with participants in the UA Study depended wholly on co-researchers, specifically graduate co-researchers. They added dimension, not only through phone calls but also through the interviews that became windows into students' lived realities. For our study, as with most longitudinal research, interviews were the most extensive and time-consuming method of data collection (Fishman 2012; Roozen and Lunsford 2014).

One of my favorite memories involves Kenny Walker, an RA for two years in the study. In spring 2014, he stopped at my open office door and exclaimed, "I had the best interview!" He went on to describe the joy and pleasure of talking with a particular student on the phone. By contrast, others popped into my office to lament difficult interviews. It was through their voices that I experienced relationships with student participants. As I reflect on those first years, I often feel absent when remarking on the interview process of the UA Study because, like Amy, I did not conduct a single interview. I came to know student participants through the transcripts and reflections of graduate students. Relevantly, the UA Study protocols required research fellows to audio-record reflective memos immediately after completing an interview. These reflective memos offered an archive of this crucial labor, attuned to participants' lives and the obligation interviewers may have felt to build relationships. Similar to researcher reflections in qualitative studies (see Merriam and Tisdell 2016), memos shared graduate student co-researchers' thinking and feeling in context. A review of these second year memos, even now, reflects an array of emotional labor. When interviewing sophomores, some interactions were affirming while others felt obligatory. Some student participants seemed generous. Other students remained reticent. Co-researcher reflections revealed how some participants treated the interview as a market exchange—trading stories for money—rather than an invitation to share their voice, a pattern in several sophomore interviews. These memos give voice to emotional labor not captured in interview transcriptions:

> Here's another student who seems pretty busy and was attempting to really help us out. I think someone called her first but then she, maybe, initiated the call back and set up this interview and I was able to text her this morning, just this morning to set up this interview. So yes, she was invested in helping us out, which is great.—Ana Ribero

> It's pretty generous of her I think to set up the phone interview and to conduct the interview while driving to work. It just reminds me of how complicated the lives of our students are and it can be easy to forget some of those things so just the fact that she squeezes [an interview] in for us and it's really, really generous.—Kenny Walker

> I just finished Participant's interview. She was really, she seemed really reticent to talk I guess. I felt like it was pulling teeth to get her to expand on some stuff . . . although she did state that she had really good experiences with first year writing and that she felt prepared this second year because of that first year.—Eric House

> In general, he wasn't very forthcoming, he didn't seem very interested in the topic and I really tried to pull some things out and I asked more specific questions, so this is one of the tougher interviews. This one was just harder. He didn't want to give me much, and I didn't really know what to do with that, except kind of keep pressing, keep asking certain questions.—Anushka Peres

> As far as notable responses go, she didn't—it was a little bit difficult to get her to talk about question two, a piece of writing from the past year that she was proud of. She didn't seem like she really was proud of anything she had done in the past year . . . She seemed like she hadn't written anything she wanted to talk about that she was proud of, so I didn't want to push in that sense.—Jenna Pack Sheffield

Graduate students often adapted to relational needs, cognizant of affect and the embodied experience of interviewing. Co-researcher reflections allowed principal investigators to become aware of undergraduate students' complex and multidimensional experiences.

TO KNOW THEM AT A DISTANCE: TEAM RESEARCH STUDIES

Over the six years of data collection, the most frequent conversation in my office was about my and Amy's distant roles in study interviews. Kenny often argued, "You should really conduct an interview, just to experience what it's like." Subsequent RAs echoed this sentiment. However, Amy and I never conducted a single interview, feeling our administrative posts and positionality as white, middle-aged, cisgender women might undermine student participant trust. The UA Study, in turn, depended on RAs. We came to know and see student writing experiences through the labor of graduate students. In *Time to Know Them*, Sternglass (1997, 300) writes, "I believe strongly in the benefit of knowing research subjects personally . . . I was able to develop close enough relationships with [research participants] that they became increasingly comfortable about revealing aspects of their personal lives that would help me interpret their academic progress." Sternglass names a long-standing tenet of feminist rhetorical research when advocating for personal relationships. Feminist rhetorical research, according to Jacqueline Jones Royster and Gesa E. Kirsch (2012, 67), is "dialogic, dialectical, reflective, reflexive, embodied, and anchored in an ethos of care, respect, and humility." In the UA Study, graduate co-researchers fulfilled this relational labor of knowing. In retrospect, the success of the second year was less about incentives or reciprocity as value exchange and more about *knowing* participants in a profoundly relational and feminist sense (Gilligan 1982; Harding 1987; hooks 1990; Sullivan 1996; Kirsch 1999; Powell and Takayoshi 2004). The UA Study co-researchers activated a "relational ethic" (Ellis 2007, 4), and that ethic made even impossible things seem possible. As Sternglass warns, "I doubt that students would reveal much about their private lives if they were interviewed by a number of research assistants over the years" (300), and I agree. If RAs are just RAs performing a superficial task, then not much will come of it. What I learned from the UA Study was that research with people, research that builds from a relational ethic, no matter its size, can supersede ranks and roles. Caring research need not exclude research teams.

In our study, establishing relational ethics with participants was the exclusive labor of graduate co-researchers. In the remaining years, these relations took different forms, while the question of reciprocity persisted. Graduate co-researchers were positioned to care for participants and listen to them empathetically. Graduate student research assistants grappled with these jointly constructed pressures, bearing witness to their labor of reciprocity. Often underreported in published accounts, such labor was fundamental to the UA Study.

Deepening Relations and Collaborations: Generative Inefficiencies

It's September 2014. I'm calling Cynthia in the dean's business office. I need to figure out how to pay for gift cards, again. As in Year Two, gift cards are a small incentive to encourage students to complete a short survey confirming their ongoing participation. This turned out to be no simple feat. In Year Three, I'm working with the lead business manager in the dean's office because my department needs to hire a new business manager after a recent retirement. There's also one more wrinkle: the English department has transitioned from the College of Humanities to a new academic home in the College of Social and Behavioral Sciences. It is a year of transitions. I barely know Cynthia, yet I speak with her daily to navigate the institutional bureaucracy involved in procuring gift cards, a process I had mistakenly assumed would be simple. I receive a direct deposit into my personal bank account after a good five hours of phone conversations, emails, and paperwork. I then purchase electronic Starbucks' gift cards, as necessary. By November 2014, we've only spent $150 of the $250 I originally requested. At the end of the semester, I write a check to the campus for the outstanding $100 not spent on gift cards and hand it over to the new department business manager. I think, "There must be a more efficient way to do this."

The need to become flexible in response to institutional context became a theme of Year Three, which we believed was also a crucial transition for our study participants who, as juniors, were taking more classes in their majors and possibly learning more disciplinary writing. These changes combined with ongoing attrition necessitated a strategic adaptation of data collection tools, a process navigated most adeptly behind the scenes by Ana Ribero and Anushka Peres, who became essential actors in Year Three. Throughout the summer of 2014, Ana and Anushka made the vital argument that interviews reflected only a glimpse of our participants' lifeworlds. Their point was an important one, and together we explored ways to learn more from participants without further burdening them. Our aim was to approximate, however distantly, a sense of community for student participants. We adapted tools to include Google+ and to add video logs, text blasts, surveys, and interviews as part of data collection. Year Three depended significantly on Google+ to communicate with participants, to remind them to complete tasks, and to interact during the academic year. These flexible communication practices revealed additional ways of knowing student participants. As a social media platform, Google+ afforded quick and easy communication with participants and allowed protections for privacy. Ana and Anushka invited participants to post vlogs in fall 2014. As the UA Study centralized communication with research participants, research assistants took sole responsibility for coordinating communication on the site. Ana and Anushka circulated surveys through Google+, and they posted deadlines for activities as well as reminders to schedule interviews.

Importantly, over time, Google+ became more than a space for Ana and Anushka to maintain relationships with our remaining thirty participants. The site represented our relational methodology in action. In a longitudinal study, with cycles of recruitment, attrition, data collection, data management, and data analysis often co-occurring, open collaboration with graduate student co-researchers afforded us the most possibilities. In this way, collaboration and relationships allowed for flexible methods and experimenting with different tools. Julie Lindquist (2012, 662) writes, "Consider, for example, that collaboration on long-running, hypothesis-generating qualitative research projects can be interpretively generative, but (or rather, therefore) it adds, rather than reduces, inefficiency in the interpretive process." Likewise, a relational methodology prizes flexibility and makes room for inefficiencies in both the mundane processes (gift cards) and the sustained interactions with people. For the UA Study, Year Three collected the most diverse data because our research assistants pushed us to listen to students' voices. We needed to make space for generative inefficiencies. Ana and Anushka taught us to do so.

Similar to the interviews of Year Two, the knowing of student participants in Year Three of the UA Study depended on co-researcher collaborations. Tenets of strong team collaborations are akin to ethical care with research participants. Katrina M. Powell and Pamela Takayoshi

(2012, 13) argue that "when we see research practice as a site of collaborative knowledge-making where rhetorician-critics or local intellectuals are learning but also teaching, we might naturally build more reciprocal and balanced relationships with participants." Longitudinal research, a capacious endeavor, has the luxury of time to sustain dialogue and engender collaborative meaning making that builds more reciprocal and balanced relationships with graduate student researchers and alternative track colleagues.

New Editions of Researcher Relations: Longitudinal Mentoring

It's April 2016. Into my already tight schedule of meetings, I have squeezed in a meeting with the new RA, Tanya Tercero. Our outgoing RA, Ana, previously met with Tanya to share Dropbox passwords, UABox files, the Google+ community, and the annual interview protocol. Despite our best efforts, Ana and I confused Tanya, who is trying to consider her own professional needs in relation to the position. For Tanya, everything was new information. For me, I was on repeat—a new version of old conversations about collecting data, organizing data, and trying to select data to analyze. Tanya probably felt like a stranger in the research context, just as I had in fall 2012.

Almost a year later, in spring 2017, Tanya asked, "Are you planning to have an end-of-the-study event? The participants are *so* interested in hearing about the study, some of the findings." I stared at her blankly, becoming numb to emotions rising in my chest, warmth in my cheeks. I hadn't made space to acknowledge a concluding cycle of the study. I was still concerned about how to ensure that participants committed to participating in follow-up surveys. Amy and I had asked Tanya to collect emails, anticipating that we could reach out to students in the 2017–18 academic year. As in Year Two, I still wasn't thinking about reciprocity *with* our student participants; nor did I prepare for the emotions of concluding this stage of the study. A few weeks later, a research fellow crossed my path near UA's Second Street garage. He asked, "What are you guys finding in these interviews?" I shrugged and muttered something about feeling overwhelmed by the sheer amount of data and the decreasing amount of time, a recurring tension. I think of countless presentations on the progress of the UA Study in which we outlined methods as a linear progression of data collection and analysis without equivalent attention to the embodied, lived realities of large-scale longitudinal research. Yet UA Study researcher relations remained dynamic, multidimensional, and imbued with affect.

Slow Research and Meaning Making in Longitudinal Relations
It's May 2018. Months after a final "Where Are You Now" survey in fall 2017, I'm meeting with a new RA, Amy Takabori (Amy T.). Her summer job: organize data from the twenty-two participants who remained in the study for six years. Explaining that I want her to sort and tag the information we collected, I feel like I'm on repeat, echoing my prior conversations with Tanya. With Amy T., our research emphasizes data analysis to capture patterns in the entire cohort of remaining students: what can we see in the data we collected from the group over five years? I describe my purpose: "I need a quick glance of how this cohort responded on surveys over time." I want to capture the longitudinal dimensions of our data. I use an online project management platform to coordinate Amy T.'s activities during the summer, and her work contributes to our initial ability to observe how student participants changed across five years. Data organized and analyzed by Amy T. helped us observe characteristics of GPA, confidence, self-assessments, and changes in degree majors. As was true with Kenny, Ana, Anushka, and Tanya, I looked forward to meetings with Amy T., even though I often felt stretched thin. I also often felt less prepared to guide her work. As with RAs before her, I learned with her as she moved from at first being overwhelmed by the amount of data and then becoming flexible and adaptive to co-researchers' needs and our study's goals.

Indeed, each graduate co-researcher experienced the research study differently and generatively. Each RA experienced a distinct cycle of study protocols and distinct experiences of meaning making. With Jenna in Year One, our focus was on assessment scores. For Kenny and Ana in Year Two, much of our discussion related to metacognition and affect. With Anushka and Ana in Year Three, we emphasized community and new data collection tools. With Tanya in Year Four, we emphasized case studies and identity profiles. For Amy T. in Year Five, we analyzed longitudinal data trends of the twenty-one participants. Most recently, with Emily Jo, we returned to literature on metacognition and writing development. Each year had its own theme while I gained the benefit of perspective, coming to recognize patterns across both our data and our graduate co-researchers' relations. I recognize that while Kenny and Jenna experienced the study as a tale of attrition and recruitment, research fellows who conducted interviews experienced the study as relationships with participants; subsequent RAs, like Ana, Tanya, Amy T., and Emily Jo, saw the study through the filters of data organization and analysis.

With the benefit of hindsight, I recognize how co-researcher relations sustained the UA Study. Everything about the UA Study exemplified the tensions, obligations, and needs of a larger, public land-grant institution. It felt untenable to experience in the moment. I was often overextended with administrative duties, helping to administer a writing program serving around 6,000 students each semester: more university undergraduate students required more resources; less funding from the state required administering the program without adequate resources. There were numerous harried research meetings where I was pulled in to manage a student or teacher complaint. We began the UA Study hoping to redress such issues, but longitudinal research proved to be as ambivalent a process as writing program administration. Co-researchers often shepherded the research, helping the team maintain a path and not veer too far from our goals. I know they felt exasperated at times, absent transparent and direct guidance. Our research assistants sustained our project across successive cycles of data collection, organization, file management, and analysis. Dialogue with research assistants persisted, repeatedly saving our study from crumbling into a data avalanche.

MORE SIMPLE GIFTS AS CARING RELATIONS

The most important lesson I learned from the UA Study is that the embodied, lived realities of complex co-researcher relations are equally precious gifts of research. My story only occurs with/amid the relations of people in this research, and the same is true for all co-researchers. Yet few accounts of large-scale, team-based research discuss researcher relations. When I invoke Paul Anderson's (1998) "Simple Gifts," I mean to resist flattening the relations of the UA Study. Anderson reminds teacher-scholars to prioritize ethical relations with research participants, arguing for an ethic beyond legally sanctioned protocols of human research. "No matter how we proceed in our discussion of research ethics, no matter what outcome we devise," he demands, "let it be our goal to assure that both individually and as a discipline we treat these gifts—and their givers—justly, respectfully, and gratefully" (83). Likewise, our graduate student co-researchers represent gifts not to be ignored. These co-researcher gifts are so much more than time. Lewis Hyde's seminal book *The Gift* (1983), for instance, argues that art, and therefore artistic practice, is not for marketplace economies since art comes to artists in the form of a gift and, as such, is in the tradition of gift exchange. In anthropology, Marcel Mauss (1966) elaborated gift giving for various purposes. One of the more influential cultural practices of the gift is its role in providing a social contract, suggesting that gifts are not neutral; they can feel obligatory at the same time they might function to cement social relations (for more, see Parry 1986). Claude Levi-Strauss (1969) later posited gifts as reciprocity. Forwarding Indigenous knowledges, Robin Wall Kimmerer (2013) paints a fuller picture of gifts as reciprocal relations. In the example of the Three Sisters, a practice of planting corn, beans, and squash together, Kimmerer describes, "The gifts of each are more fully expressed when they are nurtured together than alone" (140). Gifts, then, are relations between givers. As Jennifer Clary-Lemon (2019) explains, it is "the possibility of the gift as a way of relating."

By suggesting more simple gifts, in homage to Anderson (1998), I am telling a story about ethics in collaborations with people whose labor is gifts of creativity, obligation, and reciprocity. Crucial to our actions with these encumbered gifts is an ethic of care (Gilligan 1982; Noddings 1984). In Carol Gilligan's (1982) seminal work, a caring ethic privileges relationships because methods of research are relational and inductive rather than objective accounts of a singular reality.[1] An ethic of care challenges hierarchical relationships between the researcher and researched by honoring participant (emic) voices, reciprocal learning, empowerment, self-reflexivity, an action orientation, transparency, multidimensionality, and attention to affect (Harding 1987; Kirsch and Mortensen 1996; Newkirk 1996; Kirsch 1999; Lather 2001; Adams 2018). These same principles underscore researcher relations that honor relationships, collaboration, reciprocity, reflexivity, participatory action, attention to power relations, co-interpretation, and embodiment (Gilligan 1982; Harding 1987; Kirsch 1999; Ellis 2007; Powell and Takayoshi 2012; Royster and Kirsch 2012; Adams 2018). As I call for *more* simple gifts, I mean to bring fervent attention to these feminist relational ethics with research teams.

I echo Lindquist (2012, 660), who in a retrospective account of LiteracyCorps Michigan invokes the value of collaboration as "an important form of support not only in the opportunities it offers for triangulation, but also in its capacity to more efficiently distribute the labor of data." Whereas Sharon James McGee (2012) has explained the benefits to graduate students of collaborations with faculty—especially learning to navigate the intricacies of research, from IRB approval to kairotic responses to budget cuts and participant needs—few team-based, large-scale longitudinal studies capture the evolving relations of people cycling in and out of research studies. Of note, the Stanford Study of Writing (2008), Harvard's study (Sommers 2008), the University of Montana's study (Downs and Schlenz 2014), and the University of Michigan's study (Gere 2019) demonstrate the magnitude of longitudinal studies as a living web of relations.

We principal investigators (PIs) and mentors are obligated to attend to these generative relationships. Mentors are uniquely situated to enact caring relations with graduate student assistants, undergraduate student assistants, and alternative-track faculty as co-researchers. I recommend three principles:

Transparency. PIs need to include co-researchers in discussions of ongoing goals of the research project, especially awareness of the stages and cycles of data collection and analysis. This leads to reciprocal learning. There were moments in the UA Study when open conversations about the problem of attrition led to generative opportunities. There were also moments that lacked transparency, which occluded collaborative decisions.

Open dialogue. An infrastructure for easy and relevant feedback from graduate students to PIs can sustain generative flows of communication and learning. While such feedback can take many forms, such as reflection, the purpose is to foster thinking through research activities, including open feedback about ongoing tensions and complexity. Researchers can remain aware of and nimble in response to social and material forces impacting the study's researcher relations.

Attention to affect. In the same way Lindquist calls for slow research and generative inefficiencies, PIs can model how to attend to emotional dimensions and embodied realities of longitudinal research. Over the years, the UA Study would have benefited by acknowledging and naming our emotions and anxieties. Doing so strengthens an ethic of care.

Admittedly, an ethic of care complicates Richard Haswell's (2000) call for research to be feasible, replicable, and meaningful because a caring ethic situates research as constructed, inductive, contextual, and unpredictable—especially in response to the needs of participants, researchers, and communities. Yet standards of rigor in qualitative studies require thick description to demonstrate validity and trustworthiness in data collection and analysis procedures (Merriam and Tisdell 2016); we must offer a record of design for others to replicate and adapt in their own context with an openness to what is feasible. Along with a record of data procedures, however, an ethic of care requires attention especially to the fuller set of relationships. My reflective account offers a window into principles of an ethic of care in team research.

FINAL THOUGHTS

Gifts engender creativity, obligation, community, and reciprocity. In this chapter, rather than offer readers a neat grid of tools, funding ideas, data collection, data analysis, and reporting, I bring into sharp focus dynamic, embodied co-researcher relations as a gift of the UA Study, which depended on hundreds of people—most significant, twelve graduate students. Reflecting on the labyrinth of graduate students' labor in the UA Study, I realize that co-researcher collaborations add depth to our research narratives. They are gifts in the *how* of longitudinal research.

Exhausting and frustrating in turns, longitudinal research is also deeply affirming, not least because it brings us closer to writers writing. Longitudinal studies enable us to bear witness to writing processes in ways we have only begun to tap as writing teachers, scholars, and administrators. Telling stories about longitudinal research means grappling with issues of labor, relationships, and ethics with multidimensionality —relationships to participants, to research assistants, to funding organizations, to upper administration, and to scholars in our field. Stories of longitudinal research are more than quantity, the weight of papers collected, the number of archived artifacts, or analyzed data; rather, research is the social, emotional, and ethical dimensions imbuing every interaction with lasting impact. My story is not a guide to surviving the burdens of longitudinal research; it's a story of embracing a fuller set of relations as more simple gifts.

NOTE

1. Feminist designs are a "critique of objective, positivist methods, especially research on women" (Kirsch 1999, 1).

REFERENCES

Adams, Megan. 2018. "Post-Research Engagement: An Argument for Critical Examination of Researcher Roles after Research Ends." In *Composing Feminist Interventions: Activism, Engagement, Praxis*, ed. Kristine L. Blair and Lee Nickoson, 19–33. Fort Collins and Boulder: WAC Clearinghouse and University Press of Colorado. https://wac.colostate.edu/books/perspectives/feminist/.

Anderson, Paul. 1998. "Simple Gifts: Ethical Issues in the Conduct of Person-Based Composition Research." *College Composition and Communication* 49 (1): 63–89.

Beaufort, Anne. 2007. *College Writing and Beyond: A New Framework for University Writing Instruction*. Logan: Utah State University Press.

Carroll, Lee Ann. 2002. *Rehearsing New Roles: How College Students Develop as Writers*. Carbondale: Southern Illinois University Press.

Clary-Lemon, Jennifer. 2019. "Gifts, Ancestors, and Relations: Notes toward an Indigenous New Materialism." *Enculturation: A Journal of Rhetoric, Writing, and Culture* 30. http://enculturation.net/gifts_ancestors_and_relations.

Downs, Doug, and Mark Schlenz. 2014. "Learning Transfer from Metacognition-Enhancing Writing-about-Writing FYC Courses: A Longitudinal Study." *CCCC Research Initiative Grant*. https://dougdownsteaching.files.wordpress.com/2016/10/cccc-ri-proposal-2014.pdf.

Ellis, Carolyn. 2007. "Telling Secrets, Revealing Lives: Relational Ethics in Research with Intimate Others." *Journal of Qualitative Inquiry* 13 (1): 3–29.
Fishman, Jenn. 2012. "Longitudinal Writing Research in (and for) the Twenty-First Century." In *Writing Studies Research in Practice*, ed. Lee Nickoson and Mary P. Sheridan, 171–82. Carbondale: Southern Illinois University Press.
Fishman, Jenn, Andrea Lunsford, Beth McGregor, and Mark Outeye. 2005. "Performing Writing, Performing Literacy." *College Composition and Communication* 57 (2): 224–52.
Fleckenstein, Kristie, Clay Spinuzzi, Rebecca Rickly, and Carol Clark Papper. 2008. "The Importance of Harmony: An Ecological Metaphor for Writing Research." *College Composition and Communication* 60 (2): 388–419.
Gallagher, Chris. 2011. "Being There: (Re)Making the Assessment Scene." *College Composition and Communication* 62 (3): 450–76.
Gere, Anne, ed. 2019. *Developing Writers in Higher Education: A Longitudinal Study*. Ann Arbor: University of Michigan Press.
Gilligan, Carol. 1982. *In a Different Voice: Psychological Theory and Women's Development*. Cambridge, MA: Harvard University Press.
Harding, Sandra. 1987. *Feminism and Methodology*. Bloomington: Indiana University Press.
Haswell, Richard H. 2000. "Documenting Improvement in College Writing: A Longitudinal Approach." *Written Communication* 17 (33): 307–52.
Hesse, Doug. 2010. "Longitudinal Study of Writing." *University Writing Program* (University of Denver). https://www.du.edu/writing/research.html.
hooks, bell. 1990. "Culture to Culture: Ethnography and Cultural Studies as Critical Intervention." In *Yearning: Race, Gender, and Cultural Politics*, ed. bell hooks, 123–33. Boston: South End Press.
Hyde, Lewis. 1983. *The Gift: Imagination and the Erotic Life of Property*. New York: Random House.
Kimmerer, Robin Wall. 2013. *Braiding Sweetgrass: Indigenous Wisdom, Scientific Knowledge, and the Teachings of Plants*. Minneapolis: Milkweed Editions.
Kirsch, Gesa E. 1999. *Ethical Dilemmas in Feminist Research: The Politics of Location, Interpretation, and Publication*. Albany: State University of New York Press.
Kirsch, Gesa E., and Peter Mortensen. 1996. "Introduction: Reflection on Methodology in Literacy Studies." In *Ethics and Representation in Qualitative Studies of Literacy*, ed. Peter Mortensen and Gesa E. Kirsch, xix–xxxiv. Urbana, IL: National Council of Teachers of English Press.
Lather, Patti. 2001. "Postbook: Working the Ruins of Feminist Ethnography." *Signs: Journal of Women in Culture and Society* 27 (1): 199–227.
Levi-Strauss, Claude. 1969. *The Elementary Structure of Kinship*. London: Eyre and Spottiswoode.
Lindquist, Julie. 2012. "Time to Know Them: Practicing Slow Research in a Fast Field." *JAC* 32 (3–4): 645–66.
Lunsford, Andrea A., Jenn Fishman, and Warren M. Liew. 2013. "College Writing, Identification, and the Production of Intellectual Property: Voices from the Stanford Study of Writing." *College English* 75 (5): 470–92.
Mauss, Marcel. 1966. *The Gift: Forms and Functions of Exchange in Archaic Societies*. Translated by I. Cunnison. London: Cohen and West.
McGee, Sharon James. 2012. "Practicing Socially Progressive Research." In *Practicing Research in Writing Studies: Reflective and Ethically Responsible Research*, ed. Kathryn Powell and Pamela Takoyoshi, 143–58. New York: Hampton.
Merriam, Sharon, and Elizabeth Tisdell. 2016. *Qualitative Research: A Guide to Design and Implementation*. 4th ed. San Francisco: Jossey-Bass.
Newkirk, Thomas. 1996. "Seduction and Betrayal in Qualitative Research." In *Ethics and Representation in Qualitative Studies of Literacy*, ed. Peter Mortensen and Gesa E. Kirsch, 3–16. Urbana, IL: National Council of Teachers of English Press.

Noddings, Nell. 1984. *Caring, a Feminine Approach to Ethics and Moral Education.* Berkeley: University of California Press.
Parry, Jonathan. 1986. "The Gift, the Indian Gift, and the 'Indian Gift.'" *Man* 21 (3): 453–73.
Powell, Katrina M., and Pamela Takayoshi. 2004. "Accepting the Roles Created for Us: Ethics of Reciprocity." *College Composition and Communication* 54 (2): 394–422.
Powell, Katrina M., and Pamela Takayoshi, eds. 2012. *Practicing Research in Writing Studies: Reflective and Ethically Responsible Research.* New York: Hampton.
Roozen, Kevin. 2009. "From Journals to Journalism: Tracing Trajectories of Literate Development." *College Composition and Communication* 60 (3): 541–72.
Roozen, Kevin, and Karen Lunsford. 2014. "'One Story of Many to Be Told': Following Empirical Studies of College and Adult Writing through 100 Years of NCTE Journals." *Research in the Teaching of English* 46 (2): 193–209.
Royster, Jacqueline Jones, and Gesa E. Kirsch. 2012. *Feminist Rhetorical Practice: New Horizons for Rhetoric, Composition, and Literacy Studies.* Carbondale: Southern Illinois University Press.
Sommers, Nancy. 2008. "The Call of Research: A Longitudinal View of Writing Development." *College Composition and Communication* 60 (1): 152–64.
Stanford Study of Writing. 2008. *Stanford University.* https://ssw.stanford.edu/.
Sternglass, Marylin. 1997. *Time to Know Them: A Longitudinal Study of Writing and Learning at the College Level.* Mahwah, NJ: Lawrence Erlbaum Associates.
Sullivan, Patricia A. 1996. "Ethnography and the Problem of the 'Other.'" In *Ethics and Representation in Qualitative Studies of Literacy,* ed. Peter Mortensen and Gesa E. Kirsch, 97–114. Urbana, IL: National Council of Teachers of English Press.

8
THE PRECARIOUS METHOD
Longitudinal Research and Material Uncertainty in Professional and Technical Writing Studies

Yanar Hashlamon

I start every interview with my business writing students with the same question: Were you working in a professional environment or workplace during your time in our class? Of six participants from my 2019 course, five worked for a wage, for unpaid industry experience, or for college credit; yet they all answered with a caveat. One student worked "as an academic coach, if that would count," while another said, "the closest I would say to that was working as a research assistant." A third student worked in a data processing position and concluded, "not that it's really a professional environment." At their core, these responses signal student uncertainty about what *counts* as professional work when reflecting on their paid and unpaid work experiences, their coursework, and their postgraduate career plans. This uncertainty is as much material as it is discursive, a point that framed our discussions for an entire semester. Our course foregrounded a newly designed curriculum emphasizing social justice and accessibility frameworks in technical and professional communication (TPC).[1] In this redesigned class, I asked students to look ahead to the specialized disciplines and precarious economy they intended to enter. We examined leaked corporate strategy documents, discussed internal and external business communication, and studied histories of worker organization around issues of equity and antidiscrimination.

The interviews I conducted in 2019 were the first of several I intended to hold each year over a three-year period, following students from an explicitly anti-capitalist professional writing classroom along their academic trajectories and into their postgraduate workplaces. Ultimately, the goal of my project was to increase our understanding of the uncertainties students face in modern workplaces and the rhetorical practices they use to navigate those uncertainties. For a story in a collection on longitudinal studies, the point I find most important to consider is the precariousness I experienced in planning my project.[2] My longitudinal research was the first time I designed a study for a timeline beyond the confines of one semester, sought external funding, and navigated my position as a graduate student with shifting work roles and a developing researcher identity. Throughout the process of designing my project, I was troubled by the prospect that I might be unable to talk with my students again in a year's time. From the outset, I grew to understand that learning from and with these students was a fragile possibility, and a commitment of my time, energy, and funding alone couldn't guarantee a successful research study.

Initially, when I wrote from the precipice of my study's execution, this chapter considered how the methodological history of longitudinal studies in TPC might bear upon my story and the material-discursive uncertainty my participants and I encountered in our work. Now, two years since my first draft, my concerns have been realized. My study ended rather unceremoniously after one year and one round of data collection, as I'm sure many research studies did amid the Covid-19 pandemic. I lost what funding I had to compensate my participants, and I have since lost contact with those who were enthusiastic about entering the job market and being paid for their time to reflect and chat. Many longitudinal studies fail, and the uncertainty that comes with a long-term study design—especially for graduate students—might dissuade us from pursuing such research. However, I believe the precariousness I experienced speaks to larger systemic barriers to knowledge production that demonstrate how necessary longitudinal research is amid the broader economic and social precarity researchers and research participants experience. My survey of and intervention into TPC scholarship suggest that the field's intersections with longitudinal studies have meaningful implications for how we think about the workplace, including our own, as the site of complex and even radical rhetorical action. In particular, the field of TPC has much to gain from a methodological alignment with longitudinal studies and even more from a political alignment to social justice along with attention to precarity in workplace studies.

My own longitudinal project gave me an opportunity to bring longitudinal writing research across rhetoric and composition into generative contact with TPC, which led me to examine the rhetorical complexity and the political importance of the relationship between classrooms and workplaces in writing research. The ways structural oppressions condition and historically mediate uncertainty for precarious workers can be directly addressed by a methodology that engages with time as a factor of professional writing. The perception of professional and technical contexts as the realms of solely utilitarian, purpose- and application-based writing alienates their study from the complex rhetorical and material conditions of college-level longitudinal research. Likewise, the ways TPC can uncritically engage capitalism as a "natural" site of communicative, generic practices contributes to a sense of stability in what TPC research can look like. To intervene, I argue that the epistemological stability perceived in TPC is one key factor longitudinal work can methodologically amend. In designing my study, I found that the field's turn toward social justice and inclusion helped me frame longitudinal methods as a particularly generative way to identify and engage the precarity of modern work under neoliberalism.[3] This chapter addresses the connections I saw between TPC scholarship and broader examples of longitudinal research in the workplace. The stories that follow are twofold, interweaving disciplinary narratives told along methodological lines and my own story of becoming a longitudinal researcher in the midst of TPC's social justice turn. Writing from my marginalized position as a graduate student of color, I speak to the material conditions of work and workplace research that undergirded my longitudinal study—the design decisions, funding, and the conditions of the study's participants—that together demonstrate the precarity and possibility of longitudinal research.

THE RELATIONSHIP BETWEEN LONGITUDINAL STUDIES AND TPC

When I began drafting my study proposal, I set to work on gathering extant literature from the unique intersection of TPC, longitudinal studies, and social justice scholarship. Claiming that TPC work is often disconnected from the corpus of longitudinal studies might sound strange to some rhetoric and composition scholars. After all, many records of longitudinal writing research include reference to Dorothy A. Winsor's (1996) early example, *Writing Like an Engineer: A Rhetorical Education*. Winsor's study is a key starting point for my own work and for understanding perceptions of TPC as a knowledge-making field contextualized by work. Following what would become a familiar trajectory from school to workplace, Winsor's purpose is to examine how engineers are socialized into their disciplines through a work study program, and so her study is framed as a linear classroom-to-workplace progression. A decade later, in *College Writing and Beyond* (2007), Anne Beaufort locates her sole participant's writing in the engineering workplace as the proverbial *beyond* of the book. Although longitudinal studies can privilege such linear progression, I wanted to challenge the idea that workplaces are only sites of application for rhetoric and composition education. Instead, I wanted to bring explicit attention to students' recursive professional development both during college and after graduation. In contrast to research that assumes linearity—high school to college, college to career—the belief that professional writing education is recursive operates on the understanding that the students enter, exit, and often re-enter the university at different points of their lives with different professional goals and expectations set by a tumultuous labor economy.

The shifting constraints of labor under neoliberalism, globalization, and settler colonialism framed the rhetorical work students practiced in our course's redesigned professional writing curriculum. Globally, modern labor disturbs seemingly stable, material class structures and discursive forms of mediation. Both points can be seen in the US specifically, where legal definitions of employment fail to account for types of work in the gig economy (Steinberger 2018). Workers lose valuable protections amid unclear distinctions of what *counts* as work, drawing attention to the shifting constraints of modern labor relations. In my teaching and research alike, I found myself and my students encountering these issues on a personal level. While we read about how workers have reacted historically to shifting social and professional expectations, many students made direct connections to their current and past jobs to illustrate the contradictory positions they found themselves in. They weren't professionals, as they hadn't graduated from college, yet some had been working since they were teenagers and had amassed significant expertise in applying for jobs, maintaining employment, and navigating discriminatory situations. Others were older students whose progression in their careers was halted by their lack of a college degree. I designed my longitudinal study to attempt to address this contradiction, asking how students encountered the uncertainty of modern professional life and how their writing practices might account for its contingencies.

In addition, my study and story align rhetorical knowledge of social justice with the practices of workplace writing to advocate for a more entwined understanding of both in TPC research design. Addressing the material conditions of a longitudinal study requires a sense of the methodological and theoretical turns of TPC and the political state of the field. TPC has entered into a particularly generative moment for social justice work, as marginalized scholars have opened lines of discourse to challenge the hegemony of professional writing. Numerous scholars have written on social justice in TPC pedagogy (Scott 2004; Scott, Longo, and Wills 2006; Haas and Eble 2018; Cox 2019; Shelton 2019) and TPC theory more broadly (Walton, Moore, and Jones 2019).

However, there has yet to be a study of what a critical curricular model's *effects* could be for students moving between the classroom and the workplace. Alongside the field's pedagogical and political turn, the scale and significance of longitudinal research comes into new focus. Despite the long presence of longitudinal research in TPC's history (Taylor and Utterback 1975; Winsor 1996), longitudinal methods have yet to be applied to the critical pedagogies emerging in the field's turn to social justice. Before facing this exigence as a researcher, I had to respond to the perceived epistemological stability of TPC amid a distinctly *unstable* and precarious labor economy alongside my students in our professional writing classroom.

The anti-capitalist curriculum my study springs from was designed to invite students to understand the functions, artificiality, and ideology undergirding workplace relations along with the ways rhetorical practices can account for the precarious contingencies of market labor. We read leaked corporate documents to map out ecologies of internal and external business communication, examined how disabled activists navigate rhetorical tensions between market logics and disability justice, and analyzed coalitional rhetorics deployed by union organizers in historical and contemporary workplaces. Situating this curriculum and my study is the reality that the university itself is a site of extreme inequality and precarity. We examined coalitional rhetoric while living in a right-to-work state. We discussed accessibility while students encountered institutional ableism throughout the university. I worked to challenge neoliberal culture, but as a graduate student, I necessarily participated in its production—providing even more reason to tether my study's methodology to social justice in and beyond the confines of the university. As much as I see my study as a way to participate in TPC's social justice turn, I also want to interrogate the ebb and flow of complicity with and resistance to hegemonic power in the academy. In particular, I've thought about Audre Lorde's (1984, 111) oft-cited essay "The Master's Tools Will Never Dismantle the Master's House," where she writes: "For the master's tools will never dismantle the master's house. They may allow us temporarily to beat him at his own game, but they will never enable us to bring about genuine change." Lorde's argument has always been deeply applicable to social justice work in education but especially within TPC.

Among rhetoric and composition specializations, TPC is uniquely entwined with hegemonic power and capital, often working as a proxy to industry and employment. Sally Henschel and Lisa Melonçon (2014, 22) argue that TPC curricula should be "embracing common conceptual and practical skill sets that will prepare students to become successful professionals." In claiming anti-capitalism and social justice as guiding frameworks for my own business writing course, I've struggled with reconciling the conditions of professional writing, teaching, and research. However, my study participants' initial responses were positive. Our attention to disability justice, for example, encouraged one student to bring accessibility concerns to his supervisor when crafting media for his internship. Another student reflected on the "state of nervousness" she experienced as a queer woman in her prior career as an engineer, which she connected to a lack of coalitional support with her colleagues at the time. In these cases, students tethered social justice between classroom and workplace, but I wondered if these connections would persist as students spent more time in their internships and jobs than they did in professional writing classrooms. After all, in professional contexts, social justice work can be impractical, unprofitable, and uncommon. I believe my longitudinal study could attend to such shifts in writerly practice and precarity over time, but only because I understand the method as a tool for producing particular knowledge from and about institutions. Just as I teach the ways to repurpose professional writing practice toward social justice, my role as a graduate student is one of professionalization into institutional norms that historically keep people of color out of academia. I similarly see my longitudinal study as a way to conduct research *from* a hegemonic institution *about* hegemonic power and stability. As social justice and longitudinal methods haven't yet been paired in TPC, we must understand the stable image of TPC's epistemology presented by some of its scholarship as it relates to longitudinal studies.

THE POLITICS OF WORKPLACE STUDY

My own attention to material conditions frames normative perspectives of stability as a neoliberal perspective, allowing me to use longitudinal research to critique representations of work as stable and logical, including representations in workplace studies. All too often, when the sites of TPC—workplaces and the classrooms that teach workplace writing—are seen through hegemonic lenses, the linear development of writers is privileged along with linear notions of classroom-to-workplace pipelines. The ways my students discussed their relationships to work and education complicated these ideas as well as the way I approached my research. In this way, I join a long line of TPC scholars who have, on one hand, taken longitudinal approaches to workplace writing research and, on the other hand, sought ways to counter the linear logics and reifying progress narratives that attach to that approach.

The innovation of a longitudinal study of workplace writing in *Writing Like an Engineer* (Winsor 1996) entailed a design focused on traditional foundations of writerly identity and rhetoricity. The attention to rhetoricity in the specialized, applied discourse of the workplace formed a necessary foundation for empirical work in TPC. A much less discussed study by the same author, however, suggests a more critical way longitudinal research might produce knowledge about work. Winsor's *Writing Power: Communication in an Engineering Center* (2003) takes an ethnographic approach to writing studies, expanding on her 1996 study in key ways. First, Winsor's (2003) research questions demonstrate a more complex framing of workplace writing, positioning her study between critical rhetorical studies' framing of capitalist oppression and business communication's framing of work as hierarchical, top-down writing networks. Her research questions ask, "How are texts used to create and occupy positions of power? . . . What does this use of texts tell us about genre? . . . How does power affect the generation of text" (10). Winsor's 2003 turn to examine the complexity of workplace communication exemplifies the disciplinary position of TPC, bringing power into view as a core feature of both work and rhetorical studies. Although I found greater hold for my own research design in the precedence set by Winsor's second study, I was faced with a second problem: the innovations Winsor and other TPC scholars made to longitudinal methodology put forward perspectives on the field's politics that ran counter to my own research orientation examining precarity.

In expanding beyond *longitudinal* as a descriptor of her multi-year project, Winsor echoes other scholars conducting contemporary workplace studies in TPC. Clay Spinuzzi's methodological discussion in *Tracing Genres through Organizations* (2003, 33) offers a telling pivot, as he identifies longitudinal work with the "macroscopic" level of his data collection, which also includes "retrospective interviews, genre analysis, document analysis, semi-structured interviews, and historical research methods" (Spinuzzi 2002, 23). Spinuzzi illustrates this macro-level inquiry with his own attention to historical records at his site, but he emphasizes that it is only one of three levels of observational data collection over the course of his study. For Spinuzzi, then, it's not that his studies are not longitudinal but that they include longitudinal work in their broader methodology. For my own study, however, I needed to think about how documenting a linear progression of time could operate rhetorically at both micro- *and* macro-scales. As an object of study, precarity works at the level of the individual and that of social and economic structures, shifting in stability over time. The *assumed* stability of capitalist relations in the "big picture" of workplace activity, then, doesn't just demarcate a methodological difference of my own study's focus on professional writing but a political one as well. The precedent built by past scholars in TPC is at all times methodological and political, and while I built my own study in alignment with the innovative methodological choices made by scholars like Spinuzzi and Windsor, I also worked against the big picture of TPC those authors constructed.

As I navigated the methodological history surveyed in this chapter, I found my own critical orientation to be another layer of complexity when considering what politics have been tethered to longitudinal studies in TPC. In relating my own study to Winsor's, for example, I needed to come to terms with her orientation to power in the workplace. She remarks that she "believes capitalism's primary valuation of profit often does lead to inhuman behavior" but "that for-profit organizations often do useful work," as if the good and bad are equally distributed among stakeholder populations (Winsor 2003, 11). She centers her study between business communication's complicity with hierarchical structures and critical rhetoric's "strain" of "resistance" to them (11). This pathologizing attitude toward resistance politics marks Winsor's study as necessarily counter to the social justice turn in TPC that informs my study; yet it also suggests how political orientations are always present in workplace studies. As different as my perspective and approach are from Winsor's, my study's exigence is wrought from the political stability that she attributes to TPC and that characterizes the field outside of its social justice turn. My methodology, my teaching, my work on the assessment research and curricula design of business writing in my department—all of these elements developed from my perspective toward TPC and my feelings of exclusion in the field's scholarship. My perspective as a minority, my work in fields like critical ethnic studies, and my interest in critical pedagogy were cause for friction as I sought precedent for my study. Time and again, I found inspiration in TPC scholars' innovations in longitudinal design while pushing against the *stability* I encountered in the field's politics.

Returning to Spinuzzi's (2003) distinctions between research methods on different scales, I believe a macroscopic or long view of longitudinal work may not be long enough. The rhetorical actions of workers might defy the hierarchies of capitalist relations in the context of the workplace, but the bigger picture might frame this defiance differently. In his 2003 study, Spinuzzi's primary exigence is the "worker as victim" trope (2). He argues that this trope frames the intersection between user-centered design studies and TPC. He specifies that the trope obscures worker innovation, and he carefully pulls apart the notion that workers are subjugated to top-down communications and only innovate solutions in an effort to align with management's goals for efficiency. The worker might not be a victim in their own workplace communications, as Spinuzzi persuasively demonstrates with fine-grain micro-analyses, but we might consider how Spinuzzi's rejection of the "worker-as-victim" trope is necessarily contextualized to his site of inquiry as much as it is *decontextualized* from histories of colonialism, exploitation, and workplace discrimination macroscopically. We might also consider his claim to be "postcritical" (Spinuzzi 2008) in his later study, an orientation he argues workers and researchers should adopt.

Spinuzzi (2008, 202, original emphasis) writes that both groups must acknowledge that workplace communication is "hard work, perhaps even *unfair* work, and then [figure] out how to cope with and excel at it." Such a conceit necessarily obscures histories of oppression and decontextualizes the radical changes to workplaces that queer, disabled, and minority workers have historically enacted. Put simply, postcritical orientations cannot account for the queer student who began her response to a question I asked about her professional goals with the conditional phrase "if the world was different." They cannot account for the student of color who told me about a legal internship she wouldn't return to because the "political conversations" held around her on a daily basis were a "bad fit." It might be argued that discrimination is outside TPCs frame of workplace rhetoric, but it is undeniable that socialization, networked writing, and hierarchies of workplace communication are historically and ideologically tied up with oppressive rhetorical actions in workplaces. My story, my interests as a TPC scholar, and my conversations with my students all constellate my perspective on leveraging longitudinal methods as a proverbial "master's tool" of knowledge production. My research methods are necessarily informed by the longitudinal work of TPC scholars while my political orientation contrasts with theirs, aligning with the field's social justice turn.

When Natasha Jones, Kristen Moore, and Rebecca Walton (2016, 211–12) reflect on TPC, they write that the field struggles with "the dominant narrative that technical communication is most concerned with objective, apolitical, acultural practices, theories, and pedagogies." Their argument to turn the field to a new direction takes up the work of critical rhetoricians, such as those published in *Critical Power Tools* (Scott, Longo, and Wills 2006), an edited collection on theory, research, and pedagogy in technical writing. In all this work, scholars call for radical shifts at all levels of TPC, but the discipline's image of epistemological stability is often reified in the way social justice–oriented work is received and represented. In Deborah C. Andrews's (2007, 187) review of *Critical Power Tools*, for instance, she concludes that "we are not preparing students as well as we can to thrive as communicators in the workplace of 'fast capitalism.'" Andrews's summation that cultural studies will make more effective writers under capitalism corrals cultural studies scholars' social justice work into the same stable, purpose-based nature of TPC scholarship they seek to eschew: its "pragmatic identity that values effectiveness," to again cite Jones, Moore, and Walton (2016, 212). The reification of hegemonic ideology as the natural, stable site of rhetorical practice is not unique to TPC epistemology. However, this reification is a factor in how the application-based identity that constrains the field might foreclose it from methodological conversations and possibilities of longitudinal writing more broadly.

My prior examination of the politics of Spinuzzi's and Winsor's studies and their relationships to longitudinal methods and social justice is a discursive gesture that holds material implications. For my own study, as I wrote my funding proposals and refined my study design, I navigated the political tensions I had with extant longitudinal studies in TPC. My orientation is that modern work exploits workers and that TPC must enact an antagonistic relationship to the market logics that make work precarious, including in our longitudinal studies. Thus, I couldn't ignore Winsor's (2003) scholarship and its pathologized framing of political resistance. I couldn't ignore its problematic decontextualization of capitalism's "inhuman behavior" and "useful work" (11), which suggests that the same groups both benefit and suffer from capitalism's violence. Rather than directly informing my approach, then, extant longitudinal studies in TPC helped me position myself in contrasts. I sought to understand issues of oppression and power that workplace studies like Winsor's obscure and normalize. In framing my own work as anticapitalist, understanding the ideological character of the methodological history I draw from is a necessary step to engage the market logics my study and study participants encounter, internalize, reject, leverage, and otherwise navigate in our work.

Forces of commodity relations and ideological hegemony are necessarily at play in all academic scholarship, just as changes over time are always occurring in longitudinal data regardless of whether a scholar engaging in a multi-year study selects them as points of analysis. The perception of apolitical stability has come under scrutiny in the very same social justice scholarship that informs my own study. As Angela Haas and Michelle Eble (2018, 4) argue in outlining social justice frameworks for TPC, "We have a complicated relationship with globalization; thus, we have an obligation to critically assess that complexity." The call for reflexivity must also be attended to in methodology, and even a short survey of TPC's history with longitudinal study suggests our often short-sighted view of macroscopic forces like globalization and neoliberalism in workplace studies.

Where the stability of TPC pedagogy is continuing to be unsettled, theorizing the affordances of longitudinal work to grapple with precarity in both the classroom and the workplace is a related step for the field.[4] The place of longitudinal work in TPC has not ever just been in the classroom; perhaps now more than ever, with the field's turn to social justice, the workplace must be the subject of a politically critical longitudinal view. Longitudinal work isn't limited to an examination of the changes over time during a study but to the broader context of work and its material-discursive relations of oppression and resistance. The workplace studies I've surveyed here mark a key break from the characterization of workplace studies in composition—they illustrate socialization into a discipline, positioning the classroom and the workplace as linearly related. In the following section, I consider the precarity I experienced in designing my study and the related political and scholarly significance of social justice–informed interventions into TPC and longitudinal studies.

DESIGNING FOR A TRAJECTORY IN FLUX

The methodological history of longitudinal methods in TPC and my analysis of workplace research inform the guiding philosophy for my own study. As much of my understanding of past scholarship informs study design, so too do the material conditions that frame my work. In this section, I'll tell stories about how my own orientation has been shaped to attend to the material-discursive relations of production through longitudinal methods. Changes over time, as a dimension of research, can reveal the precarious relations that precede my study and that will continue to develop year after year for myself, study participants, and particularly marginalized students in that group—even though the study has ended. Our shared political milieu, experienced differently based on sources of privilege and interlocking oppressions across race, class, gender, sexuality, and dis/ability, historicizes rhetorical activities in professional writing.

In my study, I take neoliberalism as an endemic factor of longitudinal research. It doesn't cause whatever rhetorical actions I examine with my participants. Rather, the conditions of material uncertainty are *factors* of evolving economic structures of precarity found under neoliberalism. These factors interlock with larger forces of exploitation and colonization that can be understood longitudinally. With this guiding principle, I sought to be continually reflexive of my own researcher positionality and the positionalities of the classroom and workplace interactions I examined, combining scholarship from the social justice turn of TPC with the extant longitudinal studies methodologies. It wasn't until I began my study and gathered my first round of data that I realized how my methodological decision was fraught with risk, a point I've understood most clearly through one recent piece of TPC scholarship.

Elizabeth L. Angeli's *Rhetorical Work in Emergency Medical Services* (2019, 177), a six-year study of EMS trainees, operates along a paradigm of TPC research she refers to as "unpredictable workplace environments," which has a methodological history that includes both Winsor's 1996 and 2003 publications. Angeli's framing focuses on the distributed, complex relations of written communication illuminated by long-term observational study while emphasizing risk and unpredictability as elements of emergency medical technician (EMT) work. As I do with my own interest in precarity as an object of longitudinal study and the precariousness of my own researcher positionality, Angeli strongly foregrounds her personal connections to her workplace and researcher positionality from the first pages of her first chapter, starting her work as an EMT "at a crossroads" of her graduate work when she was "unsure whether [she] wanted to pursue an academic career" (6). One of Angeli's methods chapters is framed entirely around her material conditions as a graduate student, navigating IRB approval and graduation deadlines amid her changing goals as an academic and emergency medical technician.

It is clear in this move that longitudinal work is a deeply material process; for graduate students like myself, these conditions ground methodological decisions that might be viewed as limitations instead as the consequences of institutional timelines of programmatic funding. The conditions of graduate study afford a fragile relationship to such a time- and resource-intensive method as longitudinal study. In my first grant rejection prior to writing this chapter, I was faced with the decision to divert my funding to instead compensate research participants, many of whom are in precarious post-undergraduate positions. I wasn't willing to ask for uncompensated participation from my participants, but the multiple jobs I held as a graduate student while also progressing through my program limited the time I had to apply for grant funding.

The Covid-19 pandemic further exacerbated this issue, ultimately making longitudinal study a financially untenable prospect for me. And yet, writing about these conditions is a key affordance of longitudinal work. Research design can obscure researcher conditions just as much as it can obscure relations of production in the workplace, but an emphasis on material conditions and social justice reveals longitudinal studies' potential to highlight the precarity of both researcher and research participant.

While Angeli is not alone and many longitudinal writing researchers, including several in this volume, call attention to material and social aspects of longitudinal studies, I see precarity as an element of academic research in need of privileging in our methodological discussions. Precarity is bound in history and mediated by time, both of which can be examined in longitudinal study; however, the time and resources needed to conduct longitudinal work stress the precarious positions of researcher and research participant alike. Composition scholars Gerald Nelms and Ronda Leathers Dively (2007, 216) wrote that the longitudinal studies up to that point demonstrated "the possibility that the development they chart over time may be a consequence of their own research methods." While they wrote specifically about writers' reflections and the reflexivity endemic to longitudinal work, all of the apparatuses we use to collect, examine, and analyze data have always been inculcated with ideological, political, affective, and material-discursive energies. As Karen Barad (2003, 816) argues, research apparatuses "are neither neutral probes of the natural world nor structures that deterministically impose some particular outcome." The "cuts" we perform with longitudinal methods are themselves a deeply political and rhetorical activity. The choice to engage in longitudinal research itself requires a commitment of time and labor to a methodology that is in many ways materially incongruent to the uncertainty it is so well suited to discursively track. That is, as a method, longitudinal study is paradoxically well suited to examine precarity while also creating precarity in its own right. Every grant I applied to for funding was time I took away from preparing for my candidacy exams on a program funding clock that was counting down. Every minute a former student spent speaking with me was a minute they weren't working on another demand on their time. One student commented that the only reason they could speak with me was that the compensation I provided for an hour of their time was greater than what they made driving for a delivery app. The time and effort required by longitudinal study draws attention to the precarious conditions researchers and research participants experience.

The feminist materialist philosophy attended to here is an apt place to end my story, framing TPC methodology in both its material and discursive capacities. As Brian McNely, Clay Spinuzzi, and Christa Teston (2015, 5) write, "Usability, collaboration, and motives of technical communicators are inseparable from the material environs in which knowledge work is practiced." This articulation is even more true in longitudinal work, where material conditions are constantly shifting and time must be of central concern in the design of the study and in the analysis of its data: not time in a linear progression of classroom learning to workplace application but time as itself another horizontal,[5] networked, recursive, and negotiated dimension of the workplace *and* the classroom. Simultaneously backward-facing to the histories that contextualize precarity in the long arc of workplace study and forward-looking to the radical systemic change that labor can accomplish in professional environments, time must be understood as a material-discursive relation in the workplace and in TPC research for us to pursue emancipatory politics in our longitudinal work. Further, to align social justice with research, TPC scholars must not position themselves in a spectator role toward either the politics we participate in or the genealogies of oppression suffered in the classroom and the workplace. As Jerry L. Rosiek, Jimmy Snyder, and Scott L. Pratt (2019, 5) write, in bringing Indigenous anti-colonial epistemologies to bear on feminist materialism, it is not just research instruments and subjects of study that are constantly in flux: "inquirers are also multiple and transformed in the entanglement of inquiry."

I began writing this chapter when I, my participants, the study, and the broader relations embedding these elements all occupied a precarious position. Before the first wave of the Covid-19 pandemic in 2020, with some of my study's participants still in school and some having graduated, each had professional goals and anxieties tied up with their own disciplines, writerly identities, and material needs. The uncertainty of the study itself, of the conditions each student sees themselves entering, and of my own risks in conducting the study are all materially anticipatory factors. That is, longitudinal study itself is haunted with particular risks of failure and possibility, from its planning and first stages of execution onward. What is more, the uncertainty of continuation, of longitudinality, never lessens. Instead, the economy, the environment, and other macroscopic dimensions are constantly shifting; and the researcher is not outside any of these relationalities. Consider not only how the reciprocity of research changed for me with my access to research funds but also how it would have changed if any of my participants were laid off or if the cost of living in their communities climbed higher. As researchers, we're not spectators. We are actively involved in shared struggles with our study participants—we involve ourselves, especially when we promise compensation to students who participate in our studies, who live under the weight of student loan debt, as was the case for the majority of my study's participants.

As an inquirer, longitudinal study can record my shifting entanglement in knowledge production and ethical reciprocity. This is why when Covid-19 strained every personal and professional relationship and rendered me unable to compensate my research participants, I did not hesitate to end my study. Amid the professional, political, and personal tumult the Covid-19 pandemic brought to everyday life, what was certain was that my study would end before I had hoped. However, it left me with a sense of what longitudinal research can do within TPC. Teachers of TPC enact new possibilities for social justice in theory and in the classroom—possibilities we can further enact with longitudinal study. We can examine oppression as historically mediated for the precarious communities we interact with and that many of us are a part of ourselves. Describing the precarity of longitudinal methodology and of my positionality as a researcher is the most important thing I can do during this time. After all, that is precisely what I asked my participants to do every time they shared their rhetorical practices with me—to consider the uncertainty of their labor and address the systems in place that make our lives precarious.

NOTES

1. For insight into this curriculum, see the open-source textbook used in my institution's business writing class: *Writing Our Way toward More Livable Worlds* (Teston and Hashlamon 2019). This resource emerged from assessment research and from social justice scholarship in TPC for local use at my institution.
2. In this chapter, I use Isabell Lorey's (2015) distinctions between "precariousness" and "precarity." Where precariousness is a general condition of uncertainty, precarity is a "category of order"—an unequal distribution of social and economic uncertainty as a form of structural oppression (25).
3. Neoliberalism refers to the ideology that frames market logics—commodification, exchange, and exploitation—as cultural and political norms of social life. Rendering capitalism as a hegemony implicates writing studies as complicit in its dominance and as a potential agent of its resistance. See Wendy Brown's (2015, 164) framing of neoliberalism as the "economization of politics."
4. Recent longitudinal studies in professional and technical communication have focused on the classroom in particular. Scott Warnock and colleagues' (2017) work emphasizes rigorous quantitative assessment over time in professional writing, and Sara Doan (2018) focuses on the necessity of examining instructors' pedagogical practices amid austerity in the humanities and assessment.

5. As new materialist Rosi Braidotti (2007, 68) writes of feminist methodology, "We need to adopt non-linearity as a major principle and to develop cartographies of power that account for the paradoxes and contradictions of the era of globalisation, and which do not take shortcuts through its complexities," resonating with TPC scholars' calls to interrogate "how we may be complicit in, implicated by, and/or transgress the oppressive colonial and capitalistic influences and effects of globalization" (Haas and Eble 2018, 4).

REFERENCES

Andrews, Deborah C. 2007. "Book Review: *Critical Power Tools: Technical Communication and Cultural Studies*, by J. Blake Scott, Bernadette Longo, and Katherine V. Wills (Eds.)" *Journal of Business Communication* 44 (2): 186–89.

Angeli, Elizabeth L. 2019. *Rhetorical Work in Emergency Medical Services*. New York: Routledge.

Barad, Karen. 2003. "Posthumanist Performativity: Toward an Understanding of How Matter Comes to Matter." *Signs: Journal of Women in Culture and Society* 28 (3): 801–31.

Beaufort, Anne. 2007. *College Writing and Beyond: A New Framework for University Writing Instruction*. Logan: Utah State University Press.

Braidotti, Rosi. 2007. "Feminist Epistemology after Postmodernism: Critiquing Science, Technology, and Globalization." *Interdisciplinary Science Reviews* 32 (1): 65–74.

Brown, Wendy. 2015. *Undoing the Demos: Neoliberalism's Stealth Revolution*. Cambridge: MIT Press.

Cox, Matthew B. 2019. "Working Closets: Mapping Queer Professional Discourses and Why Professional Communication Studies Need Queer Rhetorics." *Journal of Business and Technical Communication* 33 (1): 1–25.

Doan, Sara. 2018. "Building Understanding of Instructor Feedback: Laying Groundwork for Professional and Technical Communication." Presented at the 2018 IEEE International Professional Communication Conference (ProComm), Toronto, July 22–25.

Haas, Angela, and Michelle Eble. 2018. "Introduction: The Social Justice Turn." In *Key Theoretical Frameworks: Teaching Technical Communication in the Twenty-First Century*, ed. Angela Haas and Michelle Eble, 3–20. Logan: Utah State University Press.

Henschel, Sally, and Lisa Melonçon. 2014. "Of Horsemen and Layered Literacies: Assessment Instruments for Aligning Technical and Professional Communication Undergraduate Curricula with Professional Expectations." *Programmatic Perspectives* 6 (1): 3–26.

Jones, Natasha, Kristen Moore, and Rebecca Walton. 2016. "Disrupting the Past to Disrupt the Future: An Antenarrative of Technical Communication." *Technical Communication Quarterly* 25 (4): 211–29.

Lorde, Audre. 1984. "The Master's Tools Will Never Dismantle the Master's House." In Lorde, *Sister Outsider: Essays and Speeches*, 110–14. Berkeley: Crossing Press.

Lorey, Isabell. 2015. *State of Insecurity: Government of the Precarious*. London: Verso.

McNely, Brian, Clay Spinuzzi, and Christa Teston. 2015. "Contemporary Research Methodologies in Technical Communication." *Technical Communication Quarterly* 24 (1): 1–13.

Nelms, Gerald, and Ronda Leathers Dively. 2007. "Perceived Roadblocks to Transferring Knowledge from First-Year Composition to Writing Intensive Major Courses: A Pilot Study." *WPA: Writing Program Administration* 31 (1–2): 214–40.

Rosiek, Jerry L., Jimmy Snyder, and Scott L. Pratt. 2019. "The New Materialisms and Indigenous Theories of Non-Human Agency: Making the Case for Respectful Anti-Colonial Engagement." *Qualitative Inquiry* 26 (3–4): 1–16.

Scott, J. Blake. 2004. "Rearticulating Civic Engagement through Cultural Studies and Service-Learning." *Technical Communication Quarterly* 13 (3): 289–306.

Scott, J. Blake, Bernadette Longo, and Katherine V. Wills, eds. 2006. *Critical Power Tools: Technical Communication and Cultural Studies.* New York: State University of New York Press.

Shelton, Cecilia. 2019. "Shifting Out of Neutral: Centering Difference, Bias, and Social Justice in a Business Writing Course." *Technical Communication Quarterly* 29 (1): 18–32.

Spinuzzi, Clay. 2002. "Toward Integrating Our Research Scope: A Sociocultural Field Methodology." *Journal of Business and Technical Communication* 16 (1): 3–32.

Spinuzzi, Clay. 2003. *Tracing Genres through Organizations: A Sociocultural Approach to Information Design.* Cambridge: MIT Press.

Spinuzzi, Clay. 2008. *Network: Theorizing Knowledge Work in Telecommunications.* Cambridge: Cambridge University Press.

Steinberger, Ben Z. 2018. "Note, Redefining 'Employee' in the Gig Economy: Shielding Workers from the Uber Model." *Fordham Journal of Corporate and Financial Law* 23 (2): 577–96.

Taylor, Ronald, and James Utterback. 1975. "A Longitudinal Study of Communication in Research: Technical and Managerial Influences." *IEEE Transactions on Engineering Management* 22: 80–87.

Teston, Christa, and Yanar Hashlamon. 2019. *Writing Our Way toward More Livable Worlds.* Montreal: Ohio State University Pressbooks.

Walton, Rebecca, Kristen Moore, and Natasha Jones. 2019. *Technical Communication after the Social Justice Turn.* New York: Routledge.

Warnock, Scott, Nicholas Rouse, Christopher Finnin, Frank Linnehan, and Dylan Dryer. 2017. "Measuring Quality Evaluating Curricular Change: A 7-Year Assessment of Undergraduate Business Student Writing." *Journal of Business and Technical Communication* 31 (2): 135–67.

Winsor, Dorothy A. 1996. *Writing Like an Engineer: A Rhetorical Education.* Mahwah, NJ: Lawrence Erlbaum Associates.

Winsor, Dorothy A. 2003. *Writing Power: Communication in an Engineering Center.* Albany: State University of New York Press.

9
RADICALLY LONGITUDINAL, RADICALLY CONTEXTUAL
Growing Lifespan Writing Research

Ryan J. Dippre and Talinn Phillips

Longitudinal research has long been an important approach in writing studies. In her overview of longitudinal research, Jenn Fishman (2012) identifies publications near the founding of the field (i.e., Braddock, Lloyd-Jones, and Schoer 1963; Shaughnessy 1977), indicating that the long-term study of writers and their development is crucial for understanding how writers change over time and across settings. Later writing researchers took up this challenge, looking across wider spans of lifeworlds and wider swaths of time using both qualitative (e.g., Sternglass 1997) and quantitative (e.g., Haswell 2000) methods. Alluding to the rise of a range of methods, sites, and research questions, as well as possible connections between longitudinal data collection and assessment measures, Fishman is optimistic about the future of longitudinal research: "Especially if writing teachers and administrators can integrate multiyear projects into their programs and curricula, longitudinal research stands to become a cornerstone of twenty-first-century writing education" (177).

Although Fishman's quote focuses on postsecondary settings, we find that her optimism was not misplaced as researchers in writing studies more broadly are giving increasing attention to longitudinal research in a range of settings. Ten years have passed since her work was published, but in that time, longitudinal writing studies have appeared with increasing frequency across the publication venues in the field. These studies have focused on transfer across courses (Yancey, Robertson, and Taczak 2014), academic years (Driscoll 2015), entire collegiate careers (Johnson and Krase 2012; Rounsaville 2017), and postgraduate writers (Davis 2013), as well as the complexity of development across lifeworlds (Roozen and Erickson 2017). The incredible variety of sites, methods,

https://doi.org/10.7330/9781646424337.c009

questions, and analyses has demonstrated the range of uses to which longitudinal writing research can be applied.

We also find ourselves in an age when there is a more explicit need for longitudinal studies of writing. The rise of what Deborah Brandt (2015) calls "mass writing literacy" has shifted the ways many writers learn to write and go about writing compared to previous generations. The seismic social, cultural, and economic shifts that led to that rise have only been exacerbated by the Covid-19 pandemic. Now more than ever, we need to be able to follow writers as they grow throughout their lives and many literate activities.

Thus, in this chapter, we consider longitudinal research, but we do so radically to pursue the question: *how does writing change across the entirety of a writer's lifespan?* For while longitudinal and other writing research methods have shown us a great deal, we do not yet understand the implications of how writing changes from one stage of a person's life to the next, throughout the entirety of the lifespan. The diverse research methods and approaches of our fields often don't speak effectively to each other, frequently resulting in siloed, truncated, and decontextualized understandings of how and why people write. And even when methods do play well together, the field often lacks the structures and incentives to encourage researchers to play together themselves. To wit, in the last year we've been working with Lauren Bowen and Anna Smith to develop a collaborative research project across our four institutions. The design of the study itself took months, but it then took nearly as long to negotiate the bureaucracies of a jointly submitted grant application and cross-institutional IRB. Processes were opaque, counterintuitive, and clunky.

It can also take quite a bit of effort (and, in some cases, additional funding) to share or learn about the research in other areas of writing studies. We have somewhat entrenched boundaries around K–12 research, postsecondary research, and workplace research, among others, that make it challenging for researchers to fully access and engage related research contexts and findings. Yet if writing researchers could more fully grasp writers' multiple trajectories of becoming (Prior 2018) constructed through acts of writing and if they could do so in a holistic way, then we would also be better able to understand the long-term ramifications of our pedagogical choices, curricular designs, and perhaps even broader community programming. With broader, more thorough understandings of the complex connections that are built through literate action, writing teachers and researchers could thereby locate individual acts of writing on a more complex scale. Our aim here is to help those with longitudinal research experience and understand how to bring a lifespan lens to existing and future projects, as well as situate their longitudinal work in relation to lifespan writing research.

THE LIFESPAN OF LIFESPAN WRITING RESEARCH

We suggest that the studies mentioned along with the increasing maturity of writing studies as a field have put down roots that can now grow into much more substantial, complex, and interconnected research into how writers and writing change across much longer swaths of time. At the 2016 conference "College Writing": From the 1966 Dartmouth Seminar to Tomorrow, Charles Bazerman challenged writing researchers to think in radically longitudinal ways: across the entire lifetime of a writer, from the first deliberate markings on paper/screen to the last. Bazerman (2016, 3) describes this challenge as a "thought experiment":

> Longitudinal studies offer the possibility of understanding individuals following unique pathways leading to unique skills, orientations, and responses in situations rather than being normalized through cross-sectional groups of an age, educational level, or other category, with individuals being characterized as either typical or atypical. Rather, a long-term longitudinal view perceives the individual in relation to access to resources and experiences, sequences of events, learning opportunities and challenges, orientations to those opportunities, developmental sequences, formation of writing processes, emerging identities, and all other dimensions of writing . . . Thus longitudinal studies ideally should extend across the entire lifespan to see the total picture and to understand how early experiences and growth affect later opportunities, resources, and challenges, as well as how future goals may motivate earlier learning.

It is here that we began the work described in this chapter, including wrestling with the opportunities and challenges of long writing studies. Since then, we have been working with Bazerman and other members of his Lifespan Writing Development Group to turn this thought experiment into reality.

Several events and publications followed Bazerman's 2016 challenge: an edited collection on lifespan writing development (Bazerman et al. 2018), an exchange in *Research in the Teaching of English* between the Lifespan Writing Development Group and Paul A. Prior (Bazerman et al. 2017; Prior 2018), and the publication of a special issue on lifespan in *Writing and Pedagogy* (Bazerman 2019). As the co-chairs of the recently formed Writing through the Lifespan Collaboration (the Collaboration), we had recruited an international collection of more than thirty researchers interested in taking up Bazerman's challenge to understand how writing works from cradle to grave. We've facilitated

Radically Longitudinal, Radically Contextual 153

multiple conference calls to help researchers get to know one another and one another's work, and we've also hosted our first conference to bring people together, face to face, to share lifespan writing research and more fully develop the Collaboration. Our second edited collection (Dippre and Phillips, forthcoming), third conference, and a range of pilot studies will be under way by the time readers see this chapter. With the support of Bazerman and many other interested researchers, the thought experiment has grown some pretty serious roots.

Carrying the project—in all its complexity and difficulty—forward also seems increasingly vital. We drafted part of this chapter in April 2020 in what were still the "early days" of the Covid-19 pandemic. One microscopic virus has radically altered the literate action of most people around the globe, and we are unlikely ever to go back. After years of shielding our children and ourselves from the dangers of screen time, we've all been attached to our computers for much of the day, negotiating a range of new programs and interfaces at a rapid-fire pace to manage our socially distanced lives. Talinn's four-year-old began having regular video meetings with her preschool class, which she largely negotiated by herself (after years of inadvertently hitting the "hang up" button on cell phones). She also regularly "wrote letters" to her friends and teachers, demonstrating a firm grasp of the personal letter genre months before she began kindergarten. Her eight-year-old brother set up his own Zoom meetings to talk with his teachers and with his friends to discuss Pokémon and video game strategies. And no matter how much philosophical or technological resistance we may have exerted, we now have considerable online teaching experience. These shifts have been dramatic, even violent, and are permanently re-shaping our writing selves. Understanding how, to what ends, and what might need to be done about it is not a project for one researcher in a fall writing class. To understand this re-shaping will require dozens, if not hundreds, of researchers around the globe looking at all segments of the lifespan. We've taken some initial steps toward that understanding by developing a new project that will investigate how a writer's agency and identity impact writing as they work through major life transitions like Covid-19.

If lifespan writing research has grown roots and if exigencies abound, then where does it grow from here? In this chapter, we'll describe how lifespan writing research, as a framework for seeing writing at all points of the lifespan and at all levels of activity, can serve as a cohering force for multiple longitudinal studies across age spans, sites, and methods. We recognize that the scope of lifespan writing will necessitate new ideas, new methods, and new strategies—that it is, in effect, a research agenda that is always running away from us. Nevertheless, we'll conclude by suggesting two ways we see lifespan writing research continuing to grow up from these roots.

SHARED ROOTS OF LIFESPAN WRITING AND LONGITUDINAL STUDIES

First, what do we mean by lifespan writing research? In our earliest work to establish the Collaboration, we refrained from putting any real parameters on lifespan writing research or defining it in a particular way. We wanted to encourage new researchers to join in the immense task that is lifespan writing research, not make moves that would define them as outsiders.

More recently, we've worked toward a shared definition of what we mean by lifespan writing research—one that still creates a "big tent" where many researchers are welcome but that does allow us to draw meaningful distinctions between lifespan work and, for example, longitudinal methods. After virtual and in-person meetings, surveys, comments, and revisions, the Collaboration concluded that "Lifespan Writing Research examines acts of inscribed meaning-making, the products of it, and the multiple dimensions of human activity that relate to it in order to build accounts of whether and how writers and writing may change throughout the duration and breadth of the lifespan" (Writing through the Lifespan Collaboration 2019). We would describe lifespan writing research not as a particular method or even as a subfield (as a subfield implies that the findings have a narrow range of use) but as a multidisciplinary research agenda whose researchers are interested in writing broadly (and multimodally) defined. We also seek to understand writing situated in contextual knowledge of the writer—both throughout the length of the lifespan and the breadth of spheres of social participation. We are then furthermore interested in how that writing changes (or doesn't) throughout one's life. Thus, lifespan writing research encompasses a wide range of research methods and disciplines, including longitudinal methods so long as those researchers are applying a lifespan lens to their work.

Although writing teachers and researchers often talk about writing from a framework of development, the Collaboration has chosen to exclude that concept from our definition because of the ways "development" suggests normativity. Some writers will continue to write in new and better ways throughout their lives while others may go for quite a long time without developing or improving any new abilities; disuse can even trigger the loss of an ability. As Bazerman et al. (2018, 237) write, "Transitions of life conditions and writing needs, stagnation, disruptions, redirections, or deterioration of writing also are important to understand, and can occur in different ways at different points in life." Thus, "development" connotes a common trajectory, a set of shared milestones, and a continuing accretion—all of which imply a normativity we are deeply committed to avoiding. Instead, we focus our attention on change, stasis, and the factors that trigger both. In so doing, we work against any underlying assumptions that continuous writing development throughout the lifespan should be normative and, concomitantly, the implication that those whose writing plateaus or declines have somehow "failed" at life.

Our working definition also doesn't specify particular methodology(/ies), a point we'll discuss later in this chapter; however, we believe longitudinal research methods are a set of methodologies that will always be a core part of lifespan writing research. Indeed, longitudinal research is how many of the current Collaboration members have come to this work. Yet longitudinal methods, even with all they offer, are not enough to capture the depth, width, and complexity of lifespan writing. For example, Sandra Tarabochia and Shannon Madden (2018), lacking the resources to conduct a lengthy longitudinal study, developed the "parallax method" as a substitute.

As the title of our chapter suggests, we believe that lifespan writing research is, at heart, deeply radical and that it is radical in multiple ways. We use radical here first as the Middle English origins of the word suggest, referencing the "roots or origin." Lifespan writing research is committed to understanding and revealing the roots that underlie writers' changes over time—both the large, obvious, trip-over-able roots and those that are more hidden and more subtle, perhaps only becoming evident over decades or generations. Lifespan writing research builds its accounts of change over time by a continual return to the work/roots of writers and writing, by a tight focus on inscribed meaning making, but with particular interests, concerns, and orientations in mind. Ryan Dippre (2019), for instance, traces a number of inscription practices for individuals through a range of years and circumstances—in places such as college classes, writers' workshops, nuclear submarines, and private industry. Attending to how people produce order with and through writing from one moment to the next helps us understand the complex influences literate action has on the trajectories of one's life, both in mundane, day-to-day actions and in larger patterns of social participation.

But lifespan writing research is also radical in particular ways: in its attention to context and to the durations of engagement researchers have with writers. Thus, as a phenomenon of interest, lifespan writing offers longitudinal writing researchers a useful framework for thinking in what we refer to as radically longitudinal and radically contextual ways. Drawing on more contemporary meanings of radical as "extreme" (or, as the *Online Etymology Dictionary* describes it, "at the limits of control"), we use the term *radically longitudinal* to describe taking longitudinal research to its extreme by studying writing from cradle to grave and, where appropriate, across generations, as Yvonne Lee (2020), for example, does. Lauren Rosenberg (chapter 3, this volume), for instance, learns new things about the literacy development of her participant, Chief, when she revisits him years after her initial study concluded. This revisit then sparks another study that is simultaneously new and an extension of her original research. Both Shirley Brice Heath (1983, 2012) and Catherine Compton-Lilly (2017) demonstrate that new insights and knowledge continue to form as long as the researcher stays in the field. While many of us may only have the opportunity to work with participants for one or two years, there is clearly value in pursuing a radically longitudinal research agenda that sets a decade or more of time in the field as the goalpost. Our latest project aims to follow writers in multigenerational families for two years as they work through a major life transition. We don't plan to stop there, though; we hope to transition those participants and our relationships with them into a longer-term study of lifespan writing.

Participants will keep changing and will keep writing in different ways; if we have the ability to conduct radically longitudinal studies, we will continue to learn from them and revise previous understandings in light of their new experiences. Talinn's first longitudinal project followed international graduate students during the first year of their master's programs. Having formed strong relationships with two of the participants, she applied to continue following them through the remainder of their programs after her dissertation research moved into the data analysis phase. The story she would have told about one of those participants, Chozin, was very different after two years than it would have been after one year. Chozin had certainly found his footing as a graduate writer after one year but then made rapid progress in his second year, becoming far more professionalized and proficient at integrating his writing abilities across his two languages (Phillips 2014). Similarly, the ongoing work of Melissa Bugdal and Kevin Roozen has followed their writer participants into new settings and far beyond the initial scope of their projects.

By *radically contextual*, we mean envisioning writing as occurring with, in, and through the construction of context over time. Context, in lifespan writing research, needs to be seen not as a backdrop against which writing happens but as an active component of the production of text (and, by extension, writers). Paul A. Prior (2018), Kevin Roozen (2009), Stacey Pigg (2014), and others have demonstrated through various case studies the complex, interactive work environment has on the production of text. Ryan J. Dippre and Anna Smith (2020) suggest that the protean nature of context—that is, its "responsive flexibility" to the situation at hand—makes it an essential component for understanding how writing and writers change throughout a lifetime. We argue that attending to the ways context is practiced into being—through engagement by writers with talk, tools, and texts—brings forward for closer examination the smaller acts of consciousness tuning (Prior and Shipka 2003) that constructs not only a text but also the sociality of a writer writing.

Being radically contextual opens up both conscious and habitual actions that occur with writing while also making space for surprises to be uncovered—the unexpected or forgotten influences that shape participants' writing practices. When paired with radically longitudinal studies, radically contextual approaches allow researchers to examine various levels of writing activity for both the length and the breadth of the lifespan. Length of attention and quality of context are distinct benefits of longitudinal writing studies. We simply suggest that, when possible, those benefits be pursued with a lifespan lens and to their radical extremes.

HOW SHALL LIFESPAN WRITING RESEARCH GROW? METHODOLOGICAL FUTURES

The recent proliferation of longitudinal research is a beneficial development for writing studies as a whole and for the ways it supports a lifespan writing research agenda. By thinking more broadly about the lives of writers, we can develop more complex understandings of the literate action writers perform and, by extension, build more just and equitable approaches to teaching writing and supporting writers. These goals are important to those of us in the Writing through the Lifespan Collaboration, and longitudinal, qualitative research will always be an essential methodology for our work. Yet, as mentioned earlier, the Collaboration shares a common research agenda and thus hasn't tied any methodologies explicitly to our definition of lifespan writing research. We made this choice because, as a phenomenon of interest, lifespan writing is positively mammoth. It is far beyond the scope of what any one researcher or even research team can tackle. It requires all kinds of sophisticated expertise in education, neurology, psychology, sociology, biology, and more. These different disciplinary traditions have their own research traditions and methodologies, and they all have something to offer us. They all provide another tool for chipping away at this mountain of lifespan writing, even if some are not tools that, individually, we enjoy or understand particularly well.

As a Collaboration, we've then worked to cultivate what, in her informal introductory remarks at the Dartmouth Summer Seminar for Composition Research, Christiane Donahue called a methodology of generosity, or an openness to what a method might offer (even if I don't choose to use it myself). Like Peter Elbow's (1998) "Believing Game," it calls for suspending disbelief and making it a habit of mind to enter into another's point of view in an effort to fully consider that perspective. Our first edited collection, *Approaches to Lifespan Writing Research: Generating an Actionable Coherence* (Dippre and Phillips 2020), works to showcase a methodology of generosity by bringing together studies from diverse disciplines to chart a future for lifespan writing research. For example, Magdalena Knappik's (2020) chapter on the origins and uses of the literacy autobiography draws on research from both English and German contexts and from the disciplines of education and sociology to interpret and assess its appropriateness for lifespan writing research. Adopting a methodology of generosity has thus been crucial for us in creating a big tent where researchers from many disciplinary backgrounds and methodological approaches feel welcome to contribute and share what they know. It's also been crucial to knowing *more*. As we've actively listened to the perspectives and findings of researchers from different disciplines and research traditions, our understandings of writing continue to evolve in depth, richness, and nuance.

What might a big tent and a methodology of generosity mean for lifespan writing research *within* writing studies? While practicing a methodology of generosity has been extremely productive up to this point, for lifespan writing research (and our particular Collaboration) to move forward, it's essential to develop ways to organize ourselves and our projects and to build on our research strengths while also being informed by and supporting a variety of research traditions. And, as the founders of the Collaboration who are disciplinarily oriented to English and composition/writing studies, how can we move forward in ways that are accepted and valued within our particular discipline?

It would be easy, at this point, to dismiss the possibility of lifespan writing research as a lot of noise. Methodological, theoretical, disciplinary, and philosophical contrasts, gaps, and contradictions can abound in interdisciplinary and multidisciplinary work, and lifespan writing research is unlikely to be an exception. Furthermore, in the absence of multi-billion-dollar grants, the study of writing development across a century at twenty or thirty sites around the world offers little possibility of being financially sustainable. It was with these realities in mind that we, with the Writing through the Lifespan Collaboration, began working through other ways of expanding the lifespan writing research project/orientation, both for those who are beginning new projects and for those who seek to integrate a lifespan perspective into ongoing longitudinal projects. If there's one thing that's become abundantly clear to us over the last five years, it's that operating in disciplinary silos cannot possibly help us understand the multifaceted complexity of writing through the lifespan. What follows, then, are two ways that we foresee lifespan writing research, having sprouted within writing studies, beginning to grow up. We think these possibilities are particularly relevant to longitudinal researchers who are interested in either orienting their work to the lifespan or situating their work in relation to other lifespan writing research.

GROWING A RADICAL RESEARCH AGENDA: LINES OF INQUIRY

The first site for growth is our concept, *lines of inquiry*. We propose that lines of inquiry can provide a flexible structure for organizing lifespan writing work, bringing coherence to otherwise diverse projects of researchers who are interested in working across methodological, theoretical, and disciplinary orientations toward a common goal. Lines of inquiry do this by orienting researchers across sites and methods to the same problem or problems—by rigorously investigating a concept or set of concepts that can be traced throughout the lifespan and scaled from a case study to a large dataset. Both tracing and scalability are of equal importance, particularly if we are to maintain a methodology of generosity across each of the lines of inquiry we plan to develop. Lines of inquiry can thus create projects that would be big enough to attract funding organizations but nimble enough to adjust projects when necessary, to persist as a whole if individual projects/pieces failed, and to recruit a sizable but manageable number of researchers to get pilot studies off the ground. Lines of inquiry seem ideal for longitudinal researchers who can draw on local participants and continue to pursue the particular methods and questions that are most salient to the contexts they're working in while also being a part of something much larger.

While our lines of inquiry are still being drawn, a good example of a potential line of inquiry is *agency*. Agency, broadly defined, means the capacity to act. One inquiry that lifespan writing researchers might pursue in regard to the concept of agency may be, how does writing impact the agency of writers throughout their lives? This broad question could be mobilized across a range of sites, be modified to meet the needs of those sites, and be detailed in relation to particular methodological and theoretical orientations. Consider, for instance, a team of several researchers around the globe pursuing this line of inquiry. These researchers could be trained in a wide range of methodologies, from hermeneutics to corpus analysis, and could be at a range of institutions (community colleges to research universities) within widely varying communities.

One researcher, such as a longitudinal qualitative researcher trained in structuralist and poststructuralist literary theory, might recruit several participants near each researcher's home institution for a long-term series of interviews, looking for the ways structure—as understood by the actor in an effort to reduce the challenges of uncertainty—enables and constrains agency in productive and prohibitive ways. Through such a longitudinal, close study of so few subjects, the researcher is able to identify the ways the indeterminacy of language is rendered determinate for particular actors at particular places and over significant lengths of time and how those particularities impact future writing development.

Another researcher, perhaps a corpus linguist, might collect a range of writing from dozens of participants at each researcher's home institution to understand what lexical bundles give rise to other lexical bundles as young scholars work their way into the profession. This researcher might work with the data of millions of words as opposed to the qualitative researcher, but both can examine agency, albeit in different ways. Yet a third researcher, perhaps one with a quantitative lean, might make a survey across each home institution to establish how writers envision themselves as active agents in their own writing lives. Each of these researchers might deploy different methods, but working together makes possible an expanded set of resources, research subjects, and concepts. Thus, lines of inquiry, by pulling together researchers and orienting them toward a particular question, have the capacity to do more than just provide access to a wider range of participants: they allow us the freedom to pursue longitudinal studies using a range of theoretical and empirical approaches while also creating the responsibility for researchers to situate their work in conversation with other theoretical and empirical approaches. Such inherently multidisciplinary work would render lines of inquiry durable, as they are both responsible to a number of traditions and responsive to changes in those traditions.

Our first attempt at operationalizing a line of inquiry will take up both agency and identity and will do so through the lens of major life transitions. With two other researchers at four research sites around the US, we will conduct a series of interviews and collect writing artifacts within multigenerational families that are experiencing one or more major life transitions (e.g., Covid-19, job change/loss, change in ability level, graduation, retirement, 9/11, global financial crisis, 1/6). While this will begin as a not-terribly-longitudinal project (two years), we intend for it to grow and expand beyond our initial goals and to eventually incorporate new research sites and participants over longer and longer swaths of time.

GRAFTING ON TO A RADICAL RESEARCH AGENDA: ADOPTING A LIFESPAN ORIENTATION

Although we are excited by the possibilities lines of inquiry offer, we also recognize that for many, lifespan writing research will be a more limited-term research orientation in a particular project, not a lifelong research commitment. We also foresee more measured growth in lifespan writing research among researchers who are willing to adapt existing projects to a lifespan orientation or to apply a lifespan orientation to future research projects, especially those who are already engaged in longitudinal work. Ultimately, a smaller-scale shift to orienting traditional kinds of projects to the lifespan and to some degree of longitudinality may generate the most growth in our understanding of lifespan writing. We propose the questions below as a starting point for orienting a writing research project toward the lifespan. Attending to such questions, even in the absence of a line of inquiry to align multiple researchers and methods, can help researchers think along a broader swath of time when considering the literate lives of those they study. We suggest the following heuristic for adapting/orienting/grafting on to lifespan writing research.

1. What aspects of literate action change throughout the time of the study? If literate action remains unchanged, why?

    This first step seems self-evident, but in the thick descriptions that characterize much qualitative, longitudinal work, it is easy to lose sight of change in an attempt to characterize the entirety of the social activity surrounding, embedding, and being constructed by writing. We chose the term *literate action* in this question to facilitate broad thinking about change. People can change the writing on the page, the audience the writing reaches, the practices put into play to make writing happen, and similar factors. Focusing strictly on "writing" might lose some of the radically contextual factors caught up in such change.

2. What objects can be focused on and what data should be collected to render the change (or stasis) evident? Should these objects change over time?

Obviously, answering the first question of this heuristic requires that change be recognized. However, once that recognition occurs, researchers need to hone their studies to bring the change into focus. This is akin to a biologist adjusting the setting of a microscope to more easily see the phenomenon of interest. When studying the notebook writing of a submarine mechanic, for example, Ryan (Dippre 2019) noticed some broader patterns of similarities across not only different notebooks but various other forms of media as well, such as Mac's Notes feature and Twitter. The clash of recurring forms and changing media alerted him to some kind of change, and he proceeded to focus in on particular kinds of media to bring the broad patterns of change he sensed to the surface for closer examination.

3. How might these changes be connected to a writer's prior literate action?

While recognizing and focusing in on change in a particular moment is important in both qualitative and quantitative work, lifespan writing research requires attention to the broader contours of the lives research participants are living. Returning, for instance, to Ryan's study of a submarine mechanic, it would be important to understand both the notebooks kept during the mechanic's time on the submarine and the notebooks prior to the mechanic's service in the US Navy, as well as the connections between the two. Locating a given transformation within the broader trajectory of a life of writing is necessary for determining the significance of a given change. For additional examples of researchers identifying and incorporating a writer's prior literate action, see Dippre and Phillips (2020).

4. How might these changes resonate across contemporary and future instances of literate action?

Next, lifespan writing researchers must locate the transformations they see in relation to the past and in relation to co-present literate activities research participants are engaged in. A given change in literate action might have a powerful impact on all aspects of a writer's life (see, for instance, Rounsaville 2017). A given pattern of reading and writing in one setting might deeply inform reading and writing acts in others; as we suggest earlier, treating those settings as active is an important component of seeing writing through a radically contextual lens. Lifespan writing researchers, while certainly incapable of seeing all aspects of their subjects' lives, should attend to as wide a variety of literate action as circumstances permit to understand the scope of development they are witnessing. Lifespan writing researchers might also benefit from anticipating the consequences of such changes. Transformations in literate action involve contemporary and future lifeworlds: the decision to write a letter to one's congressional representative might pull one into a complex political future as a grassroots organizer, which would drastically impact the complex web of future textual activities one regularly engages in.

5. How might these changes be characterized so they connect with other writing situations and time periods throughout the lifespan?

This final question calls attention to the ways the results of studies are organized and presented to other researchers. For lifespan writing research, a finding has the requirement of being portable—that is, usable both in the particular instance and across the range of activities and society segments. We are not suggesting that a given finding needs to be (or *can* even be) completely generalizable, of course. Rather, we suggest something akin to grounded theory, which proposes that a finding be both carefully bound and straightforwardly applicable to some (though not all) situations. For example, Deborah Brandt's (2001) "sponsors of literacy" concept has explanatory power for understanding the broader social forces that come to influence literacy development, but it does not attempt to explain all of the aspects of such social forces. The concept, however, does allow researchers to begin to make sense of how literacy is acting (and being acted upon) as a result of using it. Furthermore, the continued use of the concept in new settings allows for it to be refined and otherwise be made more effective.

It is this vision of portability that we wish to suggest is of prime importance to lifespan writing research. Any single study of writing will be bound to some particulars and should not lose sight of those particulars in the development of its findings. But attention to how characterization of findings could impact studies at other points in the lifespan can lead the way, over time, to more synchronization of studies across settings and even, perhaps, methods.

Of course, decisions about characterizing findings need to be carefully made and are not without consequence. In addition to determining how findings might be more effectively characterized, lifespan writing researchers should attend to the potential consequences of such choice making. Characterizing findings in any way illuminates some things and obfuscates others. This problem is not new but rather a common one throughout empirical research. Because of its inherently multidisciplinary work, however, lifespan writing researchers must keep this problem at the front of their decision-making activities.

This heuristic, we hope, will enable interested writing researchers to turn their projects—particularly longitudinal ones—toward a lifespan orientation. The questions above direct attention to a phenomenon of interest (i.e., change in a particular research site) and lead the researcher to connect that phenomenon to other points in the lifespan and to think about those other points in the lifespan while characterizing the phenomenon. Such work can be done with case studies over long stretches of time or with large-scale, randomized design studies of large cohorts of writers. The questions provide less structure than, say, a line of inquiry, but they allow researchers interested in pursuing longitudinal research writ radical to begin their work productively.

AN UNWIELDY CONCLUSION-BEGINNING

The future work we've described carries with it an impossibility—an absurdity, even. It is immensely unwieldy. And such a massive undertaking is of the utmost importance now, amid the rapidly changing social, economic, and political landscapes of the twenty-first century. The personal, public, and professional lives of writers are undergoing significant transformation, and it is that transformation that lifespan writing research needs to seek out and understand. Lifespan writing research—longitudinal writing research writ radical—is well suited to meet these circumstances, and it is our hope that both the concept of lines of inquiry and the heuristic we provide will encourage writing researchers interested in a range of longitudinal approaches to orient their work to a lifespan perspective.

NOTE

We'd like to thank Kelly Hartwell and Elizabeth Zavodny for their helpful and thought-provoking feedback on earlier drafts of this chapter.

REFERENCES

Bazerman, Charles. 2016. "The Puzzle of Conducting Research on Lifespan Development of Writing." Presented at "College Writing": From the 1966 Dartmouth Seminar to Tomorrow Conference, Dartmouth College, Hanover, NH, August 10–12.

Bazerman, Charles, ed. 2019. "Lives of Writing," in the special issue of *Writing and Pedagogy* titled *Writing across the Lifespan* (edited by Bazerman) 10 (3): 327–31.

Bazerman, Charles, Arthur N. Applebee, Virginia W. Berninger, Deborah Brandt, Steve Graham, Jill V. Jeffery, Paul Kei Matsuda, Sandra Murphy, Deborah Wells Rowe, Mary Schleppegrell, and Kristen Campbell Wilcox. 2018. *The Lifespan Development of Writing*. Urbana, IL: National Council of Teachers of English.

Bazerman, Charles, Arthur N. Applebee, Virginia W. Berninger, Deborah Brandt, Steve Graham, Paul Kei Matsuda, Sandra Murphy, Deborah Wells Rowe, and Mary Schleppegrell. 2017. "Taking the Long View on Writing Development." *Research in the Teaching of English* 51 (3): 351–60.

Braddock, Richard, Richard Lloyd-Jones, and Lowell Schoer. 1963. *Research in Written Composition.* Champaign, IL: National Council of Teachers of English.

Brandt, Deborah. 2001. *Literacy in American Lives.* Cambridge: Cambridge University Press.

Brandt, Deborah. 2015. *The Rise of Writing: Redefining Mass Literacy.* Cambridge: Cambridge University Press.

Compton-Lilly, Catherine. 2017. *Reading Students' Lives: Literacy Learning across Time.* New York: Routledge.

Davis, Mary. 2013. "The Development of Source Use by International Postgraduate Students." *Journal of English for Academic Purposes* 12 (2): 125–35.

Dippre, Ryan J. 2019. *Talk, Tools, and Texts: A Logic-in-Use for Studying Lifespan Literate Action Development: Practices and Possibilities.* Fort Collins and Boulder: WAC Clearinghouse and University Press of Colorado.

Dippre, Ryan J., and Talinn Phillips, eds. 2020. *Approaches to Lifespan Writing Research: Generating an Actionable Coherence.* Fort Collins and Boulder: WAC Clearinghouse and University Press of Colorado.

Dippre, Ryan J., and Talinn Phillips. Forthcoming. *Improvisations: Methods and Methodologies in Lifespan Writing Research.* Fort Collins: WAC Clearinghouse/University Press of Colorado.

Dippre, Ryan J., and Anna Smith. 2020. "Always Already Relocalized: The Protean Nature of Context in Lifespan Writing Research." In *Approaches to Lifespan Writing Research: Generating an Actionable Coherence,* ed. Ryan J. Dippre and Talinn Phillips, 27–38. Fort Collins and Boulder: WAC Clearinghouse and University of Press of Colorado. https://wac.colostate.edu/docs/books/lifespan/approaches.pdf.

Driscoll, Dana Lynn. 2015. "Building Connections and Transferring Knowledge: The Benefits of a Peer Tutoring Course beyond the Writing Center." *Writing Center Journal* 35 (1): 153–81.

Elbow, Peter. 1998. *Writing without Teachers.* 2nd edition. New York: Oxford University Press.

Fishman, Jenn. 2012. "Longitudinal Writing Research in (and for) the Twenty-First Century." In *Writing Studies Research in Practice,* ed. Lee Nickoson and Mary P. Sheridan, 171–82. Carbondale: Southern Illinois University Press.

Haswell, Richard H. 2000. "Documenting Improvement in College Writing: A Longitudinal Approach." *Written Communication* 17 (3): 307–52.

Heath, Shirley Brice. 1983. *Ways with Words: Language, Life, and Work in Communities and Classrooms.* Cambridge: Cambridge University Press.

Heath, Shirley Brice. 2012. *Words at Work and Play: Three Decades in Family and Community Life.* New York: Cambridge University Press.

Johnson, J. Paul, and Ethan Krase. 2012. "Articulating Claims and Presenting Evidence: A Study of Twelve Student Writers, from First-Year Composition to Writing across the Curriculum." *WAC Journal* 23: 31–48.

Knappik, Magdalena. 2020. "Making a Sense of a Person's Literate Life: Literacy Narratives in a 100-Year-Study on Literacy Development." In *Approaches to Lifespan Writing Research: Generating an Actionable Coherence,* ed. Ryan J. Dippre and Talinn Phillips, 67–80. Fort Collins and Boulder: WAC Clearinghouse and University of Press of Colorado.

Lee, Yvonne. 2020. "Toward an Understanding of the Multidirectional Nature of Family Literacy Development." In *Approaches to Lifespan Writing Research: Generating an Actionable Coherence,* ed. Ryan J. Dippre and Talinn Phillips, 127–42. Fort Collins and Boulder: WAC Clearinghouse and University of Press of Colorado.

Phillips, Talinn. 2014. "Developing Resources for Success: A Case Study of a Multilingual Graduate Writer." In *WAC and Second Language Writers: Research towards Linguisti-*

cally and Culturally Inclusive Programs and Practices, ed. Michelle Cox and Terry Myers Zawacki, 69–91. West Lafayette, IN: Parlor Press.

Pigg, Stacey. 2014. "Emplacing Mobile Composing Habits: A Study of Academic Writing in Networked Social Spaces." *College Composition and Communication* 66 (2): 250–75.

Prior, Paul A. 2018. "How Do Moments Add Up to Lives: Trajectories of Semiotic Becoming vs. Tales of School Learning in Four Modes." In *Making Future Matters*, ed. Rick Wysocki and Mary P. Sheridan. Logan: Computers and Composition Digital Press and Utah State University Press. ccdigitalpress.org/book/makingfuturematters/index.html.

Prior, Paul A., and Jody Shipka. 2003. "Chronotopic Lamination: Tracing the Contours of Literate Activity." In *Writing Selves/Writing Societies: Research from Activity Perspectives*, ed. Charles Bazerman and David R. Russell, 180–238. Fort Collins, CO: WAC Clearinghouse.

Roozen, Kevin. 2009. "From Journals to Journalism: Tracing Trajectories of Literate Development." *College Composition and Communication* 60 (3): 541–72.

Roozen, Kevin, and Joe Erickson. 2017. *Expanding Literate Landscapes: Persons, Practices, and Sociohistoric Perspectives of Disciplinary Development*. Logan: Computers and Composition Digital Press and Utah State University Press.

Rounsaville, Angela. 2017. "Worlding Genres through Lifeworld Analysis: New Directions for Genre Pedagogy and Uptake Awareness." *Composition Forum* 37. https://compositionforum.com/issue/37/worlding.php.

Shaughnessy, Mina P. 1977. *Errors and Expectations: A Guide for the Teacher of Basic Writing*. New York: Oxford University Press.

Sternglass, Marilyn. 1997. *A Time to Know Them: A Longitudinal Study of Writing and Learning at the College Level*. Mahwah, NJ: Erlbaum.

Tarabochia, Sandra, and Shannon Madden. 2018. "In Transition: Researching the Writing Development of Doctoral Students and Faculty." *Writing and Pedagogy* 10 (3): 423–52.

Writing through the Lifespan Collaboration. 2019. www.lifespanwriting.org.

Yancey, Kathleen Blake, Liane Robertson, and Kara Taczak. 2014. *Writing across Contexts: Transfer, Composition, and Sites of Writing*. Logan: Utah State University Press.

10
BECOMING HISTORY

Jenn Fishman

Telling time in longitudinal writing research is tricky. Individual studies usually span not weeks or months but years, which researchers experience as an ever-present present spent with writers who are always in medias res. Longitudinal projects also have relentless forward drive in a discipline eager for findings that can be applied to instructional and administrative problems. Since it is not uncommon for a decade to pass between data collection and scholarly publication, especially with monographs, longitudinal writing research also occupies a significant time lag. Now, time does not always matter in writing studies—and we don't always clock it the same way. Instead, we continually attune to various socio-cultural and material changes while we count on the apparent timelessness of some praxes and claims. From my own deep entanglement in this quandary, I am drawn to the possibility of reorienting longitudinal research. Although it may seem contrary to suggest a change of course, given the momentum longitudinal inquiries have gained over the last decades, it may also be past time to consider longitudinal writing research as a generative site for historical work. *What will we discover*, I wonder: *what might we see if we approach longitudinal writing research differently?*

Looking at my own history, I may be primed to pose these questions. In high school, Nancy and Bill "Doc" Sprague seeded my curiosity about the past in combined English and history classes, and then something clicked in college when Deborah Laycock introduced me to the so-called dark side of the Enlightenment. Reading newspapers, legal treatises, letters, and diary entries alongside long eighteenth-century novels and plays, I saw how historical knowledge could re-shape our relationship to an era's writing and to the worlds writing helps us imagine, including our own. Several years later, I was living a double life. In one, I completed a dissertation about the contribution public theater made to the development of print literate culture in England, and I taught

https://doi.org/10.7330/9781646424337.c010

historical rhetorics. In my other life, I conducted longitudinal writing research, first as part of the Stanford Study of Writing research team and later as co-principal investigator (PI) of the Embodied Literacies Project and PI of Vernon Writes.[1] Although flagship conferences bring these disparate pursuits together, as do occasional courses and publications, many of us distinguish our history pals from our comp buddies. We teach empirical and historical methods separately, and when it's time, we carefully choose where to circulate our work: the Conference on College Communication and Composition (CCCC), Council of Writing Program Administrators (CWPA), and certain journals for some projects and Rhetoric Society of America (RSA), FemRhet, and a host of particular publications for others.

So far, longitudinal studies of writing have been firmly anchored in the domain of prospective empirical inquiry, and they have aligned with our discipline's desire to seek and share knowledge that writing educators can put to use. At the college level, at least in the US, case-based multi-year studies provide a counterbalance to cross-sectional research (Haswell 2000, 311), and we have been conducting them almost continuously since the mid-1980s when Lucille McCarthy (1985, x) asked, "What happened next" after her students completed first-year writing (table 10.1).

All these years later, I wonder what might happen next if we were to approach McCarthy's study—or any of the studies listed below—as sites of historical inquiry. In some cases, we might have only formal scholarly publications to work with. In other cases, we might have not only articles and books but also institutional records (e.g., IRB applications, listserv messages), public records (e.g., news articles, project websites), and researchers' personal papers. Imagine the questions we might ask and the critical insight we might gain by examining data collection protocols from McCarthy to Hashlamon or if we read across extant correspondence among researchers. Consider what we might learn by triangulating public and scholarly writing for any given study with original project data. In some cases, we might also be able to examine project artifacts, including items distributed to participants as incentivizing SWAG.

Especially when diverse materials are available, there is great potential for new work based on previously conducted longitudinal studies of college writing. To begin, we might add to extant histories of longitudinal research (Haswell 2000; Rogers 2010; Fishman 2012c). We might also review past studies with an eye toward the praxes they make visible from methods of data collection and analysis to mentorship, academic management, and leadership. Alternatively, we could select random samples of student writing from several studies and examine familiar topics such

Table 10.1. Case-Based Longitudinal Studies of College Writing, 1983 to Present

1983–84	McCarthy, Loyola Maryland University
1986–90	Haas, Carnegie Mellon University
1987–90	Chiseri-Strater, University of New Hampshire
1989–93	Herrington and Curtis, University of Massachusetts Amherst
1989–93	Wolcott, University of Florida
1989–94	Winsor, GMI Engineering and Management Institute
1989–95	Sternglass, City College
1990–97	Beaufort, unnamed major US university
1994–98	Carroll, Pepperdine University
1997–2001	Sommers, Harvard University
2000–2005	Roozen, Auburn University
2001–6	Lunsford, Stanford University
2004–6	Wardle, University of Dayton
2007–10	Hesse, University of Denver
2007–14	Halbritter and Lindquist, Michigan State University
2009–23	Hassel and Giordano, University of Wisconsin Colleges
2010–	Driscoll, Indiana University of Pennsylvania
2011–13	Fishman, Vernon College
2011–16	Gere, University of Michigan
2012–18	Kimme Hea and Mapes, University of Arizona
2014–17	Downs, Montana State University
2014–19	Rifenburg, University of North Georgia
2014–	Serviss and Lucero, Santa Clara University
2019–20	Hashlamon, the Ohio State University[2]

as patterns of error or citation practices as they occur over time. Or we might investigate less considered issues, such as the presence and rhetorical purpose of affect in college writing or the appearance and function of particular idioms and syntactical patterns. Alternatively, we might analyze texts by specific writers from different decades in an effort to historicize our ideas about specific phenomena (e.g., knowledge transfer). We might also sample certain genres or academic discourses to learn whether and how they change, at least in college contexts; or we might choose texts by writers from particular demographics, interested in what we can learn through their writing about their experience in higher education.

Previously conducted longitudinal studies of writing might also be approached as archival collections rife with opportunities for historical inquiry. Erika Lindemann (2005), for example, demonstrates how student writing from the nineteenth century illuminates then-pressing academic and social issues, while Nathan Shepley (2016) mines the early twentieth-century archives at Ohio University and the University of Houston to show how college writing is inflected by local people, ideas, and locations. What might we learn about writing in the late twentieth and early twenty-first centuries if we reconsider datasets from longitudinal research as archives? To be sure, the focal points of our inquiries would shift. For example, place often falls under erasure in empirical studies, where longitudinal researchers may use generic institutional identifiers to name their sites of data collection. References to a "private research university" (Haas 1994, 50) or a "major U.S. university" (Beaufort 2007, 5) not only help protect participants' confidentiality; they also affirm the idea that study findings can be generalized and broadly applied. Deliberately emplaced historical work with the same data could be complementary. In fact, mixed methods that include place-based historical considerations might help us improve our collective ability to study writers and writing across both human and nonhuman lifespans (e.g., the lifetime of a college or university, the duration of a shaping state or national policy). By mixing methods according to quantity and quality as well as time or tense (e.g., past, present), we might gain new angles on everything from research sites to study designs, and we might find ourselves better positioned to acknowledge and embrace a greater range of research traditions.

Ultimately, approaching longitudinal research historically involves changing our minds along with our mind-sets. Picture a line drawing of a duck that from another focal point looks like a rabbit, or think of the Boring figure, which portrays both a young woman turning away from the viewer and an old woman looking forward and down. Ludwig Wittgenstein and others famously contemplated these double images, which exist simultaneously but can be perceived only one at a time. In writing studies, we have grown used to seeing longitudinal research in a particular way. I picture a team of divers poised and ready to enter the deep sea of ever-contemporary literacies. To envision longitudinal research historically, we must change our focus. Looking at the same scene in a new way, we might see a team of divers who have already dived. Instead of clouds and sky, underwater outcroppings and fishes surround them. Elsewhere, I have suggested that we should see longitudinal research as a tool for advocacy (Fishman 2012c), and this volume includes stories about the critical contributions longitudinal research can make to community colleges and the social justice turn in technical and professional communication (chapters 4 and 8). In the remainder of this chapter, I explore the possibility of using past longitudinal research for new, historical inquiries by returning to two of my own research projects. Diving back into the Stanford Study of Writing and Vernon Writes, I try to model ways we might regard our always growing catalog of longitudinal writing research as a resource for historical work, a monumental treasure buried in plain sight.

MY TURN(S)

My own "historical turn" as a longitudinal writing researcher involves a return to two projects. Conducted a decade apart, the Stanford Study of Writing and Vernon Writes share a broad definition of college writing as well as several data types (e.g., survey responses, interviews, writing samples). The two studies, like their host institutions, also differ in significant ways, starting with scale. The Stanford Study cohort included 189 students from the 1,876-person Class of 2005 (Stanford Report 2005), while the 12 seniors who participated in Vernon Writes were 12 out of 1,646 students enrolled at Vernon College. Over five years, the Stanford Study collected more than 13,000 electronic texts in total, and a subgroup of 38 volunteers participated in one or more interviews annually. By contrast, each Vernon Writes participant spent one year retrospectively collecting approximately three dozen writing samples, which they discussed with me during onetime, one-to-one interviews that took place in their last week of college. I joined the Stanford Study research team as a graduate student shortly before participants were consented, and more than a decade later I designed and led Vernon Writes. If the Stanford Study is well-known and regularly cited, Vernon Writes belongs to a class of smaller, institution-based research that includes thesis and dissertation studies, teacher research, writing program and writing center research, and inquiries anchored by portfolio assessment protocols.

My reasons for making a historical return to these two studies—and for encouraging a broader historical turn to longitudinal research—are distinct from other, more established reasons for circling back to past research. Most notably, the logic of RAD (replicable, aggregable, data-driven research) asks us to repeat previous studies, whether our own or others', to test and extend original findings. It is also not uncommon for writing and literacy researchers to keep up with project participants over long periods of time. Some casually stay in touch, while others maintain lifelong friendships with former human subjects. There are also a select few projects with extended *durée* that invite other forms of looking back, among them the Peer Writing Tutor Alumni Research Project (2020), which began in 2006, and the long arc of research and relations that stretches across Shirley Brice Heath's *Ways with Words* (1983) and *Words at Work and Play* (2012). In addition, there is a unique sense of return and reappraisal involved in what Lauren Rosenberg terms "revisiting." Elsewhere in this volume (chapter 3), she describes sharing her book *Desire for Literacy: Writing in the Lives of Adult Learners* (Rosenberg 2015) with George, a writer who participated in her research. At first they visited, she explains, catching up and celebrating their mutual accomplishment. But their conversation shifted, and Rosenberg recalls suddenly finding herself in the middle of a new project that was an unexpected extension of the earlier one. By contrast, the kind of historical return to prior longitudinal research that interests me does not involve a direct reconnection with participants; further, it does not extend the original research per se. Instead, my curiosity centers on whether and what we might learn anew, whether we focus wholly on the past or trace new chronological pathways through previously collected longitudinal data.

Certainly, I experience the pulls of the Stanford and Vernon archives differently. The former study began only weeks after 9/11, an instantly historic event that now sits squarely at the intersection of living memory and the annals of modern history while we live in our own unexampled times. When I teach writing from the Stanford Study, students are interested, at least in part, in comparing themselves with their Class of 2005 counterparts. They are also interested in what college was like "back then," and they are curious to learn about 9/11 itself from the writing of their past peers. Although Vernon Writes also has a relationship to notable world events, including the Great Recession, its archive is differently significant. Vernon College boasts a storied reputation for writing, not least because it is home to the esteemed literary journal the *Vernon Review*. Vernon also has almost none of the apparatus we currently associate with college writing (e.g., writing programs, writing curricula), and the college has never hired a tenure-track faculty member in writing studies. Against this backdrop, the original study was something of a boutique longitudinal project that promised a rare glimpse into an otherwise inaccessible educational context. Considered historically, it may have more to offer, particularly for scholars interested in the interwoven threads of writing and liberal education and for all who are concerned with evidencing the value of liberal arts education.

Returning to the Stanford Study of Writing
Twenty years ago, give or take, I was sound asleep in Northern California, and the phone was ringing. I could almost hear the answering machine pick up. The first time or two, I couldn't make out the voice or what it was saying, but it was my housemate calling from work. She was telling me to get up—she was shouting at me to get up and turn on the radio. (We had no TV.) In my memory there is a time lapse, and then I am listening to Bob Edwards and Jean Cochran reporting live between taped segments of *Morning Edition*. Cut to later that same day, September 11, 2001. I am in Moffitt Library, where I have gone to read the news and watch odd moments of stilted streaming video. Two weeks later, the Class of 2005 arrives on Stanford's campus, where I am a doctoral candidate; one month later, I meet some of the first-year students who agree to join the Stanford Study of Writing. The kickoff is a fancy, banquet-style dinner designed to make our project tangible as well as meaningful and important to our n: to Mark and Beth, who become our coauthors; to Amrit, Anna, and Satoko, who become our co-presenters at conferences; to Cathy, Esther, Suresh, Diane, Arun, and the others we acknowledge by pseudonym in our scholarship; and to the cohort we continue to know through their chosen codenames: Voyager'sEMH, 24681012, BrittanySpears, MRSPUNKY, and so on.

Both 9/11 and the Stanford Study of Writing are now history in the most basic sense: they belong to the past. Although I may consider 2001 the relatively recent past, most of my students see the turn of the millennium as history because they cannot remember it. They were either too young or had not yet been born. The Stanford Study seems older to me, more past, when I think about the data. We circulated surveys, conducted interviews, and collected electronic writing samples for five years, from the fall of 2001 through the spring of 2006. When we began, AOL's Instant Messenger was popular, and Napster was in the news; when the study concluded, we mailed everyone leather portfolios and CDs of their writing. Today, when I teach the Stanford Study, I have students Google "AOL Instant Messenger" as well as "Napster," and we notice that none of us has a computer that reads and writes compact disks.

Looking back, there was always a kind of historic swagger to the Stanford Study. I picture the Grand Manner portraiture of John Singer Sargent and Augustus John. After all, the Stanford Study helped herald what Marvin Diogenes (Diogenes and Fishman 2011, 1) describes as "the Decade of Yes"—the era at Stanford that witnessed the rise of the Program in Writing and Rhetoric, the opening of the Hume Center for Writing and Speaking, and countless other achievements led by Andrea A. Lunsford and her signature "yes." The Stanford Study began as Nancy Sommers's four-year study at Harvard was ending, and it stood out for not only its electronic data collection but also its uniquely broad embrace of college writing. On the ground, such details were easily eclipsed for us by practical issues like retaining participants and administering surveys on time. There was also a steady parade of singular events: a major grant deadline, a report to the faculty senate, a database switch, and so on. Although longitudinal research is a method or an approach rather than a subfield such as community writing or lifespan studies, there is an unofficial but active support system for long-haul writing researchers. Most of its members discourage reporting on early findings because so much can and does change during data collection, and we generally heeded their advice. Between 2001 and 2006, we gave presentations with titles that promised perspectives, reflections, lessons, observations, and tales. Only later did we deliver general findings or the outcomes of thematic investigations, and we published two articles: "Performing Writing, Performing Literacy" (Fishman et al. 2005) and "College Writing, Identification, and the Production of Intellectual Property" (Lunsford, Fishman, and Liew 2013).

Nonetheless, the Stanford Study made history. It was the first college-level longitudinal study in our discipline to collect academic and nonacademic writing, and "Performing Writing, Performing Literacy" is the first article coauthored with undergraduate writers to receive the Richard Braddock Award. The Stanford Study also had an impact outside the academy, and the study website (2008) is the project's most frequently cited reference. There is also still notable public commentary thanks to the interviews in which Andrea wielded study findings to counter bad ideas about digital literacies, especially that instant old chestnut: texting is the death of good writing. Clive Thompson (2009) offered one of the most compelling pull quotes in his *WIRED* piece: "When Lunsford examined the work of first-year students, she didn't find a single example of texting speak in an academic paper." That same year, a grateful blogger picked up this point and several others, citing Thompson when he pronounced the Stanford Study "the research to end all research" (Trunk 2009). Fast-forward five years. Coauthors of a Rhode Island School of Design report referenced the Stanford Study (via Thompson) as evidence of "the vivid presence of writing in millennial culture thanks in great part to social and digital media" (Law and Galvez 2014). Concurrently, a digital healthcare platform in the UK cited the Stanford Study (also via Thompson) to contest "the myth that text-only communication lacks the self-expression required for useful therapy" (SilverCloud 2014). Education researcher Jay Hurvitz stands out because he added a timestamp. In a column on his personal website, *From the Boidem* (*attic* in Hebrew), he cautioned, "In internet terms [the Stanford Study is] already perhaps ancient history" (Hurvitz 2015). Clearly torn, Hurvitz (2015) found himself equally drawn to the project (also thanks to Thompson's article) and concerned "that [the] quote from Lunsford . . . may already be outdated."

In the freeze-frame of my mind's eye, I imagine the history of the present we might have composed if we had written more in that same period. Working at the convergence of current events, history, and rhetoric and composition/writing studies, we might have borne witness to the complexity we saw every day and in our data (Ash 1999, xviii). Cathy N. Davidson (2017, 91) all but cites our unwritten monograph in *The New Education*, which spotlights Andrea and "the most famous and extensive" of her research projects: the Stanford Study of Writing. Really, Davidson draws from the study website, an episode of *The Agenda with Steve Paiken*, and a follow-up conversation with Andrea as well as a sampling of her scholarship. Davidson weaves together what she gleans from these sources to ground one of her own central arguments: "You teach students to be literate in a digital age by doing, by interacting, by evaluating technology—not by banning it in formal education" (90). Notably, *The New Education* is addressed to the second generation of digital writers, students who could be assigned the book as part of a Common Read program. As Davidson explains: "It's been a full generation since April 22, 1993, when a new world was born" with the web browser Mosaic 1.0 (5). The Stanford Study belongs to that earlier era, and as such it is less an antique, as Hurvitz (2015) suggested, than an artifact from a time Davidson urges us to learn from in order to remake higher education for current and future students.

Perhaps this is the central paradox of the Stanford Study and also why I see it as so ready for historical inquiry: the same conditions that made it hyper-relevant also made it abruptly obsolete. Social media provides another set of tidemarks. As our cohort was finishing college, many migrated to Facebook, which was first available to anyone with a dot.edu email address. Within five years, however, it was no longer novel for college courses to include both Facebook and Twitter assignments, and smartphones were ubiquitous in face-to-face classrooms. Today, we continue to discover how cultural and material changes to college writing affect the continuities we perceive, and time will tell what we learn from longitudinal writing research conducted during the early years of

TikTok or the 2020 pandemics. For all that the march of time motivates us to continue designing prospective longitudinal research, past longitudinal studies have a great deal to offer, which becomes visible as soon as we dive in.

Returning to Vernon Writes

At a CCCC annual convention more than a decade ago, I gave a talk titled "Writing Is as Writing Does" (Fishman 2009). With performance theory as my frame, I showcased some of the ways Stanford Study participants used writing as a means of invention and agency. According to my notes, I concluded with some version of these observations: "Things are changing fast, and our original motives are not as relevant. If things are interesting in our study, in many cases it's not for reasons we originally intended" (8). Next to those lines, I wrote the phrase "Historian of the contemporary" followed by another set of observations: "We want to conduct research with findings that are directly applicable. But really, we're historians" (8). I might have started that line of thinking in conjunction with my contribution to *Writing Studies Research in Practice*, which I was working on at that time (Fishman 2012c), and I might have pursued it further if present-tense and future possibilities hadn't distracted me. Specifically, through my work as a consultant on the development of pre-orientation writing workshops at Vernon College, I saw an emerging opportunity, and I proposed a longitudinal study of the first workshop participants.

Although my initial proposal was turned down for lack of funding, I received a concrete invitation a year later. In an email, the Vernon College president explained: "I believe that the assessment of writing at Vernon—from the points of view of both students and faculty—could be a very valuable step for the College." Although she was not wrong, Vernon was not well situated for writing assessment. With high expectations for students' written communication but no systematic approach to instruction or evaluation (e.g., outcomes, curricula, portfolios), the college could not sponsor the kind of locally grown evaluation that would yield meaningful results (White, Elliot, and Peckham 2015, 72). As an alternative, I proposed Vernon Writes, a longitudinal study framed by faculty and student surveys and designed to produce descriptive information, including case studies of student writers. When I shared these plans with disciplinary colleagues, they saw something else. "Oh," I heard repeatedly, "you're going to make sure Vernon finally gets a writing program." I was surprised—and taken aback. After all, what researcher worth her salt starts a project with the outcome so squarely in mind? By the fourth or fifth time I heard the same comment, I diagnosed MDP (misplaced disciplinary pride): not overconfidence in the knowledge of our field or egoism about the structures we built while accruing it but brazenness about the broad applicability of both. Instead of hypothesizing that Vernon needed a familiar set of resources to "fix" whatever might be wrong, I started with more basic questions: at Vernon, what constitutes college writing? And how does Vernon, as a whole, meet students' needs as writers?

Because the funding for Vernon Writes had a clock on it, the longitudinal study I designed was a retrospective one. To date, most longitudinal research on writing is prospective, meaning data collection takes place in real time, synched to the unfolding of participants' lives. This approach demands a high degree of engagement as well as a multi-year budget, and both participant attrition and limited funding are common problems. Prospective studies also encourage intense collaboration between researchers and participants, which makes personal relations part of the fabric from which findings are ultimately cut. By contrast, retrospective longitudinal studies entail less time spent on data collection, and they stage a different kind of concentrated cooperation. In my case, I worked with the Vernon Writes cohort for a single year following a semester of survey data collection. At our only meeting as a full group, I introduced myself along with a worksheet that served several purposes. It clarified what would count as writing, namely, "all of the different kinds of texts you create to communicate with yourself and others," from "handwritten and word-processed documents" to "statistical reports, 3-D images, still photographs, videos, and sound files," as well as performances of writing in "music, dance, or other formats." The worksheet also guided participants through the process of creating their personal archives by selecting examples of not only academic and extracurricular texts but also writing "that sounds like you" and "writing you are proud of" (Fishman 2012b, 2). Last, the worksheet structured our end-year interviews, which were wide-ranging, one-to-one conversations about the materials participants archived.

In the end, Vernon Writes was not just retrospective by design; external factors also converged to make it a thing of the past while it was still in progress. Most notably, I finished my interviews as Vernon welcomed new leadership, a president and provost eager to pursue new priorities, including an ambitious capital campaign and a revitalization of the sciences. In this changing context, Vernon Writes was not a good fit. The issues it addressed were no longer exigent, and the case studies I planned did not generate real interest. Instead, the new provost wanted a report that identified action items and made related recommendations. In response, I turned to the survey data; and I worked with a Vernon math professor and one of his students, an undergraduate researcher, to offer what I could. The resulting document, "Vernon Writes: Looking Back, Looking Ahead" (Fishman 2014a, 2014b), describes how much writing was assigned and what kinds, according to both faculty and students; it also depicts respondent attitudes toward writing, writing instruction, and available campus resources. I set some information into scholarly context and provided brief discussions of standout details, such as the disparity between faculty priorities for teaching (e.g., subject-specific content) and student learning (e.g., language and citation conventions, digital writing). Last, I made a short list of recommendations, starting with the establishment of college-wide learning outcomes for student writers and a system for clearly demarcating courses that emphasized writing. Regardless of whether my suggestions were taken, I hoped that their articulation along with discussion they generated might enrich writing at Vernon.

If story arcs like mine are not unusual, they still sting, and my sense of my own bad timing was amplified by the hours I spent transcribing interviews while I worked on the report. Although I completed several rounds of coding before the first draft was done, that document was not the place to present preliminary case study observations, and there were signs all around me that the project was timing out. Vernon colleagues were losing interest, and I had mounting writing program administrator (WPA) obligations on my own campus, where a multi-year core curriculum revision was starting. Going forward, the present-tense priorities on my to-do list seemed only to increase, as did the premium placed on usable findings from my research. As a result, the value of Vernon Writes grew increasingly opaque although I returned periodically to the data, even giving an occasional presentation about them. Then I came across my old conference notes. Although I started Vernon Writes as a diver hoping to collect data that Vernon faculty might put to use, why couldn't I shift perspectives? What if Vernon Writes could provide other kinds of insights?

Perhaps the rest, as they say, is history.

DIVING IN

Longitudinal writing research comes with an abundance of cautions. Imagine a clutch of warning signs pitched just behind divers who are preparing to jump. There are alerts about the potentially high cost of data analysis and curation, cautions against reporting data too early, and a bold statement against over-generalizing about findings—especially from projects conducted at elite universities. For divers immersed in historical research with longitudinal data, there may be no equivalent signage. However, the advice of historical scholars in writing studies may apply. Their words of wisdom include strategies for assessing collections of documents and artifacts, advice about identifying what is available and what is absent, and suggestions for revising research questions and praxes accordingly. An intrepid group with a strong DIY spirit, these colleagues also know a great deal about working where one is not necessarily invited. As Lynée Lewis Gaillet (2012, 39, 50) observes, historical researchers in our discipline "often investigate materials not originally assembled with writing instruction or instructors in mind," and a "new breed" of archivist-researchers has been making their own archives, whether by regrouping materials across holdings or by starting their own collections from scratch.

The image of immersion is itself a message of sorts. On one hand, immersion is a close cousin of absorption, fascination, and thrall; and all three can seem like symptoms of archive fever, the malaise Jacques Derrida (1995) associates with the paradoxically destructive human impulse to conserve. For qualitative researchers, immersion also has negative connotations. It suggests subjective interpretation rather than preferred, systematic methods of data analysis (Geisler and Swarts 2019). On the other hand, Linda Ferreira-Buckley (1997) and other rhetoric and writing scholars regard immersion as more productive than pathological, and they encourage it as part of a rigorous research protocol that combines intensive work with primary materials and extensive engagement with additional resources. For Ferreira-Buckley, immersion involves examining "all extant materials" (26), in particular college archives, instead of reviewing only records from the classes of direct concern. Such work can be "slow and painstaking," Ferreira-Buckley (1997) confirms, but David Gold (2008, 15) is not alone in echoing her advocacy when he asserts that "researchers must loose—and lose—themselves in the era they are studying." Richard L. Enos (1999, 17) links immersion with nothing less than "recovering the lost art of researching the history of rhetoric"; Carol Mattingly (2002) argues that immersion is essential to recovering women's rhetorical histories; and Liz Rohan (2013) connects immersion with feminist research ethics, particularly the importance of responsibly bearing witness from the archives to other people's lives.

Table 10.2. Finding Aid for the (Envisioned) Vernon Writes Collection

Higher education—liberal arts	Research design
Higher education—small liberal arts colleges	Writing—about Vernon Writes
Vernon College—administration	Writing—academic
Vernon College—attitudes toward writing	Writing—co-curricular
Vernon College—campus life	Writing—extracurriculum
Vernon College—curriculum	Writing—personal
Vernon College—history	Writing—sites
Vernon Review	Writing—workplace

In practical terms, historical immersion into longitudinal research can take many forms. Just as one can dive in open water or at night, in caverns or under ice, so, too, do different longitudinal writing research archives invite different kinds of deep engagement.

Dive No. 1: Vernon College

When divers investigate a shipwreck or a plane that crashed into the sea, they start with careful attention to ecology. What constitutes this site, they ask: what objects, what organisms, and what relations among them? To address parallel questions in historical work on Vernon Writes, we would not approach Vernon as a generic four-year college in the Midwest. Instead, our work would be enriched by embracing it as an almost 300-year-old small liberal arts college with Episcopal roots, a physical site with signature architecture and landscapes, and an amalgam of academic and nonacademic communities that shape student life and, by extension, student writing.

Both diving and historical work involve visualization. For researchers, this is important whether they ultimately visit physical sites associated with the materials they study or they work remotely. Although there is not yet a Vernon Writes Collection in any institution's digital repository, we can envision such a resource as an ideal place to launch a historical deep dive. Researchers might start by clicking through an online finding aid with subject headings that divide evenly between writing and Vernon itself (table 10.2).

Swimming through the collection, researchers might be drawn to the report "Vernon Writes: Looking Back, Looking Ahead." Under "Writing—about Vernon Writes" they would find two versions: an abbreviated, thirty-six-page document and the full text, which was sent directly

• **It sets a tone and an expectation,** which makes our work as professors easier. • This "long and storied tradition of writing" lulls students into thinking that they know how to write well when most in fact do not. We need to inform them of this right when they arrive and help them to remedy it. • The tradition is a good recruiting engine. • I think it's the myth of the Kenyon Review period. It's a coterie notion of writing. • **I think it varies tremendously across the college.** While Kenyon certainly treasures writing, I think we sometimes take it for granted. So I'd like to see us build on the strong core that we have to elevate the culture of writing on campus, to connect writers across disciplines, to increase further the visibility of writing on campus, to keep us apprised of developments in writing pedagogy. We are doing all these things to some degree, so it's a matter I think of being more systematic and thoughtful about our overall culture of writing. • **But the last thing we need is a requirement or program or first year seminar that constrains how departments teach writing.** I much prefer an approach that gives departments tools and encouragement. We are fantastic at teaching writing, and need to move forward in a distinctly Kenyon way. • One still has a strong writing tradition. On the whole, Kenyon students come to the college with a better preparation and better writing skills than students I have taught at other colleges. That said, I too often find students most focused on using writing for self-expression rather than developing and clarifying ideas and concepts. • Writing takes place in virtually every academic discipline, and is strongly supported in extracurricular activities. **It is viewed as "the" privileged medium of expression,** common to all disciplines, and accessible to all individuals. • I guess I would say that I believe writing is a significant component of the learning process. One can't really write coherently about a topic unless he or she truly

Figure 10.1. Faculty responses. The wallpaper includes a sampling of Vernon faculty members' narrative responses to a survey prompt asking them to describe the role of writing at Vernon. Bolded text includes "It sets a tone and an expectation," "I think it varies tremendously across the college," "But the last thing we need is a requirement or program or first year semester that constrains how departments teach writing," and "It is viewed as 'the' privileged medium of expression."

to Vernon Writes stakeholders (Fishman 2014b). In reviewing both versions, researchers might pause over pages wallpapered with statements about writing (see figure 10.1), and some might recognize them as faculty responses to the survey prompt: "Vernon has a long and storied tradition of writing. Describe the primary role you believe writing plays today in the overall life and culture of the College." Researchers also might recall seeing cognate questions in the student interview protocol (Fishman 2012a):

- When you came to Vernon, did you already know about Vernon's reputation for writing?
- The majority of students who filled out our survey [last year] also agreed or strongly agreed that Vernon values writing. Does that surprise you? What does that mean to you?
- We know we asked you last year in the survey to comment on Vernon's reputation for writing. What would you say now: what sums up writing at Vernon (for you)? Do you think other people would agree/see it the same way?

Diving deeper, some researchers might go on to locate and code students' responses, paying attention to emerging ideas about the mythos of writing at Vernon. Others might triangulate their results with college documentation (e.g., admissions literature, cached webpages), public commentary, and scholarship about perceptions of writing at small liberal arts colleges.

This imaginary foray into the wreckage of Vernon Writes mirrors my own preliminary work on a monograph that explores what we can learn from the study archive. In the context of my current work, place and emplacement over time matter. They are important to understand how Vernon operates as an agent of literacy sponsorship, a concept that "connect[s] literacy as an individual development to literacy as an economic development" and brings attention to "human relationships and ideological pressures," as well as the materiality of literacy activities (Brandt 2001, 19–20). Literacy sponsors can be "local or distant, concrete or abstract" entities or individuals "who enable, support, teach, and model as well as recruit, regulate, suppress, or withhold literacy—and gain advantage by it in some way" (19). In college writing, the most recognizable literacy sponsors are the individuals who hold formally responsibility for writing (e.g., writing administrators, instructors). At Vernon, which does not have writing curricula or programs—not even by Jill M. Gladstein and Dara Rossman Regaignon's generous definition (2012)—the college itself is the most prominent sponsor of literacy, and its role in the stewardship of writing education is made visible in unique ways by the Vernon Writes archive.

Likewise, the mixed methods of historical return invite new insights into old data. At least for me, immersion in participants' writing and the stories they told about it (in interviews) casts the occasions students had for writing in a new light. Perhaps, of course, college itself prompted many of the examples students shared, whether coursework, co-curricular activities, or extracurriculars such as athletics, Greek life, or volunteer firefighting. Some examples, however, were occasioned by students' pre-college affiliations, including family and formal or informal social groups. Although everything they shared was written "during college," interviews indicate that some texts were rooted in identities and relations students had established well before they came to Vernon. In addition, some writing was occasioned by students' postgraduate hopes and plans, whether their most tangible career goals or their most ambitious and fanciful aspirations. These observations may or may not help us address pressing programmatic or pedagogical problems. However, as a historian of contemporary writing, I am interested in whether and how they might inform—and enrich—our overall understanding of college writers, college writing, and college writing education.

Dive No. 2: September 11, 2001
Immersion into the Stanford Study is more of a deep dive that starts from the platform Stanford itself provides and follows the vertical, chronological institutionalization of 9/11 since 2001. Unlike the Vernon Writes Collection, which is not yet a public resource, the Stanford Study of Writing Digital Collection was established through the Stanford Digital Repository in late 2018. To date, only student writing that could be formatted as .txt files has been cleaned, de-identified, and deposited in the collection; anyone who searches the Stanford University Libraries will find three versions, although raw data are "available only to researchers included on project protocols" and anonymized data are available only "to researchers by permission" (Stanford Study 2001–6). These limits reflect the difficulty involved in preserving study participants' privacy given the power of discovery that lies within every internet user's reach. Indeed, the same search strategies writing instructors can use to best popular plagiarism detection software—Google word strings that include three to five nouns (Schorn 2015)—can also be used to identify most of the students involved in the Stanford Study. With these concerns in mind, 147 transcripts have yet to be de-identified, and extant ephemera—including presentation scripts and slides—still need to be labeled and organized before they can be archived.

After the Stanford Digital Collection was established, a call for papers (CFP) compelled me to finally take the plunge as a researcher into the study archives. Responding to a CFP for a collection of essays about teaching 9/11, the first thing Andrea and I did was reach out to study participants to ask: "With all the experiences you now have behind you, what advice would you offer a first-year student writer at this crisis-riven moment in our history. How could somebody who is eighteen today learn from somebody who entered college at another crisis-riven moment?" The responses we received were rich with reflections on everything from college to parenthood, politics, and professional life in law, medicine, and education. Reading each message as it arrived, it was impossible not to think about writing as both a powerful means of agency and a therapeutic tool with enormous potential. For me, it was also impossible not to think of those 13,000 texts. I wondered: what can they tell current students about writing in and immediately after a time of crisis? What kinds of reflections on our own moment might they invite?

With these questions in mind, I dived. Specifically, I downloaded the anonymized texts onto my laptop, and I used Spotlight to select files that included "9/11" and "September 11." My search yielded a total of 231 individual pieces of writing, contributed by 83 (out of 189) participants. There were text messages, poems, and newspaper article drafts as well as exam essays, senior theses, postgraduate job reports, and graduate school writing assignments. I read the AOL IM that Constance labeled "from 9/11 and soon after," which stated: "I hope that you and your loved ones are safe. Take care. Please pray for peace for our country and wisdom for our leaders." I read Alicia's efforts to make sense of 9/11: "Things are getting more or less back to normal for most Americans," she reported. "But America has, indeed, been changed forever, no matter how successfully she avenges herself." I also saw 9/11 accrue symbolic value. In a paper about sexual assault, Amanda explained: "This epidemic is no different from the terrorist acts that occurred at the World Trade Center or [the] Pentagon." For Felix, immigration reform protests spoke to "not only the intense, post-9/11 convergence of militarism and nationalism" in the US but also "remarkably strong and vibrant grassroots resistance movements led by people of color and their allies across our country."

Deep dives often include more than one pass through the same artifacts, and so I read and reread the 9/11 selections, and then I read them again with an undergraduate research assistant. Together, we noticed how 9/11 was woven into study participants' writing lives—sometimes as an explicit topic of inquiry or reflection, other times as a quick point of reference. I also began inviting students in my advanced composition classes to study the 9/11 selection. One day I set a clock for forty minutes and challenged them to use available resources to learn as much as they could about the cultural references that were commonplaces to their 2001 counterparts. Almost instantly, we had a blitz research guide to turn-of-the-millennium pop culture, tech, and news media. We also had a new sense of what it might mean to read historically and what kinds of further historical research might be compelling. Students went on to edit selections from the archive, adding headnotes and annotations, and they created reading guides for different audiences (e.g., high schoolers, history majors). In addition, one student created an audio story about the archive, complete with current students reading excerpts of several selections. Another compared the Stanford Study Collection and the Coronavirus Stories Archive hosted by the WAC Clearinghouse. A double major in English and data science conducted cluster analyses of the 9/11 selections to better understand, at the level of word use, how archived writing articulated responses to 9/11; an artist in the group used her talents to create a graphic novel–style rendering of Clare's IM and the days that followed (see figure 10.2).

Becoming History   185

Figures 10.2a–c. Stanford Study of Writing illustration by Clare McGinnis. Three panels from a five-panel sequence illustrating an IM autoreply that reads "I hope that you and your loved ones are safe. Take care. Please pray for peace for our country and wisdom for our leaders."

CONCLUSION

Both diving in and immersion are familiar metaphors, even if historical diving in to longitudinal writing research is not—yet—a familiar activity. Recall the argument Mina P. Shaughnessy (1976, 238) makes in "Diving In: An Introduction to Basic Writing," where she writes that effective teaching requires us to "remediate" ourselves or "become a student of new disciplines"—namely, "students themselves." Such acts take courage, Shaughnessy emphasizes. They require teachers to leave the familiar shores of discipline and instruction to follow their subjects, their students, in the various directions they lead. By the same token, approaching previously conducted longitudinal studies historically asks us to become new students of the materials associated with them, and methodological change does not always come easy. My story—or stories—of historical turn reveal the time it took me to change my mind and my mind-set to see new possibilities for longitudinal writing research. My stories also show just two of the many ways we could pursue historical inquiries through completed longitudinal studies of writing. In addition, I hope my stories convey some of the many reasons why we might choose to swim in uncharted waters. Surely, there are as many possibilities as there are fish in the sea, and for all the complexity of historical longitudinal research, diving in is easy.

Go ahead. Choose a focal point and jump in—

NOTES

1. Vernon Writes and Vernon College are pseudonyms that I use here and in other publications to protect the confidentiality of Vernon Writes participants.
2. The sources for information listed here include McCarthy (1985, 16); Haas (1994, 51); Chiseri-Strater (1991, 184); Herrington and Curtis (2000, 6); Wolcott (1994, 15); Winsor (1996, 12); Sternglass (1997, xiii); Beaufort (2004, 145; 2007); Carroll (2002, 32–34); Sommers and Saltz (2004, 126); Roozen (2008, 7); Lunsford, Fishman, and Liew (2013, 471); Wardle (2007, 70–71); Hesse (2008, 1); Halbritter and Lindquist (2022); Hassel (2022); Driscoll (2022); Gere (2019, 13); Mapes and Kimme Hea (2018); Downs (2022); Rifenburg and Forester (2018, 55) and Rifenburg (2022); Lucero and Serviss (2016, 1265); Hashlamon (2022). There are several studies well-known from scholarly conversations but absent from this list because I was unable to verify data collection dates, including a three-year longitudinal case study conducted at Tufts in the 1990s by Ruth Spack (1997); research Kevin Roozen and Joe Erickson (2017) discuss; and the longitudinal study of STEM students mentioned by Ryan J. Dippre (2019, 125). Glancing references to case-based longitudinal studies of college writers also appear in conference talks, speaker bios, and inconsistently available online professional resources. We would no doubt learn even more if we could roam the attics, garages, and hard drives of any number of writing studies colleagues.

REFERENCES

Ash, Timothy Garton. 1999. *History of the Present: Essays, Sketches, and Dispatches from Europe in the 1990s.* New York: Random House.

Beaufort, Anne. 2004. "Developmental Gains of a History Major: A Case for Building a Theory of Disciplinary Writing Expertise." *Research in the Teaching of English* 39 (2): 136–85.

Beaufort, Anne. 2007. *College Writing and Beyond: A New Framework for University Writing Instruction.* Logan: Utah State University Press.

Brandt, Deborah. 2001. *Literacy in American Lives.* Cambridge: Cambridge University Press.

Carroll, Lee Ann. 2002. *Rehearsing New Roles: How College Students Develop as Writers.* Carbondale: Southern Illinois University Press.

Chiseri-Strater, Elizabeth. 1991. *Academic Literacies: The Public and Private Discourse of University Students.* Portsmouth, NH: Boynton/Cook.

Davidson, Cathy N. 2017. *The New Education: How to Revolutionize the University and Prepare Students for a World in Flux.* New York: Basic Books.

Derrida, Jacques. 1995. "Archive Fever: A Freudian Impression." Translated by Eric Prenowitz. *Diacritics* 25 (2): 9–63.

Diogenes, Marvin, and Jenn Fishman. 2011. "The Decade of Yes: A Celebration of the Lunsford Era at Stanford, 2000–2010." Presented at the Conference on College Composition and Communication Annual Convention, Atlanta, GA, April 6–9.
Dippre, Ryan J. 2019. *Talk, Tools, and Texts: A Logic-in-Use for Studying Lifespan Literate Action Development*. Fort Collins and Boulder: WAC Clearinghouse and University Press of Colorado.
Enos, Richard L. 1999. "Recovering the Lost Art of Researching the History of Rhetoric." *Rhetoric Society Quarterly* 29 (4): 7–20.
Ferreira-Buckley, Linda. 1997. "Serving Time in the Archives." *Rhetoric Review* 16 (1): 26–28.
Fishman, Jenn. 2009. "Writing Is as Writing Does." Presented at the Conference on College Composition and Communication Annual Convention, San Francisco, CA, March 12.
Fishman, Jenn. 2012a. "Discursive Interview Script." Unpublished research protocol, September 7, electronic file.
Fishman, Jenn. 2012b. "Vernon Writes Y2 Portfolio Worksheet." Unpublished research protocol, September 7, electronic file.
Fishman, Jenn. 2012c. "Longitudinal Writing Research in (and for) the Twenty-First Century." In *Writing Studies Research in Practice: Methods and Methodologies*, ed. Lee Nickoson and Mary P. Sheridan, 171–82. Carbondale: Southern Illinois University Press.
Fishman, Jenn. 2014a. "Vernon Writes: Looking Back, Looking Ahead." Abbreviated version. https://works.bepress.com/jennfishmanphd/86/.
Fishman, Jenn. 2014b. "Vernon Writes: Looking Back, Looking Ahead." Long version. https://works.bepress.com/jennfishmanphd/87/.
Fishman, Jenn, Andrea Lunsford, Beth McGregor, and Mark Outeye. 2005. "Performing Writing, Performing Literacy." *College Composition and Communication* 57 (2): 224–52.
Gaillet, Lynée Lewis. 2012. "(Per)forming Archival Research Methodologies." *College Composition and Communication* 64 (1): 35–58.
Geisler, Cheryl, and Jason Swarts. 2019. *Coding Streams of Language*. Fort Collins and Boulder: WAC Clearinghouse and University Press of Colorado.
Gere, Anne, ed. 2019. *Developing Writers in Higher Education: A Longitudinal Study*. Ann Arbor: University of Michigan Press.
Gladstein, Jill M., and Dara Rossman Regaignon. 2012. *Writing Program Administration at Small Liberal Arts Colleges*. Anderson, SC: Parlor Press.
Gold, David. 2008. *Rhetoric at the Margins: Revising the History of Writing Instruction in American Colleges, 1873–1947*. Carbondale: Southern Illinois University Press.
Haas, Christina. 1994. "Learning to Read Biology: One Student's Rhetorical Development in College." *Written Communication* 17 (1): 43–84.
Haswell, Richard. 2000. "Documenting Improvement in College Writing: A Longitudinal Approach." *Written Communication* 17 (3): 307–52.
Heath, Shirley Brice. 1983. *Ways with Words: Language, Life, and Work in Communities and Classrooms*. Cambridge: Cambridge University Press.
Heath, Shirley Brice. 2012. *Words at Work and Play: Three Decades in Family and Community Life*. New York: Cambridge University Press.
Herrington, Anne J., and Marcia Curtis. 2000. *Persons in Process: Four Stories of Writing and Personal Development in College*. Urbana, IL: National Council of Teachers of English.
Hesse, Douglas. 2008. "Quick Overview: A Longitudinal Study of Undergraduate Writing at the University of Denver." University of Denver Writing Program, Denver, CO. December 8. http://www.du.edu/writing/documents/Longitudinal_Study_of_Writing_at_University_of_Denver.pdf.
Hurvitz, Jay. 2015. "The Most Literary Generation?" *From the Boidem* (blog), September 28. https://www.tau.ac.il/education/muse/maslool/boidem/157more.html.
Law, Andy, and Christina Galvez. 2014. "The Thesis Grid: A Writing and Design Process." Academic Commons Program, Rhode Island School of Design, Providence. https://www.idsa.org/sites/default/files/FINAL_%28Thesis%20Grid%29_Public.pdf.

Lindemann, Erika. 2005. *What's a University? The Perspectives of UNC's Antebellum Students.* Chapel Hill: University of North Carolina Chapel Hill Press.

Lucero, Margaret M., and Patricia Serviss. 2016. "Exploring the Development of Scientific Argumentation Practices among First-Year STEM Undergraduates through a Writing-to-Learn Approach." In *Transforming Learning, Empowering Learners: The International Conference of the Learning Sciences (ICLS)*, vol. 2, ed. Chee-Kit Looi, Joseph Polman, Ulrike Cress, and Peter Reimann, 1265–66. Singapore: International Society of the Learning Sciences.

Lunsford, Andrea A., Jenn Fishman, and Warren M. Liew. 2013. "College Writing, Identification, and the Production of Intellectual Property: Voices from the Stanford Study of Writing." *College English* 75 (5): 470–92.

Mapes, Aimee C., and Amy C. Kimme Hea. 2018. "Devices and Desires: A Complicated Narrative of Mobile Writing and Device-Driven Ecologies." In *Handbook of Digital Writing and Rhetoric*, ed. Jonathan Alexander and Jacqueline Rhodes, 73–83. New York: Routledge.

Mattingly, Carol. 2002. "Telling Evidence: Rethinking What Counts in Rhetoric." *Rhetoric Society Quarterly* 32 (1): 99–108.

McCarthy, Lucille. 1985. "A Stranger in Strange Lands: A College Student Writing across the Curriculum." PhD dissertation, University of Pennsylvania, Philadelphia.

Peer Writing Tutor Alumni Research Project. 2020. The Writing Center: University of Wisconsin–Madison. https://writing.wisc.edu/peer-writing-tutor-alumni-research-project/.

Rifenburg, J. Michael, and Brian G. Forester. 2018. "First-Year Cadets' Conceptions of General Education Writing at a Senior Military College." *Teaching and Learning Inquiry* 6 (1): 52–66.

Rogers, Paul. 2010. "The Contributions of North American Longitudinal Studies of Writing in Higher Education to Our Understanding and Development." In *Traditions of Writing Research*, ed. Charles Bazerman, Robert Krut, Karen Lunsford, Susan McLeod, Suzie Null, Paul Rogers, and Amanda Stansell, 365–77. Oxford, UK: Routledge.

Rohan, Liz. 2013. "Writing about Boys: Using the Feminist Method of Strategic Contemplation When Researching Male Subjects." *Peitho* 16 (1): 8–33.

Roozen, Kevin. 2008. "Journalism, Poetry, Stand-up Comedy, and Academic Literacy: Mapping." *Journal of Basic Writing* 27 (1): 5–34.

Roozen, Kevin, and Joe Erickson. 2017. *Expanding Literate Landscapes: Persons, Practices, and Sociohistoric Perspectives of Disciplinary Development.* Logan: Computers and Composition Digital Press and Utah State University Press.

Rosenberg, Lauren. 2015. *The Desire for Literacy: Writing in the Lives of Adult Learners.* Urbana, IL: National Council of Teachers of English and Conference on College Composition and Communication.

Schorn, Susan. 2015. "Replicated Text Detection: Test of TurnItIn." https://www.insidehighered.com/sites/default/server_files/files/2015plagtest.pdf.

Shaughnessy, Mina P. 1976. "Diving In: An Introduction to Basic Writing." *College Composition and Communication* 27 (3): 234–39.

Shepley, Nathan. 2016. *Placing the History of College Writing: Stories from the Incomplete Archive.* Fort Collins, CO, and Anderson, SC: WAC Clearinghouse and Parlor Press.

SilverCloud. 2014. "UK Myth 3: Text-only Communication Lacks Self-Expression." Last modified April 2, 2014. https://www.silvercloudhealth.com/uk/blog/myth-3-text-only-communication-lacks-self-expression.

Sommers, Nancy, and Laura Saltz. 2004. "The Novice as Expert: Writing the Freshman Year." *College Composition and Communication* 56 (1): 124–49.

Spack, Ruth. 1997. "The Acquisition of Academic Literacy in a Second Language: A Longitudinal Case Study." *Written Communication* 14 (1): 3–62.

Stanford Report. 2005. "114th Commencement Events Will Bring Thousands to Campus." https://news.stanford.edu/news/2005/june8/grads-060805.html.

Stanford Study of Writing. 2001–6. SearchWorks Catalog. https://searchworks.stanford.edu/catalog?f%5Bcollection%5D%5B%5D=kf504kx8111.

Stanford Study of Writing. 2008. Stanford University. https://ssw.stanford.edu/.

Sternglass, Marilyn. 1997. *A Time to Know Them: A Longitudinal Study of Writing and Learning at the College Level.* Mahwah, NJ: Erlbaum.

Thompson, Clive. 2009. "Clive Thompson on the New Literacy." *WIRED.* https://www.wired.com/2009/08/st-thompson-7/.

Trunk, Penelope. 2009. "The Internet Has Created a Generation of Great Writers." https://blog.penelopetrunk.com/2009/10/19/the-internet-creates-an-era-of-great-writing/comment-page-2/.

Wardle, Elizabeth. 2007. "Understanding 'Transfer' from FYC: Preliminary Results of a Longitudinal Study." *WPA: Writing Program Administration* 31 (1–2): 65–85.

White, Edward M., Norbert Elliot, and Irvin Peckham. 2015. *Very Like a Whale: The Assessment of Writing Programs.* Logan: Utah State University Press.

Winsor, Dorothy A. 1996. *Writing Like an Engineer: A Rhetorical Education.* Mahwah, NJ: Lawrence Erlbaum.

Wolcott, Willa. 1994. "A Longitudinal Study of Six Developmental Writers' Performance in Reading and Writing." *Journal of Basic Writing* 13 (1): 14–40.

Epilogue
WHY WE TELL STORIES

Jenn Fishman and Amy C. Kimme Hea

There are many reasons why we tell stories about longitudinal writing research. To start, stories complement commonplace scholarly forms: the monograph, the expository academic essay, the scientific report. As a mode of academic expression, story gives us unique ways to frame information, convey experience, offer critique, and press for reflection and change. Story also invites us to pay attention differently, whether we are the storytellers or the storytold. By mediating our work in distinct ways, story enables us to see data differently and to recognize as data different artifacts of research. Thus, in this volume through story we center relations that are not always acknowledged or granted priority. We bring attention to place, embodiment, and affect. We engage duration, exploring the workings of time in expanded ways; and we attune to beliefs, values, and influences to engage elements of research that do not always count when we enumerate our findings. We also accept, even welcome the permission story gives us to mix personal reflection with formal and informal observations, flights of theory, historical records, and first principles—all in service of amplifying our ways of understanding the quality or magnitude of writing research and what it can tell us about writers and writing.

After reading some or all of this collection or skipping right to the epilogue, it is fair to press: *but to what end? Why showcase aspects of longitudinal work often occluded in traditional scholarly production?* As members of a discipline overwhelmingly dedicated to producing knowledge intended for use, we recognize that our response may be insufficient, especially since it is more aspirational than it is practicable or explicitly action-oriented. Yet we are ambitious for writing studies. We have high, even wild hopes and equally high expectations for what we can accomplish collectively. Thus, on behalf of all who contributed to this book, including the researchers who shared their stories and the writers who participated in their research, we hope this collection seeds additional

https://doi.org/10.7330/9781646424337.c011

stories along with counterstories and the kinds of critical conversations that increase our shared capacity to imagine as well as carry out feasible, meaningful, and genuinely consequential writing research.

Instead of editing this collection, we could have written a novel about longitudinal research in writing studies. It would have been a collaborative effort akin to *The Floating Admiral* (Members of the Golden Age Detection Club 1931) or *No Rest for the Dead* (Abbot et al. 2011), mysteries composed chapter by chapter, respectively, by fourteen members of the Golden Age Detective Club and twenty-six members of the contemporary Crime Writers' Association. Each installment would advance a plot thick with intrigue about what we know and what can be known about writers and writing through longitudinal approaches, while the story as a whole would tell a multi-perspective tale about how and why writing teachers and scholars have for decades undertaken long research projects that involve one or more participants, sufficient interviews to create a months' long playlist, and enough writing to wrap the planet. Instead, we edited a collection of academic stories. In sequence, the first chapters of this book examine shaping relations between researchers and research participants; the next chapters story how longitudinal research can be sparked (or extinguished) by institutional exigences; and the last chapters engage broad disciplinary and methodological concerns. Readers are also invited to make non-sequential connections that align with their interests. Across chapters, there are stories about mentorship (chapters 2 and 7), graduate students (chapters 1, 2, 6, 7, 8, 10), and writing programs (chapters 5, 6, 7), as well as stories that trace individual careers across ranks, roles, and locations (chapters 2, 4, 9, 10). Some readers will be drawn to stories set at the same public, Hispanic-serving R1 (chapters 1, 5, 7); some will concentrate on stories set outside the four-year research university (chapters 1, 3, 4, and 10); and others will make additional associations.

Extending our invitational approach, we look forward to learning at least some of the many stories that *Telling Stories* does not tell, especially narratives that counter, queer, and run crooked to the most conspicuous and frequently retold stories in our field. We expect experienced longitudinal researchers, including those cited throughout this book, to have plenty of stories to tell. Likewise, we anticipate stories from writing administrators, including writing center directors and department chairs, since they are always engaged in one or more forms of longitudinal inquiry. Others stories, we hope, will come from researchers who are new to longitudinal work and to our discipline, including early career colleagues, graduate students, and even undergraduate researchers.

We also eagerly await stories about cross- and trans-disciplinary longitudinal writing research, as well as stories that focus on writers in online courses and communities, community writing partnerships, participants in stretch and bridge programs, and more. Most of all, we look forward to stories about longitudinal studies led by researchers whose views have been unrepresented or underrepresented in our discipline and stories that center writers we have not yet had—or taken—the time to know, at least not through prior longitudinal research.

On one hand, it is easy to forecast enough stories to warrant not just another book but an entire series: More and More Stories about Longitudinal Research. On the other hand, our MO is not simply additive. Instead, we want more from a standpoint that is critical and expansive, open to the challenges that a proliferation of stories told from a multiplicity of perspectives will surely pose. For example, we imagine an early volume about failure, which would complement the chapters in this collection that address that theme. It would feature stories that illustrate some of the many reasons why some longitudinal projects stall while others never get started or do not meet the expectations and needs of different stakeholders. How much would such stories reveal, we wonder, about the material constraints and affective demands that shape longitudinal writing research? What else would they show us? Other volumes in our imagined series would offset what Chimamanda Ngozi Adichie (2009) might identify as the danger of a single chapter. What insights would we gain, and which of our assumptions would be laid bare, if we could read—or watch or virtually immerse ourselves in—a succession of stories about high school–to-college writers, adult literacy learners, students active in the armed forces, and community college or small liberal arts college writers? We imagine additional volumes that would tell stories about longitudinal research conducted at historically Black colleges and universities (HBCUs) and citizen schools, in nursing simulation labs and corporate writing centers, at after-school programs and elder care facilities, across networks of hobbyists and political organizers. What would we learn from these studies—and from the studies that neither of us can imagine but others can?

We share this utopic *copia* exercise in the spirit of serious play. By letting our imaginations run ahead but not entirely away, we work to broaden the scope this book offers; but to continue our effort, we need to get down to brass tacks. We need to imagine that our book series attracts a donor and soon thereafter receives a sizable endowment. With funding, we could pay researchers for their stories, and we could commission narratives from research participants and others who become involved in longitudinal research from outside the strange economy of academic publishing. Even more important, with large enough coffers, we could seed and sustain new longitudinal studies of writing. These ideas may cross the line between invention and magical thinking, but as a discipline, we can only weakly echo past calls for greater diversity and inclusion until we acknowledge that both researchers and research participants must be able to meet their basic personal and professional needs before they can contribute. We also must work to identify or create local (e.g., institutional, regional) and global (e.g., disciplinary, cross-disciplinary) ways of supporting the research we wish to see, and we must acknowledge and address larger structural, cultural, and social problems that contribute to the ongoing precarity and marginalization of researchers and writers whose knowledge and experiences we value.

In addition to sponsoring more stories, we need to have more conversations about why we conduct longitudinal studies of writing, and we would do well to connect such discussions with renewed reflection on why we research writing at all (e.g., for what purposes, in relation to what exigences and goals) and how longitudinal methods can best help. Paul Rogers (2010) reminds us that college-level longitudinal research fits into a larger lifespan perspective that is anchored by longitudinal studies of children's early literacy acquisition and K–12 schooling. His detailed review, which includes eleven quantitative and qualitative projects, highlights the close alignment between longitudinal studies of college writing and researchers' vested interest in writers' development, particularly postsecondary students' advancement toward specific academic outcomes and related institutional goals (e.g., retention, graduation). This trend continues over the next decade, as demonstrated by the studies listed in chapter 10, half of which were conducted after Rogers completed his survey. Most (twenty-three out of twenty-five) focus on students at four-year universities, including twenty doctorate-granting institutions, sixteen of which currently boast "very high research activity" (Carnegie n.d.). Nearly all of the principal investigators worked (and in some cases, still work) as writing administrators, and the majority of studies were designed with writing assessment or other large-scale applications to writing education in mind.

In scholarship about these studies, researchers bear witness to the complexities involved in linking longitudinal research concretely to educational praxes. One example is the revised curriculum Anne Beaufort (2012) offers. As she summarizes: "After further reading, reflection, and observation of difficulties my students have, I would rewrite Appendix A," which includes a course outline complete with readings and assignments (177–205). Note the vectors that Beaufort identifies as shaping her decision. They include not only scholarship, contemplation, and direct observation of students beyond her single case study but also her own previous research, her observations of other teachers, and her overall expertise—accrued over decades of professional experience. It takes all of these inputs to even begin to apply research findings to subsequent scenes of instruction, whether on-site immediately after a study has concluded or across a discipline ten years or more after data collection. Anne Ruggles Gere and her colleagues offer another angle, demonstrating that it can take a decade and a good dozen researchers to turn a longitudinal study into the kind of thick, multi-perspectival description offered in *Developing Writers in Higher Education* (2019). In this book, where co-researchers do more analyzing, tracking, and complicating than recommending per se, the conclusion offers a set of observations presented as a succession of statements and counterstatements. For example "curriculum shapes writing" "but students supplement or subvert curriculum" (317, 318), and "students' personal and social development is linked to writing" "but students help shape the terms of that personal/social-writing development link" (320, 322).

All longitudinal researchers must, like Beaufort and the group led by Gere, determine and bridge the distance between data and findings (and beyond), just as we all must decide how to work productively with and against the forward momentum studies gather as they progress through time. In school settings we also negotiate the verticality of educational experience, which is designed to foster not only student learning but also development and growth. Of course, as Gere (2019, 17) writes, citing Beaufort, "There is . . . 'no grand theory of writers' developmental processes'"; in fact, "there is not even an agreed on set of terms to use." As a result, longitudinal research, especially at the college level, reflects a variety of priorities and outcomes, whether tangible work products (e.g., a pedagogical approach, an assignment sequence) or more intellectual resources (e.g., frames of reference, conceptions of the referent). To visualize these patterns of activity, picture the studies listed in chapter 10 as a row of feedback loops, a lineup of Slinkies—some with small coils set close together, some stretched with bent and uneven spirals. The helix shape captures the way longitudinal writing research conducted in higher ed by higher educators always circles back to school subjects. Research participants are figured as students and specifically academic writers; the bulk of writing considered is done for academic purposes; and sites of formal writing instruction occupy the fore. There are also any number of twists and quirks: Marilyn S. Sternglass (1999,

3–4) "taking into consideration non-academic factors that influence academic performance," Anne J. Herrington and Marcia Curtis (2000) framing students as persons in process, Andrea Lunsford and her colleagues (Fishman et al. 2005) collecting students' writing all-inclusively, Gere and her colleagues (2019, 17) prioritizing student agency, and Kevin Roozen (2021, 27) embracing Paul Prior's notion of "literate activity" to study longitudinally "the incredible diversity of material and cultural practices that mediate communicative action."

Looking ahead, we hope longitudinal writing research will continue to reflect and, even more important, engage with the ever-changing prospects of writers, writing, and research opportunities. In particular, we hope researchers will maintain their characteristic "pedagogical stance," which "combines advocacy with inquiry and underscores the idea that research can—and should—support writing education" (Fishman 2012, 174). To do so, researchers may replicate previous studies to confirm, contest, or expand their findings. They may also use longitudinal research to examine the impact of new or newly prominent educational praxes (e.g., un-grading, hybrid writing instruction, dual credit, campus globalization) as well as phenomena like the so-called demographic cliff (Dent 2014) and the majoritization of once minoritized students. Since the millennium, the stance of many longitudinal researchers has mirrored the discipline's commitment to *paideia*, or writing education for community as well as academic and professional participation (Fishman 2012, 175–76). To continue in this vein, researchers interested in student writers will need to focus on more than their schooling. Post-2020 projects will be uniquely able to illuminate the literate lives of college-age writers in relation to the coronavirus pandemic, white supremacist violence, and climate crisis as well as changing, high-stakes state and federal regulations. Such work will only be strengthened if researchers also study graduate students, faculty, and staff—denizens of higher education who are not only writers themselves but also literacy sponsors, individuals who participate in the "ceaseless processes of positioning and repositioning, seizing and relinquishing control over meanings and materials of literacy" through their institutional roles and their personal actions (Brandt 1998, 173).

To pursue this orientation, writing researchers can learn a great deal from colleagues across disciplines, anywhere writing is not only used but also taught and researched over time. The full list of possibilities is long and better suited to our book series than this epilogue, but it starts with the near-field of literacy studies, where since the mid-1980s literacy has been conceptualized as a situated activity and explicitly linked to historically and culturally specific sites, institutions, and dynamics of power (Barton, Hamilton, and Ivanic 2000). From this critical vantage, literacy scholars regularly address issues of equity and social justice in powerful ways, and they model a host of approaches to examining lived experience that illuminate change over time rather than advancement, development, or progress. For example, Eric Darnell Pritchard (2017, 48) uses archival documents and interviews with self-identified Black LGBTQ people born over a fifty-year period to "form a history" as well as "a contemporary way of theorizing Black LGBTQ literacies." Likewise, to understand "how migration drives literacy learning in transnational families," Kate Vieira (2019, 11) spent five years conducting interviews with "immigrants, potential immigrants, and their family members . . . on three different continents . . . in three different languages." While neither example fits within the "family of methods" typically identified as longitudinal (Menard 2002, 2), such work may be instructive. This is not to encourage the kind of "creep" that would soon have us recognizing as longitudinal any study that covers a discernible stretch of time. Instead, we want to encourage writing researchers to consider and actively cultivate greater possibilities for longitudinal research.

What we advocate is a kind of canny borrowing, a cousin to the "performative, playful, and mischievous" methodological promiscuity that Heather Lee Branstetter (2016, 18) proposes to rhetoric researchers as a way to deviate deliberately from academic and cultural (hetero)norms. Procedurally, neither adopting and adapting resources nor enacting critique is new to writing researchers. In any telling of our history, we are practiced scavengers of the knowledge-seeking and knowledge-sharing tools we need. Both remixes and mixed methods are familiar to us, and we are not strangers to scrutinizing our own or others' praxes along with their stakes. Recent examples abound, each offering its own genealogy of methods, methodologies, and related deliberations. Take the exceptionally cross-disciplinary celebration Jason Palmeri and Ben McCorkle stage in *100 Years of New Media Pedagogy* (2021), which brings into play a network sense from Derek N. Mueller's (2017) book by the same name, procedures of close and distant reading, techniques of thick and thin description, media archaeology, multimodal performance, and established methods of corpus analysis—all inflected by ongoing discussions of access and positionality. We set their bravura demonstration of playful responsivity alongside RTM, Rhetorical Transversal Methodology, which Katherine Fredlund, Kerri Hauman, and Jessica Ouellette (2020) introduce. This rhizomatic approach to feminist recovery work enables them and contributors to their volume to cross time, geography, and media platforms to critically recuperate and connect the trans-generational rhetorical praxes of feminist activists. Compare RTM with the deliberately "far from neutral" and explicitly politicized mixed methods that Nancy Bou Ayash models (2019, 11). Her "networked ethnography," the product of multi-year cross-continental research, shows us how in a postmonolingual world teacher-activists can strive to help writers gain agency through self-aware negotiations of language ideologies.

What do these exemplars of canny methodological borrowing have in common? They share extreme openness, a profound embrace of play, and a radical responsivity to the contrasting, even conflicting needs of their disparate research subjects. We appreciate them greatly, but we did not marshal them to recommend direct application to future longitudinal research; nor are we suggesting that they should be treated as set patterns or recipes to follow by anyone planning a multi-year study of one or more writers. Instead, we offer the work of Palmeri, McCorkle, Fredlund, Hauman, Ouellette, and Bou Ayash as inspiration plus just a hint of a dare. Longitudinal research, like any long-term commitment, involves risk. Imagine if IRBs were insurance brokers. We might go to them seeking advice rather than approval for new research. If that were the case, we might ask: how do we match our curiosity about writing, the most pressing questions we share with others, and the problems with the most urgency with the affordances and constraints longitudinal research offers—not only as it has been practiced by contributors to this volume, researchers in our field, and researchers in other disciplines but also as it might be reinvented and complemented to serve new purposes?

In our mind's ear, we hear the din of conversation that breaks out in response. There are practical considerations, epistemological questions, examples from a diversity of research traditions. We listen for a while, and we take some notes. We sketch study designs. We invent and reinvent protocols. And we eagerly await more stories.

REFERENCES

Abbot, Jeff, Lori Armstrong, Sandra Brown, Thomas Cook, Jeffery Deaver, Diana Gabaldon, Tess Gerritsen, Andrew F. Gulli, Peter James, J. A. Jance, et al. 2011. *No Rest for the Dead.* New York: Touchstone.

Adichie, Chimamanda Ngozi. 2009. "The Danger of a Single Story." TED video, 18:33. https://www.ted.com/talks/chimamanda_ngozi_adichie_the_danger_of_a_single_story.

Barton, David, Mary Hamilton, and Roz Ivanic, eds. 2000. *Situated Literacies: Reading and Writing in Context.* London: Routledge.

Beaufort, Anne. 2007. *College Writing and Beyond: A New Framework for University Writing Instruction.* Logan: Utah State University Press.

Beaufort, Anne. 2012. "*College Writing and Beyond:* Five Years Later." *Composition Forum* 23. https://compositionforum.com/issue/26/college-writing-beyond.php.

Bou Ayash, Nancy. 2019. *Toward Translingual Realities in Composition: (Re)Working Local Language Representations and Practices.* Logan: Utah State University Press.

Brandt, Deborah. 1998. "Sponsors of Literacy." *College Composition and Communication* 49 (2): 165–85.

Branstetter, Heather Lee. 2016. "Promiscuous Approaches to Reorienting Rhetorical Research." In *Sexual Rhetorics: Methods, Identities, Publics,* ed. Jonathan Alexander and Jacqueline Rhodes, 17–30. New York: Routledge.

Carnegie Classification of Institutions of Higher Education. n.d. *About Carnegie Classification.* http://carnegieclassifications.iu.edu/2010/.

Dent, Harry S., Jr. 2014. *The Demographic Cliff: How to Survive and Prosper during the Great Deflation Ahead.* New York: Portfolio.

Fishman, Jenn. 2012. "Longitudinal Writing Research in (and for) the Twenty-First Century." In *Writing Studies Research in Practice,* ed. Lee Nickoson and Mary P. Sheridan, 171–82. Carbondale: Southern Illinois University Press.

Fishman, Jenn, Andrea Lunsford, Beth McGregor, and Mark Outeye. 2005. "Performing Writing, Performing Literacy." *College Composition and Communication* 57 (2): 224–52.

Fredlund, Katherine, Kerri Hauman, and Jessica Ouellette. 2020. *Feminist Connections: Rhetoric and Activism across Time, Space, and Place: Rhetoric, Culture, and Social Critique.* Tuscaloosa: University of Alabama Press.

Gere, Anne, ed. 2019. *Developing Writers in Higher Education: A Longitudinal Study.* Ann Arbor: University of Michigan Press.

Herrington, Anne J., and Marcia Curtis. 2000. *Persons in Process: Four Stories of Writing and Personal Development in College.* Urbana, IL: National Council of Teachers of English.

Members of the Golden Age Detection Club. 1931. *The Floating Admiral.* New York: HarperCollins.

Menard, Scott. 2002. *Longitudinal Research.* 2nd ed. Thousand Oaks, CA: Sage.

Mueller, Derek N. 2017. *Network Sense: Methods for Visualizing a Discipline.* Fort Collins: WAC Clearinghouse and Colorado State University Open Press.

Palmeri, Jason, and Ben McCorkle. 2021. *100 Years of New Media Pedagogy.* Ann Arbor: Michigan Publishing and University of Michigan Press.

Pritchard, Eric Darnell. 2017. *Fashioning Lives: Black Queers and the Politics of Literacy.* Carbondale: Southern Illinois University Press.

Rogers, Paul. 2010. "The Contributions of North American Longitudinal Studies of Writing in Higher Education to Our Understanding of Writing." In *Traditions of Writing Research,* ed. Charles Bazerman, Robert Krut, Karen Lunsford, Susan McLeod, Suzie Null, Paul Rogers, and Amanda Stansell, 365–77. Oxford, UK: Routledge.

Roozen, Kevin. 2021. "Acting with Inscriptions: Expanding Perspectives of Writing, Learning, and Becoming." *Journal of the Assembly for Expanded Perspectives on Learning* 26: 23–24.

Sternglass, Marilyn S. 1999. "Students Deserve Enough Time to Prove That They Can Succeed." *Journal of Basic Writing* 18 (1): 3–20.

Vieira, Kate. 2019. *Writing for Love and Money: How Migration Drives Literacy Learning in Transnational Families.* Oxford: Oxford University Press.

INDEX

Page numbers followed by *f* indicate figures, followed by *t* indicate tables, and followed by *n* indicate notes.

academic ancestors, 31–34, 41, 43
academic writing, 27, 71–72, 74, 86, 177, 180*t*, 194
Act 10 (2010), 75
Adichie, Chimamanda Ngozi, 192
Adler-Kassner, Linda, 78*n*2
adult learning centers, 6, 45, 57, 61
affect, 190; attention to, 128, 129; research about, 139, 192; rhetorical purpose of, 169
agency, 4, 85, 99, 107, 176, 183, 195, 197; and citizenship, 100–102; lifespan writing and, 153, 160–61; literacy, 57–58 alternative-track faculty, 125, 129. *See also* non-tenurable faculty
Anderson, Paul, 119, 127, 128
Andrews, Deborah C., 142
Angeli, Elizabeth L., 24, 144, 145
Anson, Chris M., 87
Approaches to Lifespan Writing Research: Generating and Actionable Coherence (Dippre and Phillips), 158
Apted, Michael, 5
Archibold, Randal C., 89
Arpaio, Joe, 89
articulation theory, 83–84
assessment, 67, 97, 118–19, 126, 140, 147*n1*, 147*n4*, 150, 171, 176, 193; program, 85–88, 90, 93*n*2, 119; self-assessment, 71, 126
attrition, 31, 90, 117, 123, 124, 126, 129; managed, 116, 120–22

Bakhtin, Mikhail M., 48, 51–57
Barad, Karen, 145
Bazerman, Charles, 152, 153, 155
Beaufort, Anne, 30, 42, 116, 135, 169*t*, 186*n*2, 193, 194
Belcher, Dianne, 41
"Believing Game" (Elbow), 158
Bentley, Lizzie, 119
Bergmann, Linda S., 30, 34, 40, 42
Bianco, Margarita, 19
Bird, Barbara, 111

Blind Side, The (movie), 72
Blythe, Stuart, 83
Borrowman, Shane, 101
Bou Ayash, Nancy, 197
Bourdieu, Pierre, 97
Bowden, Randall, 101
Bowen, Lauren, 151
"Box under the Bed" (Driscoll and Jin), 42
Boyhood (movie), 5
Braidotti, Rosi, 148*n*5
Brandt, Deborah, 48, 74, 151, 163
Branstetter, Heather Lee, 196
Brewer, Jan, 89
Brown, Robert L., Jr., 87
Brown, Wendy, 147*n3*
Brunton, Lisa, 36, 39
budget cuts, 77, 81, 84, 85, 87, 128
Bugdal, Melissa, 156

Calman, Lynn, 36, 39
Campano, Gerald, 14, 15
capital: cultural, 66; distribution of, 97; institutional, 99; professional, 99
capitalism, 135, 139, 140, 147*n3*; decontextualization of, 142; violence of, 142
Carpenter, William J., 101
Carroll, Lee Ann, 116, 169*t*, 186*n*2
Castanheira, Maria Lucia, 51, 52
CCCC. *See* Conference on College Communication and Composition
change, 3, 21, 25, 34–38, 47–48, 60, 66–67, 75, 76, 126, 150–51, 154–55, 161–63, 190; institutional, 81, 86–88, 107, 117; methodological, 49–50, 167, 170, 185; systemic, 137, 141, 142–43, 146
Chiseri-Strater, Elizabeth, 68, 169*t*, 186*n*2
Christen, Julie, 105, 112
citizenship: institutional, 106–11, 112–14; metaphor, 100–102; precarity and, 99, 102–3
City College at City University of New York, study at, 116. *See also* Sternglass, Marilyn S.

INDEX

Clary-Lemon, Jennifer, 128
Cochran, Jean, 173
coding (data), 112, 178; collaborative, 40; open, 39
collaboration, 17, 56, 59, 65, 68, 78*n*3, 116–17, 128, 146, 158, 177; cross-institutional, 151; with graduate students, 38–41, 43, 99, 119–23, 124–25; with NT faculty, 99, 106–7; with participants, 22, 48, 54–55, 59, 61. *See also* Writing through the Lifespan Collaboration (Collaborative)
Collaborative. *See* Writing through the Lifespan Collaboration
College of Education (UA), 118
College of Humanities (UA), 123
College of Social and Behavioral Sciences (UA), 93*n*3, 119, 123
college writing, 9, 63, 65, 70, 168, 169*t*, 171, 172, 174, 177, 182, 193
"College Writing": From the 1966 Dartmouth Seminar to Tomorrow (conference), 152
College Writing and Beyond (Beaufort), 30, 135
"College Writing, Identification, and the Production of Intellectual Property" (Lunsford, Fishman, and Liew), 174
colonialism, 136, 141, 144, 148*n*5
Commission on Professional Service (MLA), 100
Common Core State Standards, 105
communication, 74, 85, 102, 124, 129; business, 133, 137, 139, 140, 141; ethical, 51; personal, 61; professional, 147*n*4, 171; workplace, 139, 141; written, 144, 176. *See also* technical and professional communication (TPC)
community, 19, 47, 51, 58–60, 126, 129; and campus relationships, 85, 87, 93*n*2; engagement, 85, 151, 192, 195; home, 90–91; professional, 101, 107, 108
community college, 10, 69, 74, 160, 171, 192. *See also* two-year college
community literacy, 46
community writing, 174, 192
composition, 7, 65, 70, 104, 184; multimodal, 93*n*2; pedagogy, 105; textbook, 104. *See also* first-year composition (FYC); rhetoric and composition
Composition Forum, 39
Compton-Lilly, Catherine, 156
Conference on College Composition and Communication (CCCC), 104, 119, 168, 176; Research Grant, 107, 120; Writing Program Certificate of Excellence, 66

contingent faculty, 6, 98, 111. *See also* contingent faculty; non-tenurable (NT) faculty; non-tenure-track (NTT) faculty
contingent researchers, 111, 112. *See also* contingent faculty; non-tenurable (NT) faculty; non-tenure-track (NTT) faculty
copia exercise, 192–93
Core Writing Program (MSU), 97, 103–4
Coronavirus Stories Archive, 184
Council of Writing Program Administrators (CWPA), 93*n*2, 101, 104, 119, 168
Covid-19 pandemic, 77, 88, 134, 145, 146, 147, 151, 153, 176, 195
Crawford, Teresa, 51
Crime Writers' Association, 191
Critical Power Tools (Scott, Longo, and Wills), 141, 142
critical race theory, 8
culture, 28*n*4, 90, 175, 195, 196; college, 69, 181; millennial, 174, 184; neoliberal, 137; of writing, 86; print literate, 167
curriculum, 66, 67, 133, 176; anti-capitalist, 137; professional writing, 136; revised, 193; ROTC, 16, 24; TPC, 133, 137, 147*n*1; university writing, 21; writing program, 63, 85, 93*n*2
Curtis, Marcia, 68, 169*t*, 186*n*2, 195
CWPA. *See* Council of Writing Program Administrators

Danko, Nita, 101
Dartmouth College, 4
Dartmouth Summer Seminar for Composition Research, 158
data, 6, 14, 70, 89, 182; anonymized, 183; ethnographic, 90; management, 88, 116, 124–27, 128, 129; quantitative, 70, 147*n*4. *See also* interviews; longitudinal data; replicable, aggregable, data-driven research (RAD); surveys; writing samples
datasets, 36, 39, 40, 41, 42, 43, 82, 159, 170
Davidson, Cathy N., 175
Del Principe, Annie, 69, 70
demographics, 8, 169, 195
Derrida, Jacques, 179
Desire for Literacy: Writing in the Lives of Adult Learners (Rosenberg), 172
Developing Writers in Higher Education (Gere), 194
development, 4, 37, 39, 61, 64, 69, 71, 150, 154–55, 163, 196; curriculum, 93*n*2; economic, 182; faculty, 78*n*3, 104; linear, 138; ongoing, 14, 43, 47, 48, 65, 73, 145; professional, 30, 65, 76, 86, 93*n*2, 97, 103, 136; program, 66, 68, 75; research,

119; teacher, 85, 88. *See also* literacy development; writing development
dialogue, 49, 52, 53, 55, 56, 110, 125, 127, 129
Diana Hacker Two-Year College English Association Outstanding Programs in English Award, 66
Diogenes, Marvin, 173
Dippre, Ryan J., 11, 155, 157, 162, 186*n*2
discourses, 46, 83, 86, 90, 136; academic, 91, 169; dominant, 90, 92; racist, 88; oppressive, 83–84; workplace, 139; xenophobic, 88
Dively, Ronda Leathers, 145
Dixon, Carol N., 51
Doan, Sara, 147*n*4
Donahue, Christine, 158
Downs, Doug, 6, 10, 99, 169*t*, 186*n*2
Driscoll, Dana Lynn, 9, 110, 169*t*, 186*n*2
Duffey, Suellynn, 101

Easley, Nate, 19
Eble, Michelle, 142
education, 5, 20, 35, 53, 55, 56, 91, 137, 138, 175; adult, 50, 69; college writing and, 182; general, 19, 35, 78*n*3; graduate, 6; liberal arts, 172; literacy, 54, 74; narrative of, 55; open-access, 68; policymakers, 7; postsecondary, 68; professional writing, 136; rhetoric and composition, 136; writing, 10, 91, 136, 150, 182, 193, 195. *See also* higher education
Edwards, Bob, 173
Elbow, Peter, 158
Embodied Literacies Project, 168
emergency medical technicians (EMTs), 144
empirical research, 5, 78*n*2, 118, 139, 160, 163, 168, 170
English: classes, 20, 64, 70, 71, 72, 74, 78*n*1, 86, 89, 117, 167; department, 64, 72, 119, 123; developmental, 70, 74, 76; graduate program, 104, 105, 114*n*2; language, 3, 4, 31, 34, 71, 73, 155, 158; skills program, 63; speakers, 89; subject, 63, 70, 158, 167, 184
English as a second language (ESL), 63, 71, 76, 93*n*2
Enos, Richard L., 179
Enos, Theresa, 101
equity, 67, 100, 107, 133; addressing, 196; educational, 27
Erickson, Joe, 186*n*2
ESL. *See* English as a second language
Esposito, Jennifer, 25
ethic of care, 122, 124, 128, 129

ethic of humility, 25, 122
ethnic studies, 89, 140
ethnography, 19, 28*n*4, 49, 60, 80, 139; data, 90; interactive, 51–57; networked, 197. *See also* institutional ethnography (IE)
experience(s), 35, 36, 37, 48, 56, 57, 58, 60, 73, 84, 91, 126, 152, 156; educational, 5, 69; life, 54, 72–73; literacy, 45, 52, 57, 58, 60, 63, 66, 69, 72, 78*n*2, 78*n*3, 86, 90, 91; participant, 47, 51, 59; professional, 65, 133, 194; writing, 18, 35, 45, 46, 82, 86, 90, 91, 122
extracurricular, 19, 23, 177, 180*t*, 182; all-inclusive, 195; extra-academic, 71, 72, 73

faculty responses, 181*f*
feminist ethics, 51, 128, 179
feminist materialism, 146, 148*n*5
feminist methods, 33, 122, 130*n*2, 196
feminist researcher, 46
Ferreira-Buckley, Linda, 79
first-year composition (FYC), 6, 7, 41, 65, 70, 97, 103, 143, 168; pedagogy, 97, 103
Fishman, Jenn, 11–12, 17, 116, 150, 169*t*, 186*n*2
Floating Admiral, The (Members of the Golden Age Detection Club), 191
Forester, Brian G., 186*n*2
Fort Benning, 23
Fort Knox, 25
Fort Stewart, 22
Fracturing Opportunity (Gildersleeve), 26
Fredlund, Katherine, 196, 197
Freire, Paulo, 54
From the Boidem (Hurvitz), 175
"from-through" perspective, 50
"from-to" framing, 50
funding, 75, 104, 106, 111, 113, 116, 117, 121, 129, 146; cuts, 66, 127, 134, 176, 177; grant, 18, 46, 75, 105, 107, 109, 111, 120, 144–45; pursuit of, 83, 103, 134, 142, 144, 145, 157, 159, 174
FYC. *See* first-year composition

Gaillet, Lynée Lewis, 179
ganas, 19
gender, 17, 90, 143
generosity, methodology of, 158–59
George, 45, 46, 52–61, 172
Gere, Anne Ruggles, 169*t*, 186*n*2, 194, 195
Gift, The (Hyde), 127
Gildersleeve, Ryan Evely, 26, 27, 28*n*3
Gilligan, Carol, 128
Giordano, Joanne Baird, 10, 65, 67, 76, 169*t*

INDEX

Gladstein, Jill M., 182
globalization, 136, 143, 148n5, 161, 193, 195
Gold, David, 179
Golden Age Detective Club, 191
Gonzalez, Lynn P., 101
Google+, 124, 125
Grabill, Jeffrey, 83
graduate students, 31, 32–34, 35, 37, 76, 93n2, 97, 106, 113, 114, 116, 119, 128, 129, 130, 191, 195; international, 156; marginalized, 135; of color, 137. *See also* collaboration
graduate teaching assistants (GTAs), 93n2, 118
Grant Study, 5
Green, Judith L., 51
Grossberg, Lawrence, 84

Haas, Angela, 142
Haas, Christina, 169t, 186n2
Halbritter, Bump, 5, 169t, 186n2
Hall, Anne-Marie, 81, 84, 85, 86, 117, 119
Hall, Stuart, 83
Harvard Happiness Study, 5
Harvard Longitudinal Study, 5
Harvard Study of Adult Development, 5
Harvard Study (Sommers), 86, 116, 128, 169t, 174
Hashlamon, Yanar, 11, 147n1, 168, 169t, 186n2
Hassel, Holly, 10, 65, 67, 76, 169t, 186n2
Haswell, Richard H., 116, 129
Hauman, Kerri, 196, 197
HB 2221 (Arizona), 86, 89
Heath, Shirley Brice, 156, 172
Henderson, Kelly Limes-Taylor, 18, 25
Henderson, Sheila, 33, 42
Henschel, Sally, 137
Herrington, Anne J., 68, 195
Hesse, Doug, 116
higher education, 63, 66, 68, 69, 71, 72, 74–75, 76–77, 98, 101, 113, 158, 169, 175, 180t, 195
history, 14, 48, 103, 133, 136, 141, 146, 172, 173, 176, 183, 196; case, 7; family, 5, 19–20; oral, 5; methods, 14, 33, 83–84, 139, 142–43, 144, 168, 169, 171–72, 175–76, 179–80, 182, 184; personal, 52, 56, 60, 78n2, 104, 167, 171; research and scholarship, 8, 137, 139, 140, 142, 167, 168, 170–71; TPC, 134, 137, 140, 143, 170, 179–80; writing, 12, 196
Hmong speakers, 63, 71, 78n3
Holland, Janet, 38
Hoover, Kimberly, 99, 104, 105, 107, 111, 112

Horne, Tom, 89
House, Eric, 119, 121
Hume Center for Writing and Speaking, 173–74
Hurvitz, Jay, 175
Hyde, Lewis, 127

identity, 15, 16, 34–35, 75, 91, 152, 153, 161, 162; campus, 86, 87; formations of, 90–91; professional, 40; researcher, 21, 98, 134, writerly, 139, 146
ideology, 10, 137, 142, 145, 147n3, 182; language, 197
IE. *See* institutional ethnography
Ihara, Rachel, 69, 70
immersion, 50, 179, 180, 182, 183, 185
immigrant(s), 19, 63, 196; anti-immigrant, 89, 90
immigration laws, measures, and policies, 10, 89, 184
institutional ethnography (IE), 10, 82–83
institutional review board (IRB), 49, 82, 197; application, 16, 18, 22, 27, 168; approval, 6, 9, 128, 144; cross-institutional, 151
interviews, 14–15, 19, 22, 25, 30, 31, 32, 33, 35, 36, 37, 39, 41, 51, 55, 57, 84, 91, 103, 112, 116, 119, 120–122, 124, 126, 133, 160–161, 171, 173, 177, 182, 191, 196; annual, 32, 125, 171; data, 56; dialogic, 20; extract, 52; follow-up, 51, 58; monthly, 16; protocol, 125, 181; retrospective, 17, 19, 20, 26; semi-structured, 139; structured, 45; transcript(s), 36, 41, 51, 52, 59, 179
IRB: *See* institutional review board
Isaacs, Emily, 101

Jacobson, Brad, 9, 110, 119
Jain, 9, 16–21, 25–27, 28n2
Jamieson, Sandra, 6
Jane, Patrick, 28n2
Jin, Daewoo, 41, 42
John, Augustus, 173
Jones, Natasha, 141, 142
Journal of Adolescent and Adult Literacy, 105
Journal of Response to Writing (Powell and Driscoll), 41
JUMP+, The, 6–7

Kasmin Gallery, 3
Kehler, Devon, 119
Kimme Hea, Amy C., 10, 92, 117, 121, 122, 169t, 186n2
Kimmerer, Robin Wall, 128
Kirsch, Gesa E., 51, 122, 130n1

Kitzhaber, Albert R., 4
Knappik, Magdalena, 158
knowledge, 5, 25, 33, 42, 54, 82, 101, 156, 193; acquisition, 48; base, 92; building, 33, 48, 54, 125, 196; community, 28*n3*; contextual, 154; disciplinary, 7, 12, 38, 68, 69, 177; historical, 167; new, 19, 24, 82; of social justice, 136; production, 8, 15, 28, 48, 51, 54, 59, 92, 100, 103, 106, 125, 134, 135, 138, 139, 141, 146, 147, 168, 190, 196
Koshnick, Damian, 78*n2*

labor, 11, 117, 121, 123, 128, 130, 145, 146, 147; academic, 10; advocacy, 107; critical, 8; economy, 136, 137; emotional, 76, 121; equitable, 93*n2*; graduate student, 122, 123, 130; invisible, 119; NT, 101; pedagogical, 67, 98
LaFrance, Michelle, 82, 83
Lamonica, Claire C., 101
Laycock, Deborah, 167
leadership, 8, 81, 168, 177; positions, 66, 67; writing program, 85, 93*n2*
learning, 26, 48, 50, 65, 68, 70, 74, 75, 88, 90, 123, 125, 129, 152; classroom, 146; communities, 60; domains of, 48; experience, 26, 71; literacy, 58–59, 70, 87, 90, 196; needs, 63, 71, 74, 78*n3*; outcomes, 89, 97, 106, 278; reciprocal, 128, 129, 134; requirements, 74; skills, 63; student, 86, 97, 103, 178, 194; transfer, 9, 31, 34, 37, 39, 41, 104
learning centers. *See* adult learning centers
Lee, Yvonne, 156
Leech, Nancy, 19
Levi-Strauss, Claude, 128
Liew, Warren M., 186*n2*
lifespan, 50, 151, 152, 153, 154, 155, 157, 159, 161, 163; approach, 11, 48, 57, 59, 152, 157, 159, 164, 193; orientation, 159, 161–64; writing, 153, 154, 155, 156, 157–58, 161; writing research, 11, 46, 50, 150, 152, 153, 154–57, 158–59, 160, 161, 162–63, 164
Lifespan Studies, 11, 12, 49, 174
Lifespan Writing Development Group, 152
Lindemann, Erika, 170
Lindquist, Julie, 5, 6, 124, 128, 129, 169*t*, 186*n2*
lines of inquiry, 159–61, 164
Linklater, Richard, 5
literacy, 45, 46, 51, 52, 53, 54, 58, 59, 60, 63, 75, 83, 87, 88, 90, 92, 163, 182, 195; adult learners, 9, 47, 58, 192; Black

LGBTQ, 196; education, 54, 61, 74, 78*n2*, 87, 193, 194; experiences, 45, 52, 57, 58, 63, 66, 69, 72, 78*n3*, 86, 91; histories, 60, 75; mass writing, 151; narratives, 5, 158; needs, 64, 70; practices, 56, 69, 91, 182; research, 49, 51, 69, 171, 196; social violence and, 54; studies, 49, 51, 195; videos, 90–91. *See also* agency
LiteracyCorps Michigan, 5, 128
literacy development, 60, 65, 68, 69, 71–73, 156, 163, 196
literacy sponsors, 40, 182, 195
Logan, 9, 16, 22–24, 25, 27
longitudinal (term), 3, 65
longitudinal data, 5, 12, 16, 22, 24, 38, 42, 51, 82, 85, 88, 113, 116, 118, 125–26, 142, 162, 168, 170, 171–72, 173, 175, 178–79, 182, 183; analysis, 4, 14, 16, 18–19, 27, 38–41, 70, 111–12, 116, 118, 125–27, 129, 145–46, 156, 168, 179, 190; collection, 3, 4, 15, 17, 30, 34, 36, 38, 42, 50, 51, 73, 90, 111, 116, 117–18, 119, 120–22, 123–25, 127, 129, 134, 139, 144, 145, 147, 150, 162, 167, 168, 170, 174, 177, 186*n2*, 194. *See also* interviews; surveys; writing samples
Longitudinal and Life Course Studies (journal), 4
longitudinal research, 3–5, 33, 35–38, 41, 42, 43, 50, 65, 69, 91, 98–99, 112–13, 135, 141–43, 145, 154–55, 161, 193
longitudinal studies, 6, 14, 16, 22–23, 26, 30, 45–47, 49, 77, 83, 86, 87, 90, 97, 99, 112–14, 116, 124, 128, 129, 130, 134–38, 139, 154, 159, 160, 161, 164, 167, 168–70, 169*t*, 174, 176–77, 194, 196; radically, 156–57, 164. *See also* City College at City University of New York, study at; Pepperdine University, study at; Stanford Study of Writing (Lunsford); University of Arizona Longitudinal Study of Student Writers (UA Study); University of Denver, study at; University of Michigan, study at; University of Montana, study at; Vernon Writes (Fishman); Washington State University, study at
longitudinal writing research, 4, 6–8, 9–12, 15–16, 25–28, 30, 34, 38, 48–49, 52–53, 68–70, 72, 86, 98, 102, 103–104, 105–8, 112–14, 120, 125, 127, 130, 134–35, 138–39, 147, 150–52, 157, 164, 167, 174, 190–97; challenges, 73–74, 111; at community or two-year colleges, 68–70, 74–75; historical, 170–71, 171–72, 176, 178,

180–86; in technical and professional communication (TPC), 135, 37, 138–40, 141–43, 143–47; related scholarship, 110, 116, 135; relational approaches, 17–21, 26–28, 48, 82, 122, 190
longitudinal writing researcher(s), 4, 6, 7, 10, 11, 12, 26, 34, 35, 40, 49, 52, 53, 56, 82, 98, 135, 145, 147, 156, 159, 160, 170, 171, 191, 194, 195; experience, 114*n*2; team(s), 88, 93*n*2, 98, 99, 104–107, 109, 111–12, 113, 117–19, 122–24, 127–29, 158, 160, 168, 170. *See also* graduate students; non-tenurable (NT) faculty; non-tenure-track faculty
Lorde, Audre, 137
Lorey, Isabel, 147*n*2
Lu, Min-Zhan, 74
Lucero, Margaret M., 169*t*, 186*n*2
Lunsford, Andrea A., 74, 116, 169*t*, 174, 175, 183, 186*n*2, 195

Madden, Shannon, 155
Majewski, John, 78*n*2
Mapes, Aimee C., 10, 11, 82, 88, 92, 98, 169*t*, 186*n*2
"Master's Tools Will Never Dismantle the Master's House, The" (Lorde), 137
Mauss, Marcel, 127
McCarthy, Lucille, 168
McCorkle, Ben, 196, 197
McGee, Sharon James, 87, 128
McGinnis, Clare, 184; illustration by, 185*f*
McLeod, Susan H., 98
McNely, Brian, 146
Melonçon, Lisa, 137
Menard, Scott, 4, 196
Mentalist, The (television show), 28*n*2
mentor(s), 9, 18, 24, 30–31, 34, 37, 39, 41, 129
mentoring, 9, 24, 34, 38–41, 43, 87, 103, 125–29, 129, 168, 191
methods, 6, 11, 25–26, 31, 40, 50, 111, 125, 150, 151, 160, 161, 163, 196; articulation, 82–84; course, 30, 32, 37, 41–42; empirical, 168; ethnographic, 49, 51; historical, 139, 168; lifespan, 154; longitudinal, 69, 112–13, 135, 137, 138, 140–42, 143, 144, 145, 151, 153, 154–55, 157, 174, 193; mixed, 82, 170, 182, 196, 197; new, 153; parallax, 155; planned attrition, 120; qualitative, 157; quantitative, 150; traditional, 51
methodology, 50, 139–40, 143, 155, 157–59, 160, 191, 197; change, 185; counter-story, 8; experimentation, 27; feminist, 33, 130*n*1, 148*n*5; generosity, 158, 159;

longitudinal, 4, 26, 134, 135, 136, 139, 140, 142, 144, 147, 154; precarious, 134, 140–41; promiscuity, 196; qualitative, 17, 33; relational, 124, 128; revisiting, 48, 172; Rhetorical Transversal Methodology (RTM), 196; social justice, 137, 142; storytelling, 7–8. *See also* institutional ethnography (IE); longitudinal research; technical and professional communication (TPC)
Mexican American Studies Program, 89
Miles, Libby, 83
Minnix, Chris, 81
Modern Language Association (MLA), Commission on Professional Service of, 100
Moffit Library (Berkeley), 173
Molassiotis, Alex, 36, 39
Montana State University (MSU), 103, 104, 105, 112, 113; Core Writing Program of, 97; research at, 98
Moore, Kristen, 141, 142
More and More Stories about Longitudinal Research (series), 192
Morning Edition (radio program), 173
Motha, Suhanthie, 28*n*3
motivation, 19, 42, 46–47, 52, 107–8, 110
MSU. *See* Montana State University
Mueller, Derek N., 196
multidisciplinary work, 154, 159, 160–63

Nadeau, Jean-Paul, 69, 70, 74
Nares, James, 3
narratives, 6, 16, 24–25, 57, 58, 75, 135, 191, 192; changing, 88, 92; dominant and non-dominant, 7–8, 14, 28, 81–92, experience, 51; faculty, 181*f*; linear, 26; literacy, 5, 60; progress, 138; research, 116, 130; re-spinning, 58; written/spoken, 60
National Writing Project, 104
Navy Junior Reserve Officers Training Corps, 23
Naylor Report, 6
Nelms, Gerald, 145
neoliberalism, 135, 136, 143–44, 147*n*3
New Education, The (Davidson), 175
9/11. *See* September 11th
No Rest for the Dead (Abbott et al.), 191
Nogales, Arizona/Nogales, Mexico, 88–89
Nolte, Miles, 10
non-tenurable (NT) faculty, 97–98, 103, 114*n*2, 117; citizenship and, 99–102, 106–14
non-tenure-track faculty, 10–11, 65, 67, 109, 117, 134–35

obligation, 11, 46, 100–101, 119–20, 121, 126–28, 129–30, 142–43
Office of Professional and Instructional Development (UW), 75
100 Years of New Media Pedagogy (Palmeri and McCorkle), 196
Online Etymology Dictionary, 156
open-access: education, 68; institutions, 63, 64, 66, 69, 73, 78n2; instructors, 73; pathways, 65; research, 70; student writers, 68, 73; writing programs, 70
openness, 21, 25, 129, 158, 197
Ouellette, Jessica, 196, 197

Palmeri, Jason, 196, 197
Paltridge, Brian, 28n4
Paris, Django, 20, 21
partnerships: institutional, 117; research, 23, 24, 63, 69; writing, x, 47, 49, 192
Patel, Leigh, 9, 14–15, 16
Pawlowski, Madelyn Tucker, 119
pedagogy, 67, 83, 152, 182, 196; anti-capitalist, 11; critical, 87, 140; TPC, 136, 141, 143; WAW, 103, 104, 105, 107; writing, 97, 98, 103–106
Peer Writing Tutor Alumni Research Project, 172
Penrose, Ann, 101
Pepperdine University, study at, 116. *See also* Carroll, Lee Ann
Peres, Anushka Swan, 91, 93n4, 119, 121, 124, 126
"Performing Writing, Performing Literacy" (Fishman et al.), 174
Phillips, Nathan, 15
Phillips, Talinn, 11, 153, 156
Pigg, Stacey, 157
Pirsig, Robert, 111
PIs. *See* principal investigators
politics, 3, 10, 84, 92, 100, 134, 137, 140, 143, 145, 147, 164, 183; activism, 8, 134, 163, 192; of education, 54, 134, 145, 146; empancipatory, 146; local/regional, 86, 92; of research, 136, 137, 139–43, 145, 197
Porter, James E., 83
portfolios: assessment, 93n3, 171; research, 98, 99; writing, 173, 176
Powell, Katrina M., 124–25
Powell, Roger, 38, 39, 40, 41
power, 17, 31, 53, 83, 87, 89, 139, 142, 148n5; differences, 9; dynamics, 9, 10, 15–16, 25, 196; hegemonic, 137–38; imbalance, 25, 61; relations, 17, 54, 92, 128
Pratt, Scott L., 146

precarity, 10–11, 85, 87, 99, 101–2, 108–9, 112–14, 117, 134–35, 137–47, 174n2, 193
principal investigators (PIs), 9, 11, 82, 88, 99, 117, 119, 122, 129, 168, 193
Prior, Paul A., 48, 152, 157, 195
professional development, 30, 65, 76, 86, 93n2, 97, 103, 136
professional writing, 6, 134–35, 136–38, 140, 143, 147n4; anti-capitalist, 133. *See also* technical and professional communication (TPC)
professionalism, 34–35, 40, 72, 85, 137–38
Program in Writing and Rhetoric (Stanford), 173
Promise and Perils of Writing Program Administration (Enos and Borrowman), 101
Proposition 203 (Arizona), 89
publication, 6, 17, 31, 42, 47, 65, 93n2, 99, 114; lifespan studies and, 152–53; longitudinal research and, 110, 150, 167–68; relationships in, 33, 38–41, 57–58

qualitative research, 14–15, 17, 20, 25, 27, 31, 33, 42, 45, 48–49, 121, 124, 129, 150, 157, 160–62, 179, 193
quantitative research, 70, 147n4, 150, 160, 162, 193

race, 17, 90, 143. *See also* critical race theory
RAD. *See* replicable, aggregable, data-driven research
radically contextual, 156, 157
Ratcliffe, Krista, 51
Read/Write/Now Adult Education Center, 45–46
reading, 20, 22, 41, 59, 64–65, 67–72, 78n3, 90–91, 104, 162, 183–84, 193, 196; aloud, 57–60,: circle, 64, 103; close, 51–52, 56, 196; college-level, 65, 69, 70, 74; critical, 64, 66; developmental, 63, 70; experiences, 46; rereading, 36, 184
reciprocity, 9, 11, 16–18, 20–21, 23–25, 28, 46, 119–20, 123–29
reflection: activity, 57, 58, 60, 174, 183, 190, 193; genre, 21, 27, 33, 68, 72, 105, 116, 117, 121–22, 129, 145
reflexivity, 33–34, 37, 42, 52, 122, 128, 143, 145; self-, 9, 14, 17–18, 128, 144
Regaignon, Dara Rossman, 182
relational: approach, 17–21, 26–28, 48, 82, 122, 190; ethic, 12–13, 128; methodology, 124, 128
relationships, 7, 8, 11, 48, 129, 138, 156, 182, 190; caring, 127–29; community, 85, 93n2; personal, 9, 49, 84, 122, 147, 177,

182; to production, 143, 145–46; professional, 10, 68, 147; research, 9, 10, 14, 16–21, 22–24, 25, 27, 30, 31–34, 35, 38, 39, 40, 41, 42, 43, 45–47, 48–51, 52–57, 61, 110, 117, 119–21, 124–28, 129–30, 156, 172, 177, 191; to writing, 86, 91, 144, 167; workplace, 137, 138, 140, 142. *See also* power (relations)
replicable, aggregate, data-driven (RAD) research, 129, 118, 171
research. *See* collaboration; empirical research; ethnography; history (methods); institutional ethnography (IE); institutional review board (IRB); Lifespan Studies; literacy (research); longitudinal research; longitudinal studies; longitudinal writing research; methods; methodology; principal investigators (PIs); qualitative research, quantitative research; relational; teaching and; writing research
Research Initiative Grant (CCCC), 107, 120
rhetoric: coalitional, 137; Greco-Roman, 7; historical, 168, 179; workplace, 141
rhetoric and composition, 11, 134, 135, 136, 137, 158, 175. *See also* writing studies (discipline)
Rhetoric Society of America (RSA), 168
Rhetorical Transversal Methodology (RTM), 197
Rhetorical Work in Emergency Medical Services (Angeli), 144
Rhode Island School of Design, 174
Ribero, Ana Milena, 91, 92, 93*n4*, 119, 120, 121, 124, 125, 126
Rifenburg, J. Michael, 9, 110, 169*t*, 186*n2*
Rives Engler, Ashley, 10, 114*n1*
Rogers, Paul, 68, 193
Rohan, Liz, 179
Roozen, Kevin, 26*n1*, 150, 156, 157, 169*t*, 186*n2*, 195
Rose, Mike, 74
Rosenberg, Lauren, 9, 46, 47, 49, 55, 110, 156, 172
Rosiek, Jerry L., 146
Royster, Jacqueline Jones, 51, 74, 122

Saidy, Christina, 27
Saldaña, Johnny, 39, 50
Saltz, Laura, 186*n2*
Santa Cruz, Nicole, 89
Sargent, John Singer, 173
SB 1070 (Arizona), 86, 89
Schell, Eileen E., 100
Schlenz, Mark, 10, 114*m1*, 128

scholarship of teaching and learning (SoTL) study, 64
Schwaller, Emily Jo, 119, 126
September 11th, 161, 172, 173, 183–85
Serviss, Tricia, 6, 169*t*, 186*n2*
Shaughnessy, Mina P., 185
Sheffield, Jenna Pack, 117, 119, 122, 126
Shepley, Nathan, 170
simple gifts, relations and, 119, 127–29
"Simple Gifts" (Anderson), 120, 127
Smagorinsky, Peter, 40
Smith, Anna, 15, 50, 151, 157
Smith, Dorothy, 83
Smitherman, Geneva, 74
Snyder, Jimmy, 146
social justice, 65, 196. *See also* technical and professional communication (TPC)
Sommers, Nancy, 116, 128, 169*t*, 174, 186*n2*
Spack, Ruth, 186*n2*
Spinuzzi, Clay, 139, 140–41, 146
Sprague, Bill "Doc," 167
Sprague, Nancy, 167
standardized placement tests, 65
Stanford Digital Repository, 183
Stanford Study Collection, 184
Stanford Study of Writing (Lunsford), 12, 86, 116, 128, 137, 168, 171, 172, 173–76, 183; illustration of, 185*f*
Stanford Study of Writing Digital Collection, 183
Starfield, Sue, 28*n4*
Stephens, Patricia, 97, 100
Sternglass, Marilyn S., 42, 116, 122–23, 169*t*, 186*n2*, 194–95
Stornaiuolo, Amy, 14, 15
storying, 9, 12, 15–17, 21–28
storytelling, 7, 8, 54, 58–59, 86, 190
strategic plans, 8, 81–86, 88, 92, 93*n2*, 93*n3*
Strengths, Weaknesses, Opportunities, and Threats (SWOT), 85
Stuckey, J. Elspeth, 54, 55
Student Surveys of Instruction, 67
Sullivan, Patricia A., 28, 83
surveys, 88, 91, 116, 124, 125, 126, 154, 173, 174, 176, 178

Takabori, Amy, 119, 126
Takayoshi, Pamela, 124–25
Tarabochia, Sandra, 155
Tardy, Christine, 28*n4*
teaching, 63–65, 66, 70, 75–76, 99–100, 106, 140, 157, 178, 185; ban on ethnic studies, 89; contracts and, 103, 108–9, 111, 112; dynamics of, 9; 9/11 and, 183; online and, 153; research and, 98, 136, 138

Teaching-for-Transfer (TFT), 78n2
technical and professional communication (TPC), 11, 24, 133–38, 139–43, 144, 147n1, 171; methodology, 146; pedagogy, 136, 143; social justice turn, 133, 135–38, 140–43, 145–47
technology, 85, 175; digital, 93n2; information, 67
tenured and tenure-track or tenure-line faculty, 6, 24, 37, 39, 46, 63, 65, 76, 97, 99, 104, 108, 172
tenured researcher, 107
Tercero, Tanya, 119, 125, 126
Teston, Christa, 146, 147n1
TETYC, 78n2
Thomas, Ebony Elizabeth, 14, 15
Thompson, Clive, 174
Thompson, Linda, 33
Thomson, Rachel, 38
thought experiment, 152
Three Sisters, 128
time-reflexivity-relationship triad, 34
Time to Know Them (Sternglass), 122
Tinberg, Howard, 69, 70, 74
Tohono O'odham, 89, 90
TPC. *See* technical and professional communication
Tracing Genres through Organizations (Spinuzzi), 139
transfer: *See* knowledge; learning; Teaching-for-Transfer (TFT)
transparency, 6, 128, 129; as reciprocity, 20–21
trust, 25, 129; building, 9, 18–19, 21, 32, 120, 122; of stories, 7
Tucson High School, 89
two-year college, 10, 63–77. *See also* community college

UA. *See* University of Arizona
UA Study. *See* University of Arizona Longitudinal Study of Student Writers
Undergraduate Teaching and Learning Grants, 75
UNG. *See* University of North Georgia
University of Alaska System, 77
University of Arizona (UA), 9, 10, 82, 84, 87, 88–89, 90, 92, 117
University of Arizona Longitudinal Study of Student Writers (UA Study), 81–82, 83, 86–88, 90–92, 116–27, 129–30, 169t
University of Arizona (UA) Writing Program, 81, 83, 85–88, 93n1, 117, 119
University of Denver, study at, 116
University of Michigan, study at, 128, 194
University of Montana, study at, 128

University of North Georgia (UNG), 9, 22, 23
University of Wisconsin (UW) Colleges Senate, 67
University of Wisconsin (UW)-Madison, 64
University of Wisconsin (UW)-Marathon County, 63
University of Wisconsin (UW) System, 10, 63, 66, 67, 75, 76
Up (documentary series), 5
US Army, 23, 27; writing assignments for, 23; writing standard by, 22
US Army Advanced Camp, 25
US Navy, 162
UW. *See* University of Wisconsin

Vernon College, 169t, 171–72, 176–78, 180t, 180–82, 186n1
Vernon Review, 172
Vernon Writes (Fishman), 12, 168, 171–72, 176–78, 180t, 180–82, 186n1
Vernon Writes Collection, 180, 183; finding aid for, 180t
"Vernon Writes: Looking Back, Looking Ahead" (Fishman), 178, 180
Vieira, Kate, 196
Villanueva, Victor, 74

WAC Clearinghouse, 184
Walker, Kenny, 117, 119, 121, 122, 126
Walker, Scott, 75
Wallin, J. E. Wallace, 4
Walton, Rebecca, 141, 142
Wardle, Elizabeth, 169t, 186n2
Warnock, Scott, 147n4
Washington State University, study at, 116. *See also* Haswell, Richard H.
WAW. *See* writing-about-writing pedagogy
Ways with Words (Heath), 172
"Where Are You Now" survey, 126
Winsor, Dorothy A., 135, 139, 140, 142, 169t, 186n2
WIRED, 174
Wittgenstein, Ludwig, 170
Wolcott, Willa, 169t, 186n2
Words at Work and Play (Heath), 172
work study program, 135
workplace, 137, 138, 180t; politics of, 138–46; research and, 134–35; writing, 24, 136, 138
WPAs. *See* writing program administrators
writers, 4, 8, 9, 10, 12, 24, 25, 27, 28, 50, 65, 68, 81, 83, 85, 90, 111, 130, 142, 145, 150–54, 157, 160, 165, 169, 170, 174, 176, 177, 182, 190, 194, 195, 197; development of, 30, 49, 64, 66, 69, 71, 73–75,

78n3, 82, 86, 138, 150, 155, 193; digital, 85, 93n2, 175; learning outcomes and, 118, 178; postgraduate, 150–51; transformation of, 88, 91, 164
writing, 4, 7, 8, 14, 16, 18, 20–21, 23–24, 35–37, 42, 45–46, 49, 53, 59, 65, 71, 83, 90–91, 135, 136, 141, 151, 152–57, 161–63, 168, 170, 174, 177, 181–82, 183, 190, 191, 194–95, 197; assignments, 22–23, 64, 178, 184; college, 9, 63–65, 71, 168–70, 169*t*, 172, 175, 176–77, 182; community, 174, 192; culture of, 86; curricula, 10, 21, 64, 68, 70, 82, 84, 86, 88; disciplinary, 31, 123; first-year, 22, 24, 31–32, 66, 74, 121; education, 10, 193, 195; history of, 12; instruction, 10, 103, 178, 179, 194, 195; instructor(s), 22, 74, 82, 97, 98, 101, 107, 130, 150, 154, 168, 182, 183, 191; partnerships, 47, 49, 192; pedagogy, 97, 98, 103–6; processes, 27, 110, 130, 152; researchers, 8, 10, 22, 28, 82, 150–51, 152, 164, 174, 195–96; school-based, 19; skills, 40; support, 18. *See also* academic writing; assessment; writing development; first-year composition; lifespan (writing); professional writing; workplace (writing)
Writing about Writing (Wardle and Downs), 104
writing-about-writing (WAW) pedagogy, 103, 104, 105, 107
writing across the curriculum (WAC), 93n2
Writing and Pedagogy (Bazerman), 152
writing centers, 8, 32, 37, 171, 191, 192
writing development, 4, 8, 14, 23, 24, 30, 31, 35, 36, 39, 42, 43, 48, 49, 50, 64, 68, 70, 71, 72, 119, 126, 150, 152, 154–155, 159, 160, 193, 194
writing in the disciplines (WID), 93n2

"Writing Is as Writing Does" (Fishman), 176
Writing Like an Engineer: A Rhetorical Education (Winsor), 135, 139
Writing Our Way toward More Livable Worlds (Teston and Hashlamon), 147n1
Writing Power: Communication in an Engineering Center (Winsor), 139
writing program administrators (WPAs), 22–23, 67, 81, 82, 84, 97, 103, 104, 106, 107, 108, 109, 113, 117, 119, 178. *See also* Council of Writing Program Administrators (CWPA)
writing program(s), 63, 72, 81, 82, 91, 97, 106, 112, 114n2, 127, 171, 176, 191; review of, 64–66, 78n3, 82, 85–88, 90, 93n2
writing samples, 30, 33, 39, 45, 51–52, 57, 58, 103, 116, 119, 122, 160, 161, 171, 173, 174, 177, 184–85, 191, 195
writing studies (discipline), 5, 7, 11, 17, 64, 68, 74, 77, 92, 102, 116–117, 147n3, 150–51, 152, 157–59, 170, 172, 175, 179, 190; scholarship, 28, 64, 74–75
writing studies (research), 4, 7, 11, 46, 139, 167. *See also* research
Writing Studies Research in Practice (Nickoson and Sheridan), 176
Writing through the Lifespan Collaboration (Collaborative), 50, 152, 153, 154, 155, 157, 159
writing transfer, 30, 36–37, 42–43. *See also* knowledge; learning; Teaching-for-Transfer (TFT)
writing workshops, 93n2, 155, 176

Yaqui, 90
Ying, 71–72

Zepernick, Janet, 42

ABOUT THE AUTHORS

Ryan J. Dippre is associate professor of English at the University of Maine. He is a graduate of Wilkes University (BA, MS) and the University of California, Santa Barbara (MA, PhD). His scholarship focuses on writing development; in particular, he is interested in how and why (1) writing development is shaped by participants, both philosophically and technologically; and (2) writers develop both on a moment-to-moment basis and over time. He is interested in how writers develop across the lifespan.

Doug Downs is associate professor of writing and rhetoric at Montana State University and the founder of its writing major; he also directed its core writing program during the years 2013–18. He served as editor of *Young Scholars in Writing*, the national journal of undergraduate research in rhetoric and writing studies, from 2015 to 2020. Doug researches public and personal conceptions of writing, reading, and writing pedagogy. He has coauthored several germinal articles, chapters, and books on writing-about-writing pedagogy and numerous chapters and articles on first-year composition, writing pedagogy, student reading practices, undergraduate research, and the disciplinarity of writing studies.

Dana Lynn Driscoll is professor of English at Indiana University of Pennsylvania, where she teaches in the composition and applied linguistics doctoral program and directs the Kathleen Jones White Writing Center. She serves as co-editor for the open-source first-year writing textbook series *Writing Spaces*, which offers free readings and instructional materials for composition courses. She has published widely on writing transfer, learning theory, writing centers, and research methods and has offered plenary addresses and workshops around the globe.

Jenn Fishman is a college writing educator whose research, teaching, and national professional leadership advance writing research, undergraduate research, and community-oriented work in rhetoric and composition/writing studies. A recipient of the Richard Braddock Award, she is a regular high school– and college-level writing consultant and the principal investigator of three grant-supported research projects. Her publications include *The Naylor Report on Undergraduate Research in Writing Studies*, *The Research Exchange Index*, and special issues of *CCC Online*, *Peitho*, and *Community Literacy Journal*. She is associate professor of English and co-director of the Ott Memorial Writing Center at Marquette University.

Joanne Baird Giordano is associate professor of English, linguistics, and writing studies at Salt Lake Community College. Her collaborative research focuses on two-year college students' literacy development, transitions to postsecondary reading and writing, and the experiences of literacy educators at open-access institutions. Her work has appeared in *College English*, *CCC*, *Teaching English in the Two-Year College*, *Pedagogy*, the *Journal of Writing Assessment*, *WPA Journal*, *Open Words*, and edited collections.

Yanar Hashlamon is a PhD candidate at The Ohio State University studying rhetoric and literacy with specific attention to critical pedagogy and material rhetorics. His work as a teacher and researcher has taken him from writing centers and professional writing classrooms to his current study of the history of rhetoric, colonization and carceral power. Yanar has individual and co-authored work published in *Praxis: A Writing Center Journal, Computers and Composition, Technical Communication Quarterly,* and *Rhetoric Society Quarterly.*

Holly Hassel is professor of English at North Dakota State University in Fargo, where she serves as the director of first-year writing. She taught for sixteen years as a faculty member at the University of Wisconsin–Marathon County, a two-year college. She is past editor of the journal *Teaching English in the Two-Year College.* Her research has appeared in many edited collections and writing studies journals.

Brad Jacobson is assistant professor of English at the University of Texas at El Paso, where he teaches graduate and undergraduate courses in writing studies and teacher education. His research focuses on academic writing development and the high school–to-college writing transition. Brad's work has appeared in the *Journal of Writing Assessment, Writing Program Administration,* the *Journal of Literacy Research, Currents in Teaching and Learning,* and edited collections.

Amy C. Kimme Hea is associate dean for academic affairs and student success as well as professor in the Rhetoric, Composition, and Teaching of English Program at the University of Arizona and co-owner of Pillar 1: Wildcat Journey of the University of Arizona's strategic plan. Her research has appeared in her own collection, *Going Wireless: A Critical Exploration of Wireless and Mobile Technologies for Composition Teachers and Researchers,* and other edited collections and peer-review journals. In addition, she serves on several editorial boards, has held elected positions including member of the WPA Executive Board and chair of the Rhetoric and Composition Consortium, and has shared the co-principal investigator position with Aimee Mapes on the UA Longitudinal Study.

Aimee C. Mapes is a teacher/scholar/administrator at the University of Arizona where she is director of Writing across the Curriculum and faculty in the Program of Rhetoric, Composition, and the Teaching of English. Since 2015, she has been co-principal investigator of the UA Longitudinal Study with Amy C. Kimme Hea. With interests in socio-cultural literacy studies, writing studies, agency, and a feminist ethic of care, her research has appeared in *CCC, Journal of Adolescent and Adult Literacy, Reflections,* and *WPA.* She serves as associate writing studies editor for *Prompt: A Journal of Writing Assignments.*

Miles Nolte works as a writer, editor, journalist, video producer, and conservation advocate at the outdoor media company MeatEater, Inc. He is a former fly-fishing guide, freelance magazine writer, and faculty member in the English department at Montana State University. Miles produces media that encourage thoughtful, nuanced, and evidence-based interactions with wilderness and wild animals and a sustainable approach to hunting, fishing, and eating. His work is available at themeateater.com.

Talinn Phillips is associate professor of English at Ohio University. Her research interests include graduate writing development, multilingual writing, writing centers, and lifespan writing research. Her books include *Supporting Graduate Student Writers: Research, Curriculum, and Program Design* (co-edited for University of Michigan Press, 2016), *Teaching with a Global Perspective* (coauthored with Dawn Bikowski for Routledge, 2019), and *Approaches to Lifespan Writing Research* (co-edited with Ryan Dippre for the WAC Clearinghouse, 2020).

J. Michael Rifenburg, professor of English at the University of North Georgia, serves as senior faculty fellow for scholarly writing with UNG's Center for Teaching, Learning, and Leadership. He authored *The Embodied Playbook: Writing Practices of Student-Athletes* (Utah

State University Press, 2018) and *Drilled to Write: Becoming a Cadet Writer at a Senior Military College* (Utah State University Press, 2022). He is a recipient of the University System of Georgia Regents' Scholarship of Teaching & Learning Award.

Ashley Rives was a non-tenure-track instructor at Montana State University for six years, primarily teaching first-year composition and an occasional upper-division writing course. She has worked on research projects concerning instructor use of peer workshops, the language of rhetoric in the Common Core State Standards, and student uptake of writing-about-writing curriculum concepts. She is focused on raising her two children.

Lauren Rosenberg is the author of *The Desire for Literacy: Writing in the Lives of Adult Learners* (NCTE, 2015). Her research focuses on the writing practices of adult populations that are underrepresented in composition studies, longitudinal methodologies for qualitative case study research, and feminist research ethics. Her coauthored essay with Stephanie L. Kerschbaum, "Entanglements of Literacy Studies and Disability Studies" (*College English* 83.4), was recipient of the 2021 Ohmann award. Lauren is associate professor of rhetoric and writing studies in the English department at the University of Texas at El Paso, where she also directs first-year composition.

Mark Schlenz is a retired teaching professor, researcher, and assistant director of the Core Writing Program at Montana State University. In his nine years at MSU, Mark taught first-year composition, advanced composition, courses in MSU's writing major, and literature courses; he also made significant contributions to the professional and institutional standing and well-being of his non-tenure-track colleagues in the writing program. He pursues virtuous form in martial arts and sea-kayaking.